D1499731

DISCARD

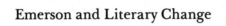

Emerson and Literary Change

Emerson
and
Literary Change

DAVID PORTER

HARVARD UNIVERSITY PRESS

Cambridge, Massachusetts
and
London, England
1978

Publication of this book has
been aided by a grant from
the Andrew W. Mellon
Foundation

Library of Congress Cataloging in Publication Data

Porter, David
　　Emerson and literary change.

　　Includes bibliographical references and index.
　　1. Emerson, Ralph Waldo, 1803-1882 — Aesthetics.
2. Emerson, Ralph Waldo, 1803-1882 — Influence.
3. Poetics.　I. Title.
PS1642.A34P6　　　814'.3　　　78-6669
ISBN 0-674-24875-9

For Lee

Preface

TEXTUAL REFERENCES are to the Centenary Edition (1903-1904) of Emerson's complete works. I have also relied on the texts of the poems in *A Critical and Variorum Edition*, edited by Carl Strauch, and *Selected Writings*, edited by William Gilman, and on the essay texts in the Gilman edition and available volumes in the Harvard *Collected Works*. Journal quotations are from *The Journals and Miscellaneous Notebooks* already published; otherwise they are from the Emerson-Forbes edition (1909-1914). Full bibliographical data can be found on the abbreviations page that follows.

The provenance of the important essay "Poetry and Imagination" at this writing remains vague. By the summer of 1872 Emerson "had got ready," to the point of having the proof sheets in his hands, the essay that is the first piece in *Letters and Social Aims*. But, according to James Elliot Cabot, Emerson's literary executor, there was an intolerable confusion of order in the piece which, owing to the fire in Emerson's house in July of that year and Emerson's subsequent trip abroad, was not faced again until 1875, when the whole business of preparation for the press was turned over to Cabot. Though the essay as it stands is no doubt of Cabot's final shaping, he says in his preface that there is nothing in it that Emerson did not write.

I am indebted to many Emerson scholars. Some of that indebtedness is acknowledged in notes, particularly to the work of Carl Strauch, Jonathan Bishop, William Gilman, Sherman Paul, Vivian Hopkins, Kenneth Cameron, Hyatt Waggoner, and Lawrence Buell. Undoubtedly, I have overlooked many others whose work is now indistinguishably part of my own thinking. I acknowledge that broad debt here.

I have benefited immeasurably from discussions with William Gilman, Carl Strauch, Everett Emerson, Archibald MacLeish, A. W. Plumstead,

Paul Mariani, Brian Fitzgerald, Gayle Smith, and Richard Noland. G. R. Thompson, Kathleen McLean, and other readers for *ESQ* provided a rigorous critique of the version of Chapter Two which was published in that journal in 1976 and which is printed here in revised form with the permission of *ESQ*. R. W. B. Lewis read the manuscript at different stages and confronted me with the most incisive kind of criticism. Maud Wilcox, William B. Goodman, and Joyce Backman provided expert counsel in editorial matters.

Staff members of the Library of the University of Massachusetts at Amherst, the Frost Library of Amherst College, and the Houghton Library of Harvard University were, as always, generous with their help. My special gratitude is owed to Nonny Burack, who civilized and typed the final manuscript, to Joan Weston and Lee Porter, who transcribed drafts at an earlier stage, to Norman and Edith Campbell for neighborly assistance, and to Thomas Porter, who verified references.

My sons Tom, Dave, and Steve were examples of the restraining grace of common sense (Emerson's phrase for the Understanding) when they may not have suspected it. Dave, by what is surely an augury, shares his birthdate with the exemplary Emerson. The book is dedicated to my wife.

A National Endowment for the Humanities Fellowship aided me greatly in the final stage of preparing the manuscript. Professional leave from the University of Massachusetts, administrative assistance from Dean Jeremiah Allen, and a grant-in-aid from the Research Council of the University were important forms of support as well.

Grateful acknowledgment is made to the Ralph Waldo Emerson Memorial Association and the Houghton Library of Harvard University for permission to publish variant readings from the Emerson manuscripts.

Special acknowledgment is also made for permission to reprint passages from the following works:

The Journals and Miscellaneous Notebooks of Ralph Waldo Emerson, vols. 1-13, ed. William H. Gilman et al., The Belknap Press of Harvard University Press, Cambridge, Mass., copyright 1960, 1961, 1963, 1964, 1965, 1966, 1969, 1970, 1971, 1973, 1975, 1976, 1977 by the President and Fellows of Harvard College.

A Critical and Variorum Edition of the Poems of Ralph Waldo Emerson, ed. Carl F. Strauch, University Microfilms, Ann Arbor, Michigan, copyright 1965 by Carl F. Strauch.

The Collected Poems of Wallace Stevens, Alfred A. Knopf, New York, copyright 1954 by Wallace Stevens.

D. P.

Pigeon Cove, Massachusetts

Abbreviations

Emerson. Edited by Carl F. Strauch. Ann Arbor: University Microfilms, 1971.

W   *The Complete Works of Ralph Waldo Emerson*. Edited by Edward Waldo Emerson. The Centenary Edition. 12 vols. Boston: Houghton Mifflin Co., 1903-1904.

Contents

If there is any period one would desire to be born in, is it not the age of Revolution; when the old and the new stand side by side and admit of being compared; when the energies of all men are searched by fear and by hope; when the historic glories of the old can be compensated by the rich possibilities of the new era? This time, like all times, is a very good one, if we but know what to do with it.

Emerson, "The American Scholar," 1837

Introduction: New Demands
on Literature

EMERSON THE ARTIST was the central man. William James distinguished the poet from the metaphysician: "Emerson's mission culminated in his style, and if we must define him in one word, we have to call him Artist."[1] He was, in addition, a poetry theorist of profound reach, a revolutionary committed to the introduction of a radical aesthetics. This aim subsumes all others in Emerson's achievement. We neglect his innovative genius if we confine ourselves simply to the ways he codified the nationalistic clichés and furnished the American consciousness with its images of identity and self-reliance. That was Emerson the culture hero. He was, however, more the exceptional artist than we have discerned. Defining that aesthetic brilliance is the purpose of this book and its justification in view of the enormous amount of learned commentary on Emerson. I agree with Jonathan Bishop: "Emerson the artist, the man of words, tends perpetually to escape the alertness of his best readers. Yet this is the Emerson that counts."[2]

This study, then, seeks the aesthetic figuration by which Emerson meant to accomplish his primary aim: "to invite men drenched in time to recover themselves and come out of time, and taste their native immortal air" (*JMN*, VII, 271).[3] It is not an orderly scheme whose development can be traced chronologically, as I remind readers later on, but rather an abiding order of perception—a latent figure without a climactic Eureka!—that must be precipitated out of its state of suspension in the intellectual solution formed over nearly three decades by the poems and essays. We find as its innermost design the deep revolutionary aesthetics commensurate with Emerson's hope for man fully alive. In the pursuit, we follow him through what he called "the profoundly secret pass that leads from Fate to Freedom" (*JMN*, XIII, 404).

The field of Emerson's poetic imagination holds even larger significance,

for Emerson's aesthetic problems were fundamental. Because he was supremely a conscious artist, he enacted the aesthetic dilemma of his age. His
achievement was a radical shift in poetic form that led out of the common
crisis. Emerson stands, therefore, not so much as the cause of a literary
revolution, or even the dominant influence, but rather as a paradigmatic
figure in whose mind, at the time of the most marked discontinuity in
American poetry, the divergent stresses pulled visibly. In an early verse-
book, in lines that foreshadow the poem "Grace," appear the incessantly
opposing vectors of convention and free movement: "Him strong Genius
urged to roam / Stronger Custom brought him home" (*VP*, 65).[4]

We follow in Emerson an explicit struggle to force the emergence of a
new poetic consciousness and expressive idiom. It was no jingoistic campaign of the Know Nothing school of poetry to promote stock symbols of
nationality like the bald eagle and the buffalo. Rather, his was a deep aesthetic penetration into the literary master-current of his epoch.

In a still larger theoretical context, he stands as an exemplary figure in
the crisis in the relationship between poetry and reality in the mid-nineteenth century. He labored at the crucial divide between a poetry that had
become deaf to the sounds of its time, deprived of the body of its surrounding reality, and the poetry that was to supersede it—open, flexible, of diminished literariness, capable of great absorption and resonance, conso-
nant with a broad and manifold reality.

This study of the Emerson idiom thus looks directly into the deep discontinuity in American poetry a century and a quarter ago, and into the new
correspondence of art and experience that emerged. His deliberate search
for a redeeming form portrays the coming-into-being of poetic structures
by which we identify the modern literary era. In the impassioned energies
of his writing and his poetic desiderata we confront the full achievement of
the American artistic imagination.

More broadly yet, we perceive the phenomenon of literary innovation:
the nature of its arrival, embodiment, and theory as tradition converges
with individual need. Inevitably we begin to uncover the root of modern
forms and attitudes. There is a glimpse of literary revolution, the structure
of which we barely understand.

One of the keys to Emerson's theoretical structures is to see how his poetics assumes its intricate expression in his prose. In the end, his defense of
poetry stands as the defense of his prose, and both the theory and the prose
represent a new grammar of enormous intake, what he meant by "being
altogether receptive." In the practical employment of his theory he was
true to his belief that theorizing, "profuse declamation" as he called it, was

nothing as compared to "new matter" itself (*JMN,* VII, 431).[5] Emerson had not resigned himself to a victoryless struggle against elusive forces. The crisis in art demanded more than railing, of which the reviews and papers were full. He actively emptied out the old vintages of Europe—the attitudes and the embellishment—and prepared the times for a liberating new fundamentalism: "We shall not have a sincere literature, we shall not have anything sound and grand as nature itself, until the bread eaters and water drinkers come" (*JMN,* IX, 422). His essays, as consciously crafted and as attentive to form as poetry—yet opening out verbal fields designed after the Musketaquid pastures—were the immediate triumphs of the new prosaicism.

The passage to these new artistic anatomies involved a deep contradiction: though the consciously deployed imperatives of his philosophy impoverished his poetry, the aesthetic sweep generated by the deep structure of that philosophy created in his prose the principle of heuristic form by which poetry after his perceived a richer and denser reality. In short, the poetry failure and the prose triumph were inseparable. Thus, for the first time, we can fully relate his poetics to his work. Such a relationship is not the common presumption in Emerson studies. The stereotyped image of an aloof Emerson, withdrawn from the sensational world into an inner imperialism, persists. A similar misconstruing of aesthetic terms exists in F. O. Matthiessen's commentary, for all the general brilliance of his treatment: "We can hardly assess Emerson's work in the light of his theory of language and art, since there is such disproportion between this theory and any practice of it."[6] Quite to the contrary, between the theory and the practice flows a profound and generative force.

So obsessive was Emerson's theoretical concern with art form and its reconciliation with experience (the journals record it from as early as 1819) and so thoroughly homeomorphic were his works that even the occasional poem "Concord Hymn," rote possession of American schoolchildren, is, as we shall see, a compact theory of poetry.

Ultimately, the poetry, the prose, and the theorizing represented a network of obsessions. The nuclei were three: first, the faith that the material world rightly seen would yield its meaning (the process is a conversion; Emerson's impatience to effect this in his poems cost dearly in texture and conviction); second, the downward thrust (what Jonathan Bishop calls "decendentalism")—a reversal of the soaring abstractness of the conversion principle—to take hold of total experience, which in the aesthetic realm was an obsession with the reconciliation of art and reality; and, third, Emerson's lifelong rejection of single systems of life and thought. "I wish to break all prisons" he wrote in his journal on October 17, 1840. Reconciliation demanded a new mathematics for taking up the full world. Liberation both made this possible and was its fundamental result. In Emerson's distillation, "the magic of liberty . . . puts the world like a ball in our hands" (*W*, III, 32).

To penetrate to the generative center of his poetry failures and then come back out by way of the poetics and the prose to his theoretical breakthrough and his major artistic achievement, I have pursued some structuralist activities. My goal, to borrow partly from a felicitous phrase of J. Hillis Miller's, has been to find in the natural synchrony of the public and private work as a whole the fundamental project of Emerson at its most elementary level and, then, to see the project in its aesthetic significance. In this pursuit, I hope to contribute to the sharpened image of Emerson emerging from the scholarship of Stephen Whicher, William Gilman, Jonathan Bishop, Carl Strauch, Hyatt Waggoner, R. A. Yoder, Lawrence Buell, and others. Bishop defined part of the goal: "to be as sure as we can of the action the chief essays and poems seek to define in the half-disguise of words."[7] I maintain that the essential nature of that action is aesthetic. I have tried to state the argument concisely because in truth the issue is a relatively simple one and, to paraphrase Whitehead, prolonged discussion is a source of confusion. Beyond this, I have tried to suggest how poetry-vision in the twentieth century down to our own day reenacts some of the illuminations in Emerson's seekings, and has been shaped inevitably by configurations similar to his thought forms. My concern, let me emphasize, has not been to map the details of Emerson's impact on individual poets who came after him.

This is a sharply focused book and therefore not exhaustive. It might have been more comprehensive, tracing out influences and a developmental chronology, indeed, looking in more detail at Emerson's work. But I have resisted elaboration beyond defining the basic structures and their transformations. The confirming linguistic analysis of the texts based on the new stylistics is already in progress by others.[8] I have also stopped short of the alluring prospect of associating the aesthetics with Stephen Whicher's developmental view of Emerson's transcendentalism steadily giving way to a fundamental empiricism. Although I have not made a poem-by-poem analysis, I trust I have succeeded in opening up the fuller dimensions of the poetry. Readers will look at the poems, perhaps, with new eyes and, one hopes, with greatly increased interest.

The basic formal discriminations in Emerson's art have been bypassed in comprehensive studies of American poetry. I am, in effect, tracing a deep faultline in the field where others find continuity. When we discuss the poems as aesthetic constructs and not mainly as philosophy or cultural products, we discover a different set of emphases, not the least important of which are the deep formal structures. Many valuable books exist on areas I touch only peripherally: origins of Emerson's ideas, his persistent themes, their development, the traces of his composition habits and revisions. Much more will be possible in the way of genetic study when the Centenary Edition of Emerson's works, although sufficiently authoritative for my present purposes, is superseded by the new Harvard edition and a variorum presentation of the complete poems. I have been single-mindedly concerned with the basic structure of his poetic theory and the nature of his formal innovation at a watershed in American poetry.

I have said the book is a journey to the center of Emerson's poetry and back out to his achievement as an artist. I begin by surveying the surface characteristics that impoverish his poetry and by uncovering the sources of those qualities in his poetic thought. I then follow the transformations of the deep structure in the poems. Finally, I trace Emerson's theoretical penetrations and the emergence of his brilliant formal innovations. Near the end I outline some of the implications of these new anatomies for modern American poetry.

The subject of poetic form after Emerson is complex and takes us to primary considerations of forms of poetry and fields of vision. The passage Emerson made from closed poetic vision to a broad reconciliation of art and reality foreshadowed the later formal undertakings of Eliot and Pound, Crane and Olson and Williams, Stevens, Lowell, and others. Although specific lines of influence are not my concern here, it is clear that the ramifications of those earlier theoretical efforts are still in motion and await a proper mapping. Emerson's relationship to the moderns will then be accurately established by the discovery, with the acute observations now possible, not of a continuity of themes but of American poetry's particular time, that is, the history of its forms.

The fundamental irony is that the Emersonian form inevitably invited the dominant modern attitudes of anxiety and disconfirmation, the darkening of the bright vision to which his own saltatory form was wholly compatible. But Emerson had said: "Since every thing in nature answers to a moral power, if any phenomenon remains brute and dark it is because the corresponding faculty in the observer is not yet active" (*W*, III, 15). The alternative we know is also valid: if language-vision is fragmented and secular, the phenomenon it perceives will also be fragmented and secular. By this consideration we touch the bedrock correlation of poetry and vision.

The world we live in is the words we use, a way of speech is a hypothesis about that world. In view of the transformation of the poet's world since Emerson's time, we may put the evolving relationship this way: a particular arrangement of language, divorced from the vision that helped to shape it, will induce about the world an attitude appropriate to the form itself and not necessarily to its philosophical origin. What remains then is the vision inherent in that form. I quote Picasso later on: "once a form has been created, then it exists and goes on living its own life." Because of this, the Emersonian composition opened up some views of the wasteland.

CHAPTER 1

Poetry Warps Away from Life

EMERSON'S POETRY was an art *in extremis*. Matthew Arnold announced on his American tour in 1883, the year after Emerson's death, that it was "touched with caducity." Though he praised Emerson extravagantly to the Americans for a clear and pure voice that brought a strain as new and moving and unforgettable as the strain of Newman or Carlyle or Goethe, Arnold came to a strict estimate: "in truth, one of the legitimate poets, Emerson, in my opinion, is not. His poetry is interesting, it makes one think; but it is not the poetry of one of the born poets."[1]

The contradiction reflects a long tradition of divided judgments about Emerson. Yet his small success as a poet, by a stunning paradox, is inseparable from the brilliant invention of form that simultaneously came into being in his work. This is the reason for turning at the beginning to Emerson's problems as an artist rather than to his achievements.

Locating infelicities in specific poems constitutes the leaden chore of a century of Emerson criticism.[2] Finding the cause of those defects, however, remains to be accomplished; it requires seeing beneath the surface awkwardnesses of individual poems to the deeper faultlines within the body of verse. From there we can establish a new perspective by which to understand how Emerson liberated his art. To know finally why his poetry has the character it has, we must see its main structural parts. The first result of this inward reading will be to see how the poetry is impoverished of life, abstracted from the reality by which its own life must finally be measured.

The hazard of abstracting, as Emerson himself recognized in the fullness of his career, is a kind of poetic forgetting: "Poppy leaves are strewn when a generalization is made . . . I can never remember the circumstances to which I owe it, so as to repeat the experiment or put myself in the conditions" (*W*, IX, 479). Kenneth Burke called it "beyonding."[3] This is not to

7

say the poems are without virtue. If they are passionless and abstract, they are also spare and not dismally sentimental. If generally they have a peculiar indeterminate quality, they are surprisingly interesting for their interior drama. But the majority critical opinion over the years has not been kind to Emerson's poetry. It has been judged cold and bloodless, excessively philosophical, mystical and nonsensical, egotistical, an icy fish. Early reviews called attention to the dismaying qualities. Ralph Rusk described Emerson's contemporary reader as "a traveler suddenly set down in an arctic landscape, immensely impressed if he could properly adjust his vision, but perhaps chilled." He continued: "intellectual pallor and the brevity and irregularity of lines and meter were the faults that impressed one most in this book [*Poems,* 1847]." Caroline Sturgis, a contemporary, warned Emerson against abstractions, advising him to make sawdust pies with his daughter and hunt rattlesnakes so as to be schooled in concrete realities (Rusk, 312, 320, 307). Matthew Arnold, whose criticism is still among the best we have, said the poems had "no evolution" but rather tended to be series of observations. Concluding a discussion of "The Titmouse," he says of Emerson: "He is not plain and concrete enough, —in other words, not poet enough, —to be able to tell us [what the titmouse actually did for him]. And a failure of this kind goes through almost all his verse, keeps him amid symbolism and allusion and the fringes of things, and, in spite of his spiritual power, deeply impairs his poetic value." More generally, Arnold said of the poetry, using Milton's terms but sounding modern and "new critical," it "is seldom either simple, or sensuous, or impassioned. In general it lacks directness; it lacks concreteness; it lacks energy. His grammar is often embarrassed; in particular, the want of clearly-marked distinction between the subject and the object of his sentence is a frequent cause of obscurity in him. A poem which shall be a plain, forcible, inevitable whole he hardly ever produces."[4] Santayana said Emerson shared with Poe and Hawthorne "a certain starved and abstract quality."[5]

The abstract moral aim of the poetry was a matter of deliberate Platonist emphasis which Emerson declared early in an 1831 journal:

> I write the things that are
>   Not what appears;
> Of things as they are in the eye of God
>   Not in the eye of Man.   (*JMN,* III, 290)

Retreating from the complicated and apparent to the abstract was the inevitable result of Emerson's enormous impatience for the clarity of large truths: "Our little circles absorb and occupy us as fully as the heavens," he said, "the only way out of it is . . . to kick the pail over, and accept the horizon instead of the pail" (*J*, X, 238).

Under the tyranny of such an abstracting design, lively particulars must lie stunned. In a kind of selective destruction, life-producing profusion is pressed by constant mental compaction into hard little aphorisms. One result is that Emerson's poetry creates no engaging dialect, holds few sounds of a private experience, and a reader finds it unnecessary, as it is with Whitman and Dickinson, to learn a special Emersonian poetry language. This is not to overlook how Emerson creates patches of rich detail, of contrast, of voices clearly heard, of modest liberties in prosody, and in his "runic" lines refreshing abruptnesses.[6] But one finds no sustained inventive activity. As readers have noted, stock images dog the poetry: rubies, drops of wine, Alpine heights, stars to deck a woman's hair, and pebbles thrown in ponds. We do not trust them because they are distant from precise reality.

But there are constitutional qualities of the sort Arnold suggested that more deeply tyrannize the poems. Not simply stylistic clumsinesses, they are part of the inescapable character of Emerson's poetry. The most prominent of these properties, beginning with the general tendencies and proceeding to the specific, are linked: the presiding voice, the controlling structures, and the habits of language.

An elevated reserve in the character of Emerson's speaker and a monotonously solemn tone pervade the poetic utterances. The voice troubles us, as it did some of Emerson's contemporaries, because it fails to alter our sense of reality, to remove barriers of reticence, to establish what seems to us important awareness, to make us strange by brute energy.

The Emersonian inertia derives in part from the passive character of the watcher-meditator who speaks in the poems. With important exceptions, it is the habitual stance of Emerson's poetic personae, appearing as early as the poem "Good-bye," written when Emerson was nineteen or twenty. The poem seems to refer to his pleasurable daily return to the Roxbury countryside from his brother's school in Boston where he was teaching. It begins without originality — "Good-bye, proud world! I'm going home":

> I am going to my own hearth-stone,
> Bosomed in yon green hills alone . . .
> [Where] vulgar feet have never trod
> A spot that is sacred to thought and God.

Assertions of a like sort repeatedly convey the static condition of Emerson's observing consciousness. In *Nature*, Emerson's first major work and the program of his thoughts, he wrote that the soul "is a watcher more than a doer, and it is a doer only that it may the better watch" (*W*, I, 60). Elsewhere he admonished the poet to stand apart to wait:

> Sit still and Truth is near . . .
> Wait a little, you shall see
> The portraiture of things to be.

That ideal passivity never disappeared from the poetry. In his intellectual development up to the American Scholar address in 1837, there is projected for *Man Thinking*, the hero of Emerson's talk, a more active role as both influential writer and teacher that he identified with Luther and Milton and that he felt himself becoming.[7] But, for all Emerson's regard for man acting, the persistent identity of his persona is the single consciousness meditating rather than acting. Emerson admired a consciousness, as he said in the poem "Woodnotes II," "Grave, chaste, contented, though retired . . . of all other men desired." In the poetry, although there are fine exceptions, little comes across of a living intensely in public view.

Part of the reason for this reclusiveness was a habit Coleridge called the "despotism of the eye."[8] Wordsworth similarly asserted it in *The Prelude*:

> the eye was master of the heart,
> . . . in every stage of life
> The most despotic of our senses.

The visualist notion of reality, brilliantly remarked by D. H. Lawrence, produced in Emerson a highly selective subject-object distinction that abstracted experience, made the observer content with a few preferred signs of infinity, and remained insensitive to the lines of reverberation and distortion between mind and object.

This confined field of vision in the poems is crucial. The perceiving imagination, because of the eye's mediation and the mind's abstract ends, took account in reality only of those experiences that were convertible into mental and moral equations. The Platonist view was limited in Emerson's poems to things seen as part of a moral system about which it could be said they are *not this but that*. In that deliberate movement toward the moral ideal, contrary compulsions had to be annihilated. These included the concreteness of things and the coarse realities of nature, the "swinish indulgences" as Emerson called them. The correlation between vision and the narrow moralizing consciousness grows quite literal in Emerson's essay "The Poet": "The sublime vision comes to the pure and simple soul in a clean and chaste body" (*W*, III, 28). This formula set severe limitations on the kinds of experience Emerson's imagination could perceive, and the narrow range of experience that could find its way into the poetry was a primary factor in its deprivation.

Still, Emerson's aim in the poems was not to particularize but rather to propel away from the particular to the essence. A reader of the poetry feels suspended, like Hawthorne's Coverdale: "I had never before experienced a mood that so robbed the actual world of its solidity." Where Hawthorne engaged the passionate and conflicting realities of the moral consciousness, Emerson "etherialized," as his contemporaries termed it. There was then little possibility that his poetry would take account of what Lawrence was later to call the "gruesome sort of fantasy" of nationalistic America or the "unravished local America," despite Emerson's call for such a downward vision. Lawrence's terms included, but outside of his journals Emerson's did not, "the great continent, its bitterness, its brackish quality, its vast glamour, its strange cruelty."[9]

Rarely on the face of this withdrawn poetry of Emerson's is there apparent the theoretic activity that would anticipate the descendant poetics of twentieth-century realism. Wallace Stevens defined the ground:

> From this the poem springs: that we live in a place
> That is not our own and, much more, not ourselves
> And hard it is in spite of blazoned days.

Nor did there seem to be a real anticipation, as there was in 1860 by Emily Dickinson, of the bleak modern view characterized by Norman Mailer in the pathological terms the late twentieth century finds so congenial: "the modern condition may be psychically so bleak . . . so plastic . . . that studies of loneliness, silence, corruption, scatology, abortion, monstrosity, decadence, orgy, and death can give life, can give a sentiment of beauty."[10]

From his programmatic moral vision as acted out by his persona came another constitutional depletion of the poetry: the assured declamatory voice of a man measuring his being in a world not of dense implacabilities but of pristine moral lines, a man not in a physical world of contingencies but of immanent moral possibilities. The tone inevitably drives the reader away from the experience of the actual, which is sacrificed to the need of the poetry to make stronger sense. Emerson was being faithful, of course, to a preacherly concept: "the higher use of the material world is to furnish us types or pictures to express the thoughts of the mind" (*W*, VIII, 14). The assertive voice that oppresses the verse is directly linked to the moral purpose. In "The Problem," for example, another poem of curious indetermination, for all its felicities of decisive language one recoils from the weight of the rhetorical questions and lecturing tone which seem excessive for a confessional poem.

> Know'st thou what wove yon woodbird's nest
> Of leaves, and feathers from her breast?
> Or how the fish outbuilt her shell,
> Painting with morn each annual cell?
> Or how the sacred pine-tree adds
> To her old leaves new myriads?
> Such and so grew these holy piles,
> Whilst love and terror laid the tiles.

This sternness, reminiscent as elsewhere of the crushing whirlwind's voice in *The Book of Job*, is relieved momentarily by a personal intrusion near the end of the poem ("I know what say the fathers wise, — / The Book itself before me lies"), but the possessing tone is public and homiletic, reflecting the frequent merging in Emerson's lines of sermon, creed, and poem.

The declamatory tone entails a structural device that may be unique to Emerson and certainly contributes to the characteristic enervation of the poetry. He said in "Poetry and Imagination" that poetry "must be affirmative [meaning not blindly optimistic but true to nature's harmony]. It is the piety of the intellect. 'Thus saith the Lord,' should begin the song" (*W*, VIII, 64-65). This moral aim induced Emerson to enlist a disembodied voice or consciousness. We encounter this curious separation of the poetic speaker almost everywhere in the poetry. Further on in "Poetry and Imagination," Emerson touches on allegory: "The poet must let Humanity sit with the Muse in his head, as the charioteer sits with the hero in the Iliad" (*W*, VIII, 66). The dissociated voice is doubly drained of its power because in the customary structure of Emerson's poems even *it* is *reported* by the speaking person. In "The Sphinx," it is "a poet" overheard; in "Woodnotes II," a pine tree. Such a companion voice, set apart always by quotation marks, effectively distances the reader one more stage from an immediate experience within the poem. This filtering effect, curiously Emersonian, will command our attention in the discussion to come. There are notable exceptions to the ministerial cast. A reader finds that the declaiming second persona succeeds powerfully in "Hamatreya." "Hear what the Earth says" introduces the "Earth-Song," a bold-voiced incantation in runic lines unfettered by obtrusive meter requirements, unabashedly prosaic, intense:

> 'Mine and yours;
> Mine, not yours.
> Earth endures;
> Stars abide —
> Shine down in the old sea;
> Old are the shores;
> But where are old men?

> I who have seen much,
> Such have I never seen.'

In "Bacchus," the primary voice is self-consciously learned and verges on the tendentious and decisive, a first-person imperative with its force not distorted by awkward slopes to its line-end rhymes: "Bring me wine, but wine which never grew / In the belly of the grape."

"All writings," Emerson said, "must be in a degree exoteric, written to a human *should* or *would*, instead of to the fatal *is*" (*W*, VIII, 30-31). That moral duty, so exclusionary for the artist, was laid early upon American poetry. Jones Very, in his 1838 essay "Epic Poetry," assumed that obligation to be the artist's as he marked, in a prescient way, the literary attention turning from outward experience to the moral battles in the interior mind. Sampson Reed formulated the coda of an age which linked poetry's moral purpose, its preoccupation with nature imagery, and its assumption of a divine ontology. "By poetry is meant," he said, "all those illustrations of truth by natural imagery, which spring from the fact that this world is the mirror of Him who made it."[11] Emerson's version was a Platonist's equivalent: "A symbol always stimulates the intellect . . . therefore is poetry ever the best reading. The very design of imagination is to domesticate us in another, in a celestial nature." And he added this: the poet "is very well convinced that the great moments of life are those in which his own house, his own body, the tritest and nearest ways and words and things have been illuminated into prophets and teachers" (*W*, VIII, 20, 36).

In willing bondage to these principles, but without the incisiveness of Milton's lines, Emerson's poetry was attenuated. It was art based not on aesthetic needs but on doctrine. It was art processed for ready consumption whose aim Bertolt Brecht was to call, a century later, the "fodder principle." Gertrude Stein was being Miltonic when she called art that sacrificed the reality of particular objects to a principle "pornographic." The hurtful irony as Emerson came to maturity is that, while this moralizing purpose was proudly American in character, celebrated as such, at the same time it was the generic element in the enfeeblement of American verse. American poets, Roy Harvey Pearce has said, "have defended man by showing that he at his best can make sense out of his world, no matter what its inherent confusions."[12] The paradox in Emerson was that the price of those noble clarifications was the vitality of the art itself.

This moral commitment necessarily deflected criticism away from aesthetic concerns, and in the process some of the strengths available to the artistic imagination were neglected. Moral insight brought on aesthetic blindness. In his study of Ruskin, Roger Stein sees the closed conceptual

circuit of Emerson's contemporaries with marvelous clarity: "By identifying the forms of art with the forms of nature and nature itself with Deity,
the transcendentalists made the criticism of art essentially a moral venture."[13] The impoverishment of poetry which approached sermonizing was
in most hands a self-generating process. One way out was the radical innovation toward which Emerson moved. After 1836, key passages show him
entertaining the redeeming view of art as intrinsically self-regarding. Here
is a significant passage in "Poetry and Imagination": "Poetry will never be
a simple means, as when history or philosophy is rhymed, or laureate odes
on state occasions are written. Itself must be its own end, or it is nothing"
(*W*, VIII, 54). The division in the mind of Emerson the artist is coming
into view.

Moral engagement was not confined to Emerson's age. Yeats wrote that
he could see that the literary element in painting and the moral element in
poetry were "the means whereby the two arts are accepted into the social
order and become a part of life, and not things of the study and the exhibition."[14] To Emerson's Platonist mind, moral concern also meant a kind of
objectivity, an avoidance of the inwardness of what he regarded as the
worst kind of romantic poetry. It remained to Lawrence, characteristically, to reveal the scandalous nature of this obsession with moral clarity:
mentalizing everything "makes a vicious living and a spurious art . . . Everything becomes self-conscious and spurious, to the pitch of madness."[15]
Part of the counterfeit derives from the inherent solemnity of moral art.
Poetry of principled order and meditation lacks saving self-deprecation
and a release from gravity; it necessarily avoids the random ironies that
digressive fullness and a reaching for actual experiences threaten.

The audience implied by Emerson's poetry is equally significant. To the
extent that the poetry delivered sermons, it presumed an audience joined
in a common moral enterprise. The audience existed not as a congregation
of individuals capable of winning through to difficult judgments but rather
as a homogeneous group to be reached by simple designs and admonitions.
Whitman, on the contrary, was to regard his audience as individuals who
could be approached one by one — "Crossing Brooklyn Ferry" is a model of
the kind — and he fashioned an intimacy of expression layered with subtle
activity. He invited private gestures rather than the passivity of a decorous
audience. The designs of poets on their audience reveal in part their primary intentions. If Whitman prepares his audience by a kind of linguistic
foreplay to receive the infusion of soul he proposes in "Crossing Brooklyn
Ferry," Emerson's design is rather to persuade his audience to a collective
intellectual discovery. Poe, more conspicuously musical than either, con-

ceived his audience as mesmerizable, seeking sonorous disembodiment and flight from rational meaning.

Unlike Whitman and Dickinson, who were ahead of their audiences, laying verbal traps, contriving snares of candor outside the conventions, Emerson joined other American poets in reinforcing the audience's ideas and playing to their expectations.[16] The construction of a moral ideal was incompatible with unprecedented experience of the noise of complexity. Poe had distinguished between *richness* in a poem — meaning suggestiveness, unexhaustible implications — and the *ideal*. They are incompatible qualities and are not to be confounded. In Emerson's poems, meaning displaced particularity, morality displaced reality, and clarity displaced body. The world was glass.

The tonal qualities Emerson addressed to this undifferentiated audience which, unlike his Lyceum audiences, he could not see, thus add their own weightiness to the poetry. The imperative mood intrudes, regularizes, limits the audience's responses. To the extent he avoided an effective particularity, he created distance, then blockage and the strict reserve of the poet as public figure. Stiffness is even notable in the Ellen poems, depending as they do on phrases drained of emotion and made sterile by the habit of a public pose. Yet Emerson's craving to make a personal cry is felt close at hand by a reader even so. It was achieved only under the terrible pressure of grief at his young wife's death in 1831. With the aid of Carl Strauch's edition of the unpublished poems, along with his invaluable discussion of them, we can see this astonishing breakout. Lines from the poem "To Ellen," first printed in the Centenary Edition, evince the public role:

> if I read the page aright
> Where Hope, the soothsayer, reads our lot,
> Thyself shalt own the page was bright,
> Well that we loved, woe had we not.

The journal poem beginning "Dost thou not hear me, Ellen," written within days of Ellen's death, still moves with a public decorum:

> Dost thou not hear me, Ellen,
> Is thy ear deaf to me,
> Is thy radiant eye
> Dark that it cannot see?   (*JMN*, III, 228)

Later in the same journal, a second Ellen poem holds Emerson's desolation directly to the light. Here we have "the fatal *is*"; the transforming power of natural symbol has collapsed and the attention turned inward, the language moving in blank verse so loosely in the middle lines that it is close to prose.

Teach me I am forgotten by the dead
And that the dead is by herself forgot,
And I no longer would keep terms with me.
I would not murder, steal, or fornicate,
Nor with ambition break the peace of towns,
But I would bury my ambition,
The hope and action of my sovereign soul,
In miserable ruin. Not a hope
Should ever make a holiday for me.
I would not be the fool of accident,
I would not have a project seek an end
That needed aught
Beyond the handful of my present means.
The sun of Duty drop from his firmament
To be a rushlight for each petty end.
I would not harm my fellow men
On this low argument, *'twould harm myself.*

Emerson relies in his finished poems on syntax, aiming at the mind more than the ear. One can say of his verse what Donald Davie said of *The Prelude,* that the syntax "presents what is really going on, meditation, not argument."[17] Syntax, especially when concentrated into epigrammatic form, gives prominence not to sensation but to logical relationship. Straightforward, inaccessible to deviation however psychologically valid, Emerson's poems are designed for the understanding rather than for the more ambiguous currents of feelings. Poetry of clarification is dutifully defined by Emerson in the essay "The Poet." Deliberately ascending above the teeming and distracting world, the poet insists upon an *understanding* of life and consequently upon a view from a distance. The Platonist removal plays a part in the narrow conception of the audience as well as the audience's expectations from the poetry. Emerson rhapsodizes at some length on the reader's liberation, beginning: "With what joy I begin to read a poem which I confide in as an inspiration! And now my chains are to be broken; I shall mount above these clouds and opaque airs in which I live, — opaque, though they seem transparent, — and from the heaven of truth I shall see and comprehend my relations" (*W,* III, 12).

Emerson reinforces the intellectual isolation in several ways: by the imperative form, by the epigrammatic reduction of experience to a strict syntactical construct, and by the habit of aphorism, incising single moral lines through complex existence. Emerson's insistence on touchstone phrases is consistent with the moral aim of his aesthetics; they are grammatically the translation of life into ideas. Even as the grammar holds technically, awkward inversions and all, the life has leaked out.

> The fiend that man harries
>   Is love of the Best.   ("The Sphinx")

> Who bides at home, nor looks abroad,
> Carries the eagles, and masters the sword.   ("Destiny")

> For He that worketh high and wise,
>   Nor pauses in his plan,
> Will take the sun out of the skies
>   Ere freedom out of man.   ("Ode")

The poetry-vision caricatures reality by reducing life to laws, language to propositions, and aesthetic development to the single trajectory of clarification. The pulpit tone, the dissociated voices, the lack of physical gesture, and the absence of a distinct dialect in the poems add up to a poetic practice that sacrifices art to meaning and experiential fullness to the goal of converting the world into idea. The full world itself is finally sacrificed to a language narrowed to the logic of propositions. Emerson's world, like his abstract audience, was inevitably the projection of the language that sought it.

DEEPER THAN the language, restraining it, is Emerson's distinctive linear schema. Its origin and effect seem clear enough. As the poems record a rationalized, most often symbolic, experience, the activity necessarily unfolds in sequence. The encounters and thoughts of the speaker-meditator proceed to a conclusion, almost without exception to a revelation. Where Whitman muses, retraces, digresses, gathers up, echoes, kneads experience, often with a fine illusion of randomness, the poems of Emerson proceed deliberately, excluding experience and particularity all along the line. They are devices of separation in the service of a vision that imposes denouements. The syntax mirrors this, as does the prosodic awkwardness of means. Perhaps Fenollosa was right, we do not always sufficiently consider that thought is successive — but there is no escaping the successive arrangement of Emerson's poetry.

In lining up the mind to seek revelatory significance, Emerson necessarily slighted what poetry has known since Homer, what Lionel Trilling called the "exquisite particulars." The returning in poetry after Emerson to the concrete, as we see it initiated by Whitman and Dickinson, evidences the collapse of faith, however unconsciously, in those universalizing processes of mind that Emerson celebrated in his poems. His occasional excursions into particularity tend to be innocuous, rarely touching human mystery with details of the psyche or body. Catalogues sometimes constitute his specifics, as does the long one in a fragment on nature that begins

> Come search the wood for flowers, —
> Wild tea and wild pea,
> Grapevine and succory,
> Coreopsis
> And liatris,
> Flaunting in their bowers.

The flowers have no visual existence, only names, and the names are there because they rhyme or almost rhyme. We pause at the line "Nerv'd leaf of hellebore" because it stands out as a visual mark. The great peculiarity of poetic language, Winifred Nowottny has said, is its power to bridge or seem to bridge the gap between what has meaning but no particularity and what has particularity but no meaning.[18] Emerson's structures led to meaning, with the particulars exploited for the purpose of reaching a philosophical revelation. An example in a familiar early poem is the closing passage of "Each and All." Despite the catalogue of forest items, their palpable being is sacrificed to the immanent revelation solemnly waiting at the end of the list. The poem marches undistractedly toward the revelation, a version of Emerson's famous eyeball experience in the final lines. Until we know more of Emerson's habitual concerns, we see only names.[19]

> The ground-pine curled its pretty wreath,
> Running over the club-moss burrs;
> I inhaled the violet's breath;
> Around me stood the oaks and firs;
> Pine-cones and acorns lay on the ground;
> Over me soared the eternal sky,
> Full of light and of deity;
> Again I saw, again I heard,
> The rolling river, the morning bird; —
> Beauty through my senses stole;
> I yielded myself to the perfect whole.

There is no accumulated conviction, but rather only an authoritative declaration. The poem is embarrassed by its spurious revelation, a moral coin not earned but simply declared like a dividend.

Henry Adams spoke in the *Education* of wanderers who have perhaps alone "felt the world exactly as it is." The abandonment of this sort of exactitude, the relishing of irrelevance and what Ezra Pound was to call local taste, created Emerson's impoverishing abstracts. His predisposition was clear and concise in a fragment collected under the title "The Poet": "What parts, what gems, what colors shine, — / Ah, but I miss the grand design" (*W*, IX, 331). Though Emerson would admonish the poet to "Hunt knowledge as the lover wooes a maid" ("Written at Rome, 1833"), the fleshed reality is not finally the poet's proper focus:

> [The muses] turn his heart from lovely maids,
> And make the darlings of the earth
> Swainish, coarse and nothing worth.

The paradox at the center of Emerson's poetics has been conspicuous to his readers. We hear the man of poetic imagination saying of the poet, "as everything streams and advances, as every faculty and every desire is procreant, and every perception is a destiny, there is no limit to his hope" (*W*, VIII, 42). Whitman gave verbal body to a comparable vision, but for Emerson it remained mostly a vision haunting his own poetry, stunted as the verse was by its linear structure, impoverished by its epigrammatic language, only rarely able to grasp the possibilities of streaming life, the procreant processes and the "everyness," all that he felt swarming outside the argument of the poems. Possessing this plenitude by language, feeling man's being in it, was to be the astonishing theoretical breakthrough finally forced by his aesthetic needs as an artist.

Whereas Whitman's poems enact a coming into being, adopting their identity as they proceed, Emerson's poems stand as a remembrance, fixed in progression, insisting on significance by the finality of the argument, mechanical in their march toward a preconceived end, non-heuristic in their careful avoidance of the sudden fascinations of random attention, and unreceptive to the pressure of the language as it breeds its own meaning. We are reminded periodically that modern poetry has to do with a person *having* thoughts, not with the thoughts a person *had*. The formulation enables us to identify another characteristic of Emerson's poetry, its reportorial quality. Emerson's poems are *about* life, testimonials to an experience elsewhere than in the poem and prior to it. They are transitive poems, concerned with the revelation they record more than with the cumulative experience along the way. Wallace Stevens makes the distinction in "An Ordinary Evening in New Haven": he can conceive of monuments as littered newspapers, that is, palpable things not about events or people—a statue about George Washington, say—but objects in themselves, as newspapers, blown by the wind, are not *about* fires, theft, rape, and war, but rather pulpy flowers tumbling at the curbs. We can notice the recurrence of the figure of the poet-as-builder in Emerson's poetry. He conceived of poems as constructed after a master plan, the final shape already in the mind of the maker before he begins. "Great design belongs to a poem," he declared, "and is better than any skill of execution,—but how rare! I find it in the poems of Wordsworth, — Laodamia, and the Ode to Dion, and the plan of The Recluse. We want design, and do not forgive the bards if they have only the art of enamelling. We want an architect, and they bring us an upholsterer" (*W,* VIII, 33). He calls for substance, not surfaces, but it is clear his formulation has no place for improvisation or for finding in irrelevant particulars the vitality of the unforeseen. It was thought's tyranny.

The fact-to-truth design of Emerson's poems constitutes their characteristic structural set. It is a grammar of monumentality, of prior thought and anticipated outcome. We recognize sharp differences between poems that transfer attention from experience to concept, and poetry that is intransitive and concerned with relationships, their permutations, the discoveries available in the contemplation of balances, the irony, and finally with the possibilities of language itself as it becomes dramatically self-regarding. Emerson's poems center on images of ideas rather than bodies. In the fragment "Transition," in the image of trees the movement characteristically disperses matter into concept. It is a summarizing image for Emerson, the leafless trees diffusing themselves into the air

> ever subdividing, separate
> Limbs into branches, branches into twigs,
> As if they loved the element, and hasted
> To dissipate their being into it.

Tension on the line that leads from fact to idea in Emerson's poems rarely develops because the success of the process rarely fails. Frost's poems, Emersonian in origin, are saved from a similar innocuousness precisely because Frost explores all the the anxieties that Emerson left out. Revelation is engagingly immanent in Frost (in "The Most of It," "Two Look at Two," "The Woodpile," even "Mending Wall"), but it is habitually denied. The man in "The Most of It" cries out for the world to signal its counter-love for him. The living creature that seems about to respond to this cry,

> Instead of proving human when it neared
> And someone else additional to him,
> As a great buck it powerfully appeared,
> Pushing the crumpled water up ahead,
> And landed pouring like a waterfall,
> And stumbled through the rocks with horny tread,
> And forced the underbrush — and that was all.

The situation trembles with possibility, but the tension is never relieved. When it is, for example in "A Tuft of Flowers," the poem's strength diminishes in ratio to the cosiness of the revelation: "men work together . . .

whether they work together or apart." Emerson's poems go on without in-
terruption and the language looks ahead, excluding the hazards of the experience and dissipating vitality as the tree in its upward divisions dissolves
in the airy elements.

Emerson constructed his poems according to his training under Edward
T. Channing in rhetoric and oratory wherein language was conceived as
the clothing of thought.[20] "I had rather have a good symbol of my thought,
or a good analogy, than the suffrage of Kant or Plato," he wrote later (*W*,
VIII, 13). His notion of thought as prior to poetry, of poetry as a "metre-
making argument," flows directly from his controlling metaphor of the
cosmic soul, which was the origin as well of so many of the dissociated
voices that enter his poetry. The poet is "an exact reporter of the essential
law. He knows that he did not make his thought, — no, his thought made
him, and made the sun and the stars" (*W*, VIII, 39). Emerson's poetry is
the language of that reporting. His syntactical organization of the essential
law involved equations and propositions. It was an arrangement of conviction, exclusion, clarification, and of a steady reluctance to indulge in the
irrelevant. It involved mental closure rather than elaboration. To be
strong, Donald Davie says, poetic syntax "must bind as well as join, not
only gather together but fetter too. The actual function of meaning,
'which calls for permanent contents,' *must* be fulfilled. Verse may be
'strong' or it may 'aspire to the condition of music': it cannot do both."[21]
Emerson yearned for music in his verse, but he insisted on meaning. He
was therefore never fully to achieve a flowing form for his own poems so
that they could sweep outward to monitor an unfinished reality. Instead,
Emerson's poems swallowed the world. They are converting systems, trimming the cumbersome world and shaping it to fit an idea already formed.

Thus not only was the poetry famished, to use Emerson's term, but so
was the correlative world that the poetry saw. His assertive and rigidly closing poems perceived a purposeful world whose significance was the object
of the poetic undertaking. The world was *exemplum* rather than reality in
a state of becoming.

Reflections of this mentalizing system show in the imperatives of Emerson's poetry, early and late. In "To Rhea," to which we shall return later,
the rudimentary pattern of conversion stands revealed by the preferences
in syntax. The not-this-but-that construction projects an obsessive sense of
the two-termed mental strategy of the paradox. Illustrative lines can be
picked almost at random: "Not with flatteries, but truths, / Which tarnish
not, but purify"; "Thy softest pleadings seem too bold, / Thy praying lute
will seem to scold; / Though thou kept the straightest road, / Yet thou

errest far and broad" (*W*, IX, 9-10). The poem stands essentially as a proposition that insists on a neat intellectualized displacement of selfish possession by divine generosity, of a small aspiration by a godly one, that is, of
the half gods by the gods. A reader will not find a fully experienced dilemma of troublesome love and disappointment. The poem proceeds instead by terms of logical discourse: not-but, if-then, thus, and whereby. To
the extent that these connectives hold the diction and direct the progression of the poem, they exclude whatever lies outside the rationalizable. In
the end, the impoverishment is linked to the poem's formulaic designs and
the distance they place between the reader and contingent reality. What
remains is intellect holding a set of equal balances, viewing life as a proposition, not this shadow but that truth.

The doubleness in "To Rhea" pervades Emerson's poetry and constitutes
one of the characteristic expressions of the conversion system that is their
primary structure. Binary patterns appear wherever an interested reader
looks. In "To Rhea," phrase after phrase shows how the incessant doubles
hammer along: "to the blind and deaf," "of gods or men," "his study and
delight," "that creature day and night," "Adorn her as was none adorned,"
"Statelier forms and fairer faces." The march of equivalences is epitomized
in the terminal proposition: "the god, having given all, / Is freed forever
from his thrall." Duality is enforced by the regularity with which these
phrasal units and line ends coincide. The poem is a toted-up column of
double propositions. Moreover, the doubleness and attendant line-end correspondence are compounded by being hammered home, for better or
worse, with rhymes.

This doubleness set the equation that resolved the world into clarity.
Even Emerson's more supple poems are overtaken by language rigid with
ideas of concord. Strong colloquial rhythm begins the "Ode: Inscribed to
W. H. Channing," with full-blooded, libertarian passion over Daniel Web-
ster's support of the Fugitive Slave Act apparent in the edgy lines.

> Though loath to grieve
> The evil time's sole patriot,
> I cannot leave
> My honied thought
> For the priest's cant,
> Or statesman's rant.
>
> If I refuse
> My study for their politique,
> Which at the best is trick,
> The angry Muse
> Puts confusion in my brain.

The poem falls into a drumming march, however, as it looks to its conclusion after reminding the reader that "There are two laws discrete, / Not reconciled, — / Law for man, and law for thing":

> Foolish hands may mix and mar;
> Wise and sure the issues are.
> Round they roll till dark is light,
> Sex to sex, and even to odd.

The language continues on in thrall to the mind's duality and its countervision of the world as a proposition even in the bitterness of its ending:

> The Cossack eats Poland,
> Like stolen fruit;
> Her last noble is ruined,
> Her last poet mute:
> Straight, into double band
> The victors divide;
> Half for freedom strike and stand; —
> The astonished Muse finds thousands at her side.

In contrast to the more flexible aspects of form which a reader would expect to flow from Emerson's basic assumption of the organic circularity of the world, his major poems were, with few exceptions, linear in their structural development, logical in moral progression, and supremely intellectual in their closures. There is a strong necessity for ordered thoughts and definable emotions, and consequently a need for formal strategies. With later Emersonian poets — Williams is a good example — we cross to the other side of the divide, where *knowing* is abhorrent, forms are nonclosing, and structure itself is significant according to the shape of its progressions or, as in Pound's cantos, refractions. With the poet's conscious intention, novel forms signify in their own nonverbal way, and the poems are the richer in experience for these formal conveyances. In the strict poetics from which Emerson was to liberate himself, the poem's formal elements were conceived as packaging devices. He said of rhyme, for example, "We do not enclose watches in wooden, but in crystal cases, and rhyme is the transparent frame that allows almost the pure architecture of thought to become visible to the mental eye" (*W*, VIII, 52). The familiar emphases are here: the architectural metaphor and the abstracting consciousness. In Emerson's conception, a poem was a transfer of knowledge, where a reader is not expected to feel his life in manifold new ways but rather to locate himself intellectually.

But in attempting to fashion those ideal transparent prosodic frames, Emerson made them all the more obvious. In the end, they formed such a rigid container that his thought in turn was caricatured. No matter how adventurously he theorized on the way out of this dilemma, he was unable to accomplish the liberation in the poetry. The obtrusiveness of the prosodic maneuvers was hauled directly to his attention by Thoreau in his famous critique: "I have a good deal of fault to find with your 'Ode to Beauty.' The tune is altogether unworthy of the thoughts. You slope too quickly to the rhyme, as if that trick should be performed as soon as possible, or as if you stood over the line with a hatchet and chopped off the verses as they came out, some short and some long . . . It sounds like parody . . . Yet I love your poetry as I do little else that is near and recent, especially when you get fairly round the end of a line, and are not thrown back upon the rocks" (*W*, IX, 431-432). The conventions that constituted the prosodic boulders on which Emerson planted his feet were to his mind the literary signs of his poetry. In the prose, where his radical aesthetics took form, we see a heady repudiation of such literariness. But his evident need for those poetry signals bound Emerson to a cartoon of poetic form: conspicuous rhyme, strained sonorities, balanced ideas, cadence overpowering diction, paradox in the service of conversion, and all of the prosodic regularities that led to those moral, summing-up equations.

His mode of composition started with a prose statement of the idea to be versified. The process is of a piece with the aesthetic supposition in the idea of a meter-making argument. Edward Emerson printed the following lines as one of the "early rhythmic ventures" from which evolved "Solution," a later poem that appeared in Emerson's 1867 volume. As was often true of Emerson's exploratory lines, suspended between prose and verse, they possess stark power:

> I am the Muse,
> Memory's daughter,
> I stood by Jove at the first, —
> Take me out, and no world had been
> Or chaos bare and bleak.
> If life has worth, I give it,
> And if all is taken, and I left,
> I make amends for all.
> Long I wrought
> To ripen and refine
> The stagnant, craggy lump
> To a brain
> And shoot it through
> With electric wit.
> At last the snake and dragon
> Shed their scales,

And man was born.
Then was Asia,
Then was Nile,
And at last
On the sea-marge bleak
Forward stepped the perfect Greek;
That will, wit, joy might find a tongue,
And earth grow civil, Homer sung.   (*W*, IX, 477)

The first stanza of the poem appeared refashioned this way in *May-Day and Other Pieces*:

I am the Muse who sung alway
By Jove, at dawn of the first day.
Star-crowned, sole sitting, long I wrought
To fire the stagnant earth with thought:
On spawning slime my song prevails,
Wolves shed their fangs, and dragons scales;
Flushed in the sky the sweet May-morn,
Earth smiled with flowers, and man was born.
Then Asia yeaned her shepherd race,
And Nile substructs her granite base, —
Tented Tartary, columned Nile, —
And, under vines, on rocky isle,
Or on wind-blown sea-marge bleak,
Forward stepped the perfect Greek:
That wit and joy might find a tongue,
And earth grow civil, HOMER sung.

Several strategies of expansion fill out Emerson's final version to meet the needs of meter and rhyme. Though felicitous emendations appear, much of the direct power of the original disappears in the prolixity. The blunt prosaic temper in the notebook lines holds the page halfway between spontaneous speech and verse, a condition of immense potentiality that Whitman and later artists of the quick, suggestive line were to exploit. But in Emerson's versifying process, the spare, hard words go slack. What seems to have been the original opening, "I am the Muse, / Memory's daughter, / I stood by Jove at the first," puffs out by additional words in the first two lines of the finished poem to make an extended cliché, including the illogic of "sung alway" and the redundancy of "at dawn of the first day." The most successful emendation is "spawning slime," a phrase that lay in prose in another entry in the verse-book. But Asia is expanded artificially to include a shepherd race, as is Nile; the "sea-marge bleak" is then overloaded by Emerson's felt need of cadence to produce the redundant "wind-blown sea-marge bleak." We see the constricting process inherent in

Emerson's notion of language as the clothing of ideas. Impulsive thoughts thrown out in simple strong prose are actually devitalized by being enclosed in a self-conscious literary form which, as Thoreau saw, diluted the original strength Emerson intended. Not the least tyranny was his custom of thinking and therefore of composing separate line by separate line.

In the end, this dutiful laboring to display the strenuously wrought signals of "literature" diverted Emerson's poetry into narrow declamation. "Dissonance / (if you are interested) / leads to discovery," Williams was to say in *Paterson*. Emerson achieved a similar insight only when he sought in less formulaic prose a strategem for dramatizing the mind in a state of becoming. His impatience to make poems of revelation drove him to a prosodic regularity that closed off the dynamic verbal plays possible in a more spontaneous and less formal scheme. He was among the last of the old regime even as he contemplated the new consciousness demanded of poetics. The awareness flashes repeatedly in the Divinity School address, as he proclaims how the idioms of language and the figures of rhetoric usurp the place of truth (*W*, I, 129). The change was to involve a liberation from the idea of closure and finish, that is, from language as monument, to the idea of poetic form as a motion of spontaneous disclosure and infinite suggestion.

Emerson's poetry held insufficient space for the lived world, and yet his imagination aspired to a redeeming liberation. The compulsion occupied the imaginative center of his life and became one of the structural necessities of much that he wrote. His libertarian aesthetic vision permeated his theology: "All who hear me," he told the divinity students, "feel that the language that describes Christ to Europe and America is not the style of friendship and enthusiasm to a good and noble heart, but is appropriated and formal" (*W*, I, 131). In the historically localized meanings of "friendship and enthusiasm," popular concepts that have yet to be adequately explored as cultural bases of American literature, are bundled the impulses of spontaneity, sincerity, openness, and the escape from the confines of formalism, whether in worship or literature. Emerson's aim was ultimately to escape *generic thinking*. The impediment lay in his conventional belief that truth of such a high order was properly the subject only of poetic poems.

To DESCRIBE Emerson's poetry as verse in extremity seems in the light of these observations not too harsh. It is representative of poetry in America that had exhausted its initiative and lost its correspondence with reality. But this warping-away quality is the negative side of Emerson the poet and man of imagination. There would be only limited value in analyzing its impoverishment if the poetry did not display at the same time an intermittent but revealing aspect of his theory of mind from which, in a most fortunate paradox, there also arose the liberating thrust.

Though most of the poetry lacked the genuine resonance of a complex body of experience, a portion of it looked to a new authenticity. It is poetry on the border of prose, risking formlessness and chaos, calling up fuller realms of experience than it habitually did. In that poem of near excruciating self-revelation, "The Discontented Poet," a work neither brought to completion nor published in Emerson's lifetime, glimpses open up of the world his poetic imagination consorted with but rarely took into the poetry. Yet Emerson had suggested in the poem "Music," which was not published in his lifetime either, that even the basest of material would release its beauty under the pressure of conversion.

> in the darkest, meanest things
> There alway, alway something sings.
>
> in the mud and scum of things
> There alway, alway something sings.

Intimations of experience other than mentalized abstractions lurk in "The Romany Girl" from the *May-Day* volume:

> Go, keep your cheek's rose from the rain,
> For teeth and hair with shopmen deal;
> My swarthy tint is in the grain,
> The rocks and forest know it real.
>
> The wild air bloweth in our lungs,
> The keen stars twinkle in our eyes,
> The birds gave us our wily tongues,
> The panther in our dances flies.

In "The Adirondacs," despite Emerson's intention toward the end to extract philosophy from the camping trip ("O world! What pictures and what harmonies are thine!"), and particularly from the news of the Atlantic cable-laying (an event calling for the sort of sustained symbol analysis that has been applied to Brooklyn Bridge), the reality of the excursion ("Hard fare, hard bed and comic misery") endures. The blank verse is firm and natural, and there is an effective deliberateness that reminds a reader of passages in *The Prelude*.

> We crossed Champlain to Keeseville with our friends,
> Thence, in strong country carts, rode up the forks
> Of the Ausable stream, intent to reach
> The Adirondac lakes.

But the passages of apparently artless power are lost in the general impression of strained contrivance. Again we encounter Emerson's speaker as a vaguely concerned watcher-meditator. The consciousness actualized in the poems, subservient to the despotism of the eye, selects the experiences that are convertible into mental matter. The intractable experiences are evaded: nature's mysteries, the unimagined body, whatever resists abstraction or clarification. Emerson's exclusion is deliberate Platonism, as here in a fragment:

> You shall not love me for what daily spends;
> You shall not know me in the noisy street . . .
> Nor when I'm jaded, sick, anxious or mean.
> But love me then and only, when you know
> Me for the channel of the rivers of God
> From deep ideal fontal heavens that flow.

This kind of turning to the ideal realm, at the price of the ambiguous, is sustained by the declamatory tone in the poems and the repeated voice of the moralizing imagination. In its most intellectualized form, that tone is conveyed by Emerson's habitual overheard voices, disembodied minds summoned to testify. They are the ultimate step in the mentalizing of Emerson's poetry. Otherwise to make mortal speakers deliver such thoughts would make them insufferably tendentious or put upon the poems the obligation, which Emerson's revelation-bound forms could not meet, to create adequately dramatic personae. The result is that the speaker is a reporter of spiritual voices, and the poems consequently are doubly removed from the bodied reality from which the ideas sprang. The tone presupposes an audience possessed of communal good sense and motives, willing to be preached to, and demanding little in the way of the idiosyncrasies of life as lived. The designs of this epigrammatic poetry, then, are almost exclusively in the realm of meaning rather than particularity.

In structure, the poems are narrow and predictable because they are linear in disposition, projecting a field of consciousness rigorously discriminating in experience. We hear a voice that has organized experience so as to extract from it a revelation, figuratively passing from the cave to the sunlight. The formula is part of Emerson's persistent notion that the poetic idea stands prior to its language. This narrow idea of the craft enervated so much of Emerson's poetry because it took no account of the disorderly processes of the mind in the act of discovery. We find instead the habit of binary patterns — prosodic, syntactic, semantic, phonological — which create an oppressive symmetry. If there is an identifiable sound in Emerson's poetry, it involves this steady repetition of a bipolar pattern. The grammar of meaning comes too readily and is too little varied. It was Emerson arranging language to affirm "the applicability of the ideal law to this moment and the present knot of affairs (*W*, VIII, 31). The Emersonian poem subsumed life to principle because the vision and the language in which it found its form were corelative and inextricable. One cannot say which came first.

The result is a language that is predominantly addressed to the mind and concerned more with reporting than with creating meaning as it proceeds. It is not gestic; there is a whole realm of verbal possibility outside the habitual range of Emerson's language. We miss there what I have called after Dante the element of digression: a linguistic sweep that incorporates the irrelevant, explores for meaning in new relationships, and arranges the permutations that absorb a particular world.

Wallace Stevens said that the poet lives in the world of Darwin and not in the world of Plato. The dissociation of mind from the language of factual existence was played out in Emerson's poems. It led to Arnold's judgment that the poetry of the American he so much admired for his powerful optimism is seldom sensuous, lacks concreteness and energy, and is thus seriously impaired. A new approach to one of Emerson's major poems will illuminate more basic causes of that impairment and disclose their relationship to Emerson's deeper preoccupations as an artist.

CHAPTER 2

"Threnody": The Hidden Allegory

EMERSON'S ELEGIAC POEM "Threnody" suffers demonstrably from a failure of feeling. It lacks emotional authority and convincing particularity in its portrayal of the son who died, of the relationship of the father to his son, and of the consequent grief. Yet "Threnody" holds in its core the steady shape of Emerson's aesthetic dilemma. The poem rises out of an obsessive poetic theory embodying his concept of the structure of the poetic consciousness. It is this inner meditation on art that preempted, as it did throughout his poetry, the particulars of experience. Whitman's achievement by comparison makes Emerson's problem sharply visible. When Emerson's poetry failed, it was because the inward concern with an ideal aesthetics drained the poetry of its immediacy and personal voice. In "Threnody," the link between the interior poetics and the enervated surface of the verse comes clearly into view.

The subject of the poem is itself significant. Thoreau said "wherever a man *fronts* a fact . . . there is an unsettled wilderness . . . between him and *it*. Let him . . . wage there an Old French war . . . with Indians and Rangers, or whatever else may come between him and the reality, and save his scalp if he can."[1] In our own century, T. S. Eliot sought a comparable stark reality as a vivifying pang in a world of smug social distractions. "The possibility of damnation," he said, raising the ante characteristically to the metaphysical limit, "is so immense a relief in a world of electoral reform, plebiscites, sex reform and dress reform, that damnation itself is an immediate form of salvation—of salvation from the ennui of modern life, because it at last gives some significance to living."[2] Emerson possessed a similar craving. "There are moods in which we court suffering," he said, "in the hope that here at least we shall find reality, sharp peak and edges of truth" (*W*, III, 48). No more sharply piercing example of intractable reality could exist than the death of his son Waldo at age five in 1842, the one incontrovertible and final fact of all. In a ghastly way, Waldo's death constituted an ideal subject for Emerson's converting imagination, which, as he had explained at length in "The American Scholar," changed fact into truth. Could the fact of Waldo's death be converted to an article of faith by the Emersonian mind?

Not only did the subject present the most difficult of tests for the conversion process; it possessed in Emerson's view inherent elements for an exemplary poem. "The poet writes from a real experience, the amateur feigns one," Emerson said. "Talent amuses, but if your verse has not a necessary and autobiographic basis, though under whatever gay poetic veils, it shall not waste my time" (*W*, VIII, 31).

Waldo's death was reality intensified to the crushing point for the man, but even so, reality evaded the artist. With the grey bedrock of fact before him, Emerson had not the language to enter it: "The only thing grief has taught me is to know how shallow it is. That, like all the rest, plays about the surface, and never introduces me into the reality, for contact with which we would even pay the costly price of sons and lovers" (*W*, III, 48). What Emerson sought lay beyond the poetic language of conceptual neatness he commanded. Without a language of dense particularity, his vision was of such broad resolution that intricate reality was in effect invisible to his poems. Of his son's death, he said what might be said of the poem: "I cannot get it nearer to me . . . this calamity; it does not touch me . . . I grieve that grief can teach me nothing, nor carry me one step into real nature" (*W*, III, 48, 49). His crucial need was to fashion language that would enable him, in Wallace Stevens' marvelous phrase, to walk barefoot into reality.

The impeding elements in "Threnody" crowd so thickly they suggest an obsessive hidden negating source. Why is the poem, given the immediacy of the subject itself, far less effective than the corresponding prose passages in the journals? Why exactly does the manifest poem differ so markedly from the possible poem?

"Threnody" dissipates its power in several characteristics that appear in almost all of Emerson's poetry: vagueness, abstraction, withdrawal, and an impatient plot. In other words, the poem never has a chance for individuality because it so resembles its companions in the canon. The Emerson persona is a watcher, and his inaction makes the poem ruminatively static. To compound that inertia, the poem lacks location. Is the initial speaker seated at some distance from his house, looking over the hills, or is he alone in a quiet house, reflecting on the death of the son? The vagueness produces only a generalized way of seeing. Whitman, on the same subject, created precise setting and person with what seem the most casual of strokes:

Come up from the fields father, here's a letter from our Pete,
And come to the front door mother, here's a letter from thy dear son.

Emerson immediately set about abstracting ("Life, sunshine and desire . . . on every mount and meadow") with the purpose of converting the death to a usable idea. The eye dominates in a way characteristic of Emerson ("I see my empty house, / I see my trees repair their boughs"), and although there is a generalized sense of smell (the south wind "Breathes aromatic fire") there is nothing to compare in sharpness to Whitman: "Smell you the smell of the grapes on the vines? / Smell you the buckwheat where the bees were lately buzzing?"

Emerson's flight from piercingly felt particulars is another characteristic gesture in his poetry. Thus in "Threnody" the first speaker's single act of consequence within the meditation is to *withdraw* from the pressing reality. That disengagement takes form in the negatives, the qualifications, the reversals, and the final generalization. The mourning father says of his child:

Not mine, — I never called thee mine,
But Nature's heir, — if I repine,
And seeing rashly torn and moved
Not what I made, but what I loved,
Grow early old with grief that thou
Must to the wastes of Nature go, —
'T is because a general hope
Was quenched, and all must doubt and grope.   (lines 126-133)

A further removal, coming at line 162 just before the sudden shift to the third person, occurs even in the poem's strongest lines:

this losing is true dying;
This is lordly man's down-lying,
This his slow but sure reclining,
Star by star his world resigning.

The poem's design on us as readers is predominantly intellectual, asking our assent to each idealized formulation (for example, "love's . . . streams through nature circling go"; "see the genius of the whole / Ascendant in the private soul") as it points toward resolution in the universal. Patches of particularity (the painted sled, the gathered sticks, the snow-tower) stand precariously on the edge of sentimentality, stock images asking for stock responses. Particular experience that is not otherwise diluted in pastoral elegy conventions is stifled in clichés:

wondrous child,
Whose silver warble wild
Outvalued every pulsing sound
Within the air's cerulean round.   (11-14)

At its basic structural level, this poem, which might have uniquely real-ized the idea of a "metre-making argument," was further deprived of dis-tinction by the habitual Emersonian *plot*. The primary action of this plot is a hurrying toward a single philosophical resolution, a process defined not by the agitation of a complex emotional net but rather by an act of the mind, rational, working almost exclusively toward a release from ignor-ance. No matter what Emerson's theoretical protestations were concerning a meter-making organicism, the narrow path of this revelation-seeking im-pulse determines both the philosophical and structural formulas of the poem. Specifically, the linear plot is a conversion ritual. It begins with the poem's focal consciousness in a state of ignorance and confusion, after which it descends to helpless despair, and then, thanks to revelation, achieves consolation and finally liberation from the grip of error.

An attempt at circular closure shows feebly in "Threnody" (unrestored losses in line 6 become "ruined systems *restored*" seven lines from the end), but the linear figure dominates. Individual elements in the pattern of meditation are thoroughly conventional: the cruel paradox of human death in the face of nature's incessant rebirth (1-29); the child remem-bered, his great promise (30-97); the time and agony of his death (98-109); the lamenter questioning the purpose of this seemingly needless death (110-165); the lamentation (166-175). Only in the coerced resolution im-posed by the deep Heart in the long declamatory conclusion (176-289) do we encounter Emerson in his uniqueness.

The plot to that conclusion advances along the characteristic Emerson-ian path from ignorance that imprisons to knowledge that liberates. The initial loss ("I mourn / The darling who shall not return") is followed by confusion and ignorance ("Was there no star . . . / No watcher . . . / No angel . . . / Could stoop to heal that only child [?]"). Bitter despair results ("I am too much bereft. / The world dishonored thou hast left. / O truth's and nature's costly lie! / O trusted broken prophecy!"), but leads into the consolatory declaration of the deep Heart whose account ends excessively neatly with the balance-sheet entry "Lost in God, in Godhead found." The poem assumes, without depicting it, the speaker's acquiescence in this revelation.

So intently managed is Emerson's deliverance schema that we necessarily remark on the life it excludes. By restricting experience to what could be expressed in such a deliberate structural order, the poem closes its attention to the texture of life. Release from this narrowness by deliberate *digressiveness* appeared inevitably in the work of later poets who went about restoring the world that Emerson had annihilated. In Whitman's poem "Come up from the Fields Father," the perspective sweeps confidently into the surrounding landscape. Whitman turns his poem out to the autumn trees, the villages of Ohio, and to the rain-freshened sky, the farm, and back to the mother's hair and cap, taking account, even as it never loses concern for a young man dead too soon, of the full world:

> Where apples ripe in the orchards hang and grapes on the trellis'd vines,
> (Smell you the smell of the grapes on the vines?
> Smell you the buckwheat where the bees were lately buzzing?)

This lateral attentiveness builds the world's body, defying "clarification" and intellectual satisfaction while it provides currents of sensation which the easy unity of Emerson's typical plot excludes.

Liberation into moral clarity is what Emerson meant by calling his poets "liberating Gods." It is his version of Plato's parable of release from the cave of ignorance. In "Threnody," liberation is the promise of the deep Heart with its "higher gifts" which "unbind / The zone that girds the incarnate mind" (230-231). The inner voice bullies the father out of binding ignorance into moral understanding. For all the poem's explicit promoting of a world where life and love "radiate" and "generate" in a cosmic moral circulation system (242-244), the poem itself finally imposes its own rigid deliverance figure.

This figure terminates in a curious image that recurs elsewhere. Like most of Emerson's poems, "Threnody" recounts a past deliverance of mind and thus stands metaphorically as a monument to "man thinking," to the process by which truth is disclosed within the coarse rock of reality. At the end of "Threnody," God the Maker (one of Emerson's analogues for the poet) erects the symbolic monumental building:

> Not of adamant and gold
> Built he heaven stark and cold;
> No, but a nest of bending reeds,
> Flowering grass and scented weeds.   (272-275)

The exclusive progress of the poem as it converts the son's death into an idea contrasts sharply with Whitman's modernist poetics that aims to *preserve* the intricate mystery of experience and not to hurry its conversion into mental matter. The fundamental difference between the two modes of poetry stands out in a comparison of Emerson's compacted terminal formula "Lost in God, in Godhead found" — where life is excluded by the moral tightness of the syntax — with the close of "When Lilacs Last in the Dooryard Bloom'd." Whitman, after making his poem quite literally before the reader's eyes ("O how shall I warble *myself* for the dead one there I loved?" asks the poet) and after weighing the necessities of both public and private lamentation, concludes not with a formula of clarification but with an image of mysterious density, "in the fragrant pines and the cedars dusk and dim." Just previously, the lamenter in "Lilacs" insists by a crucial emphasis that no part of the lived experience is to be nullified by a final consolation (my italics):

> I cease from my song for thee . . .
> *Yet each to keep and all, retrievements out of the night,*
> The song, the wondrous chant of the gray-brown bird,
> And the tallying chant, the echo arous'd in my soul,
> With the lustrous and drooping star with the countenance full of woe,
> With the holders holding my hand nearing the call of the bird,
> Comrades mine and I in the midst, and their memory ever to keep.

These differences begin in the deepest generative features of Whitman's and Emerson's poetics and practice. Emerson's poetic vision is exclusive, reasonable, and syntactically compacted, where impulse falls victim to an habitual argumentative form; Whitman's mode is centrifugal, digressive, remystifying, and preservative of the complex and contradictory materials of its own making. The differences disclose the root distinction between a poetry that is bound by an inflexible revelation-seeking form, and a new kind of poetry that is experientially centered and self-regarding as an artistic enterprise, yet yielding at the same time to the corelative and sometimes vagrant demands of the language medium itself. These two poetic undertakings stand on facing promontories at the great language divide in American poetry.

Emerson's linear constructions bind poems as ostensibly different from "Threnody" as the early poems "To Rhea" and "The Snow-Storm" and the later poem "The Titmouse." Selections can be made almost anywhere, in fact, so inescapable is his linear plotting. "To Rhea" mirrors "Threnody" in both its surface and interior organization. The poem's evident attention is on how one ought to behave when love is unrequited. Even so, we encounter the now-familiar dissociated voice ("Listen what the poplar-tree / And murmuring waters counselled me") and the initial formulaic situation of agony and ignorance that leads down to despair:

> If with love thy heart has burned;
> If thy love is unreturned;

> Hide thy grief within thy breast,
> Though it tear thee unexpressed;
> For when love has once departed
> From the eyes of the false-hearted,
> And one by one has torn off quite
> The bandages of purple light;
> Though thou wert the loveliest
> Form the soul had ever dressed,
> Thou shalt seem, in each reply,
> A vixen to his altered eye.

The sort of idealized disengagement we saw in "Threnody" is advised: "thou shalt do as do the gods . . . *Who drinks of Cupid's nectar cup / Loveth downward, and not up.*" The poem drives unswervingly to the revelation, which is crowded into one of Emerson's transforming paradoxes: with the god's withdrawal from mortal infatuation, the Universe is "better and not worse." The victim has proceeded from ignorance to knowledge and freedom: "the god, having given all, / Is freed forever from his thrall." As in "Threnody," the conversion formula transforms a loss into an asset.

Once again, also, the monument that is familiar from the elegy for Waldo is constructed to commemorate the liberation. Nature, the dissociated voice, reports to the original speaker (now awkwardly *thrice* removed) what the god says:

> "This monument of my despair
> Build I to the All-Good, All-Fair.
> Not for a private good,
> But I, from my beatitude,
> Albeit scorned as none was scorned,
> Adorn her as was none adorned."

By the poem's design to turn adversity to advantage, the argument proposes that to be the victim of unrequited love is to have the opportunity to be like a god in generosity! In the press of Emerson's formal strictures, feelings are turned into mental matter, the bodied experience converted to a truth, and a monument erected to liberated reason.

The formulaic transition from ignorance to clarity and from helplessness to deliverance unfolds even in so unlikely a situation as that in "The Snow-Storm." The poem begins with furious activity, the analogue of the ignorance that begins the other poems. It takes form here in the storm's confusion and obscuring effect:

> Arrives the snow, and, driving o'er the fields,
> Seems nowhere to alight: the whited air

> Hides hills and woods, the river, and the heaven,
> And veils the farm-house at the garden's end.

Impediments, which are the corollaries of the paralyzing despair in "Threnody" and the grief in "To Rhea," multiply: "The sled and traveller stopped, the courier's feet / Delayed, all friends shut out"; the choking snow "Fills up the farmer's lane from wall to wall, / Maugre the farmer's sighs." Then occurs, typical of the Emersonian withdrawal procedure, the saving disengagement from the turmoil. The storm "when his hours are numbered, and the world / Is all his own, retiring, as he were not, / Leaves, when the sun appears, astonished Art." The inevitable dissociated voice has been transformed into a separate actor who, to complete the formula, is also a builder of monuments. He is the "fierce artificer" who has made the "frolic architecture." The poem's dramatic structure, once again, carries from confusion to clarity, converting experience into statement, moving from dim and clogged activity into the sun, and setting there a sculptured monument to natural revelation.

The poem closes schematically, as do "Threnody" and "To Rhea" ("Each and All" is perhaps the paradigm of the sort), with serene beauty the outcome of the experience, the higher truth displayed, the inconveniences (not to mention tragedies) converted by the revelation-seeking pattern. Emerson's deliverance schema presides over the poem, threatening to exclude a whole contingent world, though in this superb work, unlike "Threnody," the reality of the storm survives the impress of the structural formula.

"The Titmouse" is a late example of the form's tyranny. The speaker, lost in the snow, is confused, trapped initially in formulaic confinement, unable to act:

> I found my lukewarm blood
> Chilled wading in the snow-choked wood.
> How should I fight? . . .
> The frost-king ties my fumbling feet,
> Sings in my ears, my hands are stones,
> Curdles the blood to the marble bones,
> Tugs at the heart-strings, numbs the sense,
> And hems in life with narrowing fence.

In this confusion, the dark prospect of despair (curiously exaggerated) suddenly opens up. The speaker, on the verge of the prescriptive but here suicidal *disengagement,* contemplates death in the snow:

> Well, in this broad bed lie and sleep, —
> The punctual stars will vigil keep, —

> Embalmed by purifying cold;
> The winds shall sing their dead-march old,
> The snow is no ignoble shroud,
> The moon thy mourner, and the cloud.

But, once more, the redemptive path is signaled by a beamed-in voice:

> this way fate was pointing,
> 'T was coming fast to such anointing,
> When piped a tiny voice hard by,
> Gay and polite, a cheerful cry,
> *Chic-chic-a-dee-dee!* saucy note
> Out of sound heart and merry throat.

Hardly the deep Heart's thundering voice but a soulful surrogate even so. The poem turns then to seek from the experience the intelligible simplicities of an idea. The walker concludes:

> "I think no virtue goes with size;
> The reason of all cowardice
> Is, that men are overgrown,
> And, to be valiant, must come down
> To the titmouse dimension."[3]

The speaker here, like the father in "Threnody," is saved by the encounter. As in the other poems, the primary process is one of conversion, from the cold paralysis of resignation to revelation and then release. And, yet again formulaically, the idea into which the experience is converted becomes the inescapable Emerson monument, this time in a written version:

> I will write out annals new,
> And thank thee for a better clew,
> I, who dreamed not when I came here
> To find the antidote of fear.

Emerson's habitual linear plot replicates itself in the constrictions of his syntax and even his prosody. In notable ways, of course, "Threnody" suffers less from mechanical contrivance than other Emerson poems. There is a lower correspondence between phrase ends and line ends in the opening of the poem. There is less reaching for the meter and the rhymes by expansion or inversion, though the poem falls rather soon into a regularly thumping cadence. Generally, too, there is an increased naturalness of diction and syntax. Yet these virtues cannot disperse the oppressive *twoness,* noted in earlier discussion, in the language of "Threnody." More than one line in five teeters on paired parts of speech or phrasal structures. In the last forty-eight lines there are seventeen sets of two:

Line 242 Light is light which radiates
     243 Blood is blood which circulates
     244 Life is life which generates
     253 Beckon it when to go and come
     255 Fair the soul's recess and shrine
     259 Whose omen 't is, and sign
     261 What rainbows teach, and sunsets show
     264 Voice of earth to earth returned
     271 Up to his style, and manners of the sky
     272 Not of adamant and gold
     273 Built he heaven stark and cold
     275 Flowering grass and scented weeds
     278 Built of tears and sacred flames
     280 Built of furtherance and pursuing
     284 Broadsowing, bleak and void to bless
     288 House and tenant go to ground
     289 Lost in God, in Godhead found.

So many pairings, while ingenuously filling out the meter, indicate the crucial fact about Emerson's language-vision in the poetry: it rationalized the world according to a persistent doubleness. The simply balanced couplings programmatically misrepresent the intractable density of experience.

The same exclusive rationalizing quality marked other syntactical preferences. "Threnody" begins with a proposition: "The south wind brings Life . . . But over the dead he has no power." Neither descriptive nor sensation-evoking (compare the sensuous opening prose of the Divinity School address), the construction is as spare as it must be in the service of a purely rational analysis. Once again, Whitman's beginnings are instructive. "Out of the Cradle Endlessly Rocking" sets forth on the trajectory of an adverbial phrase — that is, a syntactical proposition that demands closure — and continues so for nineteen lines before the subject-predicate brings all the lines to ground and assigns their significance. "Lilacs" begins similarly. Where Emerson straightaway excludes experience as "Threnody" deliberately seeks revelation, Whitman's poems begin accumulating experience. Where Emerson's language excludes mystery, occasions for digression, and opportunities for spontaneous discovery and heuristic meanderings and excitements, Whitman's allows all of these. Where Emerson's syntax holds static remembrance — grammatical monuments to ideas extracted from experience — Whitman's language is gestic. It absorbs materials and energy, creates inevitable movement (all those dependent clauses seek a subject), and discovers satisfaction in activity and not in remembrance. A reader participates with Whitman in the creation of meaning in his poetry and does not simply wait, part of the passive audience implicit in the address, tone, and syntax of Emerson's poems. In Whitman, life is spontaneous and open to diversion. In Emerson, it is impatiently converted into mental accounts. So much as his syntax excludes, that is the measure by which the contingent world is diminished.

The basic plot of Emerson's deliverance design is also replicated in individual sentences in "Threnody." The persistence of this plan underscores the habitual angle by which the presiding consciousness perceives in the poem. Sentences and phrases carry the plot of conversion because they are arranged to say that reality is not-this-but-that.

> Line 23 My hopes pursue, they cannot bind him
> 27 Nature, who lost, cannot remake him
> 28 Fate let him fall, Fate can't retake him
> 129 Not what I made, but what I loved
> 138 Perchance not he but Nature ailed
> 139 The world and not the infant failed
> 210 Dearest, to thee I did not send
> 211 Tutors, but a joyful eye,
> 281 Not of spent deeds, but of doing

Conversion plots create more compacted versions in the form of paradoxes, which are the essential intellectual conceit in Emerson. The speaker in "Threnody" weighs the injustice of the paradox that nature cares for the minutest of creation — chick, weed, and rockmoss — while allowing the noble to perish, the "loss of larger in the less!" (117). At the bottom of the speaker's despair, death seems the cruelest denial of the future by the future itself; the boy is "Born for the future, to the future lost!" (175). But other conceits constructed of compensation-seeking paradoxes accumulate significance, adding up to consolation in larger perspective. Thus by line 245 the deep Heart can assert the moral harmony of nature: "many-seeming life is one."

The binary diction and syntax, the sentences that plot the not-this-but-that perceptions, and the paradoxes that expose the good concealed in the bad intersect with distilled purity in the concluding consolatory paradox: "Lost in God, in Godhead found." The syntactical binding of experience, trimming perception to a single angle, inevitably impoverished the poetry to the extent that it simplified life and ignored mystery. Habitual in Emerson's poetry, the same syntactical double knot closes many poems, early and late: "To Eva" ("fire that draws while it repels") and "Hermione" ("Follow not her flying feet; / Come to us herself to meet"); it is part of the closing equation of "Saadi" ("blessed gods in servile masks / Plied for thee thy household tasks") and in "Ode to Beauty" ("Dread Power, but dear! if

God thou be, / Unmake me quite, or give thyself to me!"). It occurs repeatedly in the late poems, in "May-Day," "Ode," "Boston Hymn," "Merlin's Song," "Waldeinsamkeit," and others. We engage Emerson's poetic consciousness most directly by way of his syntax. Narrow in articulation, it so walled-in his poetry that the blocked poetic imagination sought release by opening out the poetic form itself, to where the static language of the abstract might give way to gestic language concerned not with immanence but with process, accumulation, self-discovery, and the dramatic determination of meaning. Poetry in our own day continues to explore with this intricately observant language-instrument. Emerson's breakthrough was already potential in his radical theorizing, but, for the reasons becoming clear in "Threnody," it was not to be accomplished in the poetry.

Although his theory of poetry constrained both the language and the prosody, it manifested itself most curiously in the dissociated voice which, in one guise or another, enters almost all of the poems. It is this split-off voice that shows finally the basic construct of the poetics where the anxiety of failure was acted out. The voice beams into Emerson's poems as if pure spirit were summoned to exhort. Characteristically, as with the deep Heart's voice in "Threnody," it is meant to reverberate out of divinity itself. Its identity was established very early by Emerson in lines from an 1831 poem: "God dwells in thee . . . / He is the mighty Heart / From which life's varied pulses part. / Clouded and shrouded there doth sit / The Infinite / Embosomed in a man" (*JMN*, III, 290-291).

The basis for such separation of consciousness rested securely in Romantic metaphysics. Wordsworth, in *The Prelude,* had plotted the distinction, for example, between love that is "merely human," as between child and parent, and the love that "proceeds / More from the brooding Soul, and is Divine." In "Threnody" Emerson organized the distinction by eyesight. The deep Heart says sternly to the father: "I gave thee sight — where is it now?" (196). The vision is not of "aged eyes" that see but a "short way before" (180), but rather Platonic sight, that of "the man of eld, / Whose eyes within his eyes beheld / Heaven's numerous hierarchy span / The mystic gulf from God to man" (183-186). Superhuman, this eyesight penetrates "the masks . . . That dizen Nature's carnival" (189-190).

The double power of discernment is a basic part of Emerson's model of the poetic consciousness. It is this two-level model finally that forms the inmost structure of "Threnody." The deep Heart, once it takes over the poem, urges upon the grieving man "High omens" which produce "diviner guess," lest he of short sight, fooled by appearance, be "conned to tediousness" (229). Thus set as a conceptual armature within the poem is the

fundamental distinction between *fancy,* to use Emerson's original Cole-
ridgean terminology, in the figure of the grieving father who suffers experience but is blind to its higher significance, and *imagination* (several other
terms would suit here to reflect the stratification), which discerns by superior "sight" the truth the deep Heart proclaims. The first speaker in the
poem, the father, is the experiencer who, because of ignorance, both
doubts and misunderstands. He *mourns* and then *despairs* over the death
of his son. The deep Heart speaks for the divine imagination and reveals
the larger synthesis, argues the consoling significance of the death, and asserts the cosmic order in which the death no longer appears random or,
worse, caused by neglect. Reconciliation comes through this larger vision
that the deep Heart possesses. Emerson was to call this prized faculty
Genius or Reason, and the lower one, Understanding. The two levels of
consciousness operate thus as primary coordinates in the basic allegory of
the poem. There is no pretense of a dialogue in this confrontation between
limited understanding and the supreme imagination. Rather, the mourner's lament disappears with neither rebuttal nor consent.

The separating-out of the reconciling genius from the poet-speaker is
profoundly significant in Emerson's aesthetics. Moral insight in "Threnody" comes from without, from the deep Heart. It must be *impressed* upon
the mourner who, while he mourns, is the *mis*understander. In aesthetic
terms, Emerson's dissociated voice of the deep Heart speaks as the ideal
poet and the father-mourner is a transmuted figure of the poet without
imagination. The father-mourner, like the figure in "Days," is poetic consciousness enfeebled, unable to perform as seer, unable to penetrate, as
genius does, to the reality behind the masks, unable to sing. Emerson's terrible sense of his own poetic failure is seated precisely here. The agony of it,
which bothered him like a gadfly all his life, is measured by the gulf between the failed father in the poem and the deep Heart. It is measured by
the rupture at line 176 in the form of the poem itself.

So strong was his feeling that his verses failed always of music and frequently of genius that the acknowledgment, sporadic in his letters and
stark in the poem "The Poet," also informs his son's elegy. The failure, indeed, is manifested far more widely in the poetry than we have realized. Its
obsessive appearance must force our understanding, finally, of the enormous strength and ultimate centrality of Emerson's commitment to his art.

Identification of the mourning father as the failed poetic imagination
helps to explain the browbeating power of the deep Heart. Again, like the
arrogant voice in Job, the deep Heart is distant, stern, and unremitting in
its preachment:

Wilt thou, uncalled, interrogate,
Talker! the unreplying Fate?
Nor see the genius of the whole
Ascendant in the private soul,
Beckon it when to go and come,
Self-announced its hour of doom?   (249-254)

By projection to the point of sublimation, Emerson berates himself for his poetic failures. The force of his desperation sounds in the tone of the deep Heart's hammering rhetorical questions. At their base structure (again, as in Job and as in Blake's "Tiger") the questions are positive prononcements. Only partially disguised by the transformation, they mount a powerful verbal assault.

Two powerful elements then—the conceptual model of the divided poetic consciousness and Emerson's own dilemma as a poet—weave inextricably throughout "Threnody." The man of aspiring imagination, lacking commensurate language and artistic form, inevitably made that dilemma the under-subject of his poems. Thus we move toward an understanding of all those dissociated voices in Emerson's poems: they are the personified imagination constantly badgering the failed poet.

In this light, we understand how the potential sting of particulars in "Threnody"—the reality of death, of grief, and of the boy himself—are sacrificed to the hidden allegory of artistic failure. The obsession with inadequacy existed at a level apart from Emerson's actual grief, but the preoccupation determined the tone of the elegy. "Threnody" is a study of the failed poetic imagination, and thus it skims over the actuality of the death of the boy and ignores the particular reality because it was not concerned with them.

Emerson's poems embody a constant negotiation between this deeply imbedded aesthetic need and the surface elements of occasion, language, and prosody. Thoreau was exhilarated by the poetry, despite its woodenness, because of that powerful inward poetic imagination consorting incessantly with itself. In this rudimentary dialogue lay both the primary impetus of the poetry and the cause of its incapacitation.

Thematically, the poetics appears in "Threnody" as the Lycidas motif. Though the boy who died is Emerson's son, he is also the paradigm of the promising young poet. No wonder we seek vainly in the poem for immediacy and passionate grief. Instead there is an elaborate choreography of allegorical figures. Genius asserts itself as the deep Heart, and the poet without imagination is the mourning father. The third figure is the ideal boy-poet, and therefore, like Edward King, his death as a poet and the survival of the poetic principle become a crucial focus in the poem. "Threnody" in this way parallels *Lycidas* and other elegies which recognize that art is long while life is short, that the artist, no matter how noble his gift, is vulnerable to random destruction.

The Lycidas theme rises to view in several places. The boy is a prophetic speaker: "his lips could well pronounce / Words that were persuasions" (52-53). He transforms, as does the poet, divine insight into men's terms: "Gentlest guardians . . . Took counsel from his guiding eyes / To make this wisdom earthly wise" (56-57). He hears the celestial music sensed only by the poetic ear: "A music heard by thee alone / To works as noble led thee on" (78-79). Explicitly the boy is the poet-to-be:

> flattering planets seemed to say
> This child should ills of ages stay,
> By wondrous tongue, and guided pen,
> Bring the flown Muses back to men.   (134-137)

Placed topmost by Emerson in his poetic hierarchy, the boy is "A genius of so fine a strain" (141). The meditation on Waldo's death, then, is simultaneously a meditation on the fragility of poetic genius. Bishop has written that "Emerson had fallen into identifying too much of what was most precious and precarious in himself with the life of his son."[4] The identification of the poetic gift with Waldo shows in another perspective how thoroughly preemptive the poetic theory was.

The division between the ostensible subject of Emerson's poems and the persistent deep activity where his feelings of poetic inadequacy faced his stubborn aspiration to expressions of genius produces in the poems a submerged anxiety and at worst a fatal awkwardness. Emerson wrapped mask after mask over his dilemma. But the basic contradiction that lay beneath all the others was the disparity between the bardic power he wanted to sweep over his readers and his static meditation on the ideal aesthetic consciousness of a poet. The obsession imposed its plan on "Threnody," on its plot, and even on its syntax and diction, distracting the poem from experiential immediacy and hardening the contradiction without ever reconciling it.

CHAPTER 3

The Act of Imagination

THE THEORY OF MIND and the theory of art in recent ages have tended to be related and to employ similar metaphors.[1] In Emerson's case, the fusion of the theories of mind and art was complete. In addition, his idea of art possessed a far more comprehensive integrity than either of the other two important, more or less coherently formed, aesthetic concepts that appeared in America in the mid-nineteenth century: Whitman's emblem of the autochthon and Dickinson's emblem of the haunted house. My aim now is to look into the special character of the inward forms raised to view in "Threnody" and to locate in them the center from which each of Emerson's artistic endeavors radiated. It leads to his own curious emblem, the famous transparent eyeball.

The origins of Emerson's thought have been described by others in detailed philosophical terms.[2] Here the main outline of the familiar set of his beliefs will enable us to find imbedded in the philosophy the basic poetics, to relate the philosophy to the poetry, and then, what is most important to our picture of the revolutionary artist, to define the world Emerson saw and the language that supported his perception. The "capital secret" was the process of conversion. That crucial act, apparent in "Threnody," Emerson conceived as the goal of the nation's spiritual teachers: to convert life into truth and to show the meaning of events.[3]

Insistence on the importance of the conversion process is evident in Emerson from the beginning. In the early lecture entitled "Literature" (January 1837), Emerson dwells on "the conversion of action into thought," using "common" and "spiritual" as terms for the poles of this process. The writer, Emerson says,

> must draw from the infinite Reason on the one side and he must penetrate into the heart and mind of the rabble on the other.

> From one he must draw his strength: to the other, his must owe his
> aim. The one yokes him to the real; the other to the apparent . . .
> A defect on either side of this entire range immediately affects the
> success. Plotinus and many philosophers united with God, on one
> side, do not attain a sympathy with the crowd on the other. On the
> contrary, great numbers of persons dwell in full understanding
> with common life like Falstaff, but with slender communion with
> the spiritual source.   (*EL,* II, 62)

Emerson seemed never to exhaust his devising of ways to describe this mentalizing activity dedicated "to the pursuit of truth and to the conversion of
the world of events into ideas of the mind" (*EL,* II, 59).[4]

Not only did the perspective and the language associated with this process shape Emerson's world; it was the concept that fettered the poetry and
then, by its literal application, in turn liberated the form. American poetry
later extended that liberation by a willful adoption of similar prosaic and
antiliterary attitudes.

The axis of Emerson's belief in the possibility of man's truth-seeing is
grounded in what he called early in his career the "radical correspondence
between visible things and human thoughts" (*W,* I, 29). This equation enabled him to assume, with no substantial diminishment throughout his active thinking life, that men could transfer the world to the consciousness.
In the late essay "Fate" (1860), even while recognizing the intractability of
reality, he declared that "every jet of chaos which threatens . . . us is convertible by intellect into wholesome force" (*W,* VI, 32).

The metamorphosis involved a world of elements. Basically it transformed ignorance to understanding, but its analogues were also the change
from the inarticulate to the articulate and from confusing flux to intelligible fixity. Metamorphosis allowed emergence into language of the
intuited, paralleling the divine gift of speech and mirroring God's own language manifest in the visible universe. "I will make a lecture," Emerson declared in an early notebook, "on God's architecture, one of his beautiful
works, a Day" (*JMN,* IV, 60). The identification of verbal articulation and
architecture, both manifestations of the will, is deliberate and characteristic. It also represented to Emerson's mind the equation between God's
creation and the artist's. That identification, to be sure, is fundamental to
Emerson's thinking about the poet.

His own poetry is crowded with testaments to this converting power, perceived both in the flow of the universe and in the work of the visionary
poet. "There's a melody born of melody, / Which melts the world into a
sea," Emerson said in the poem "Destiny"; this transformation into freer
forms spiritualizes the material world, transforming the palpable into the

impalpable mind. The poet enacts the metamorphosis according to his divine power.

> As snow-banks thaw in April's beam,
> The solid kingdoms like a dream
> Resist in vain his motive strain,
> They totter now and float amain.   ("The Poet")

Digesting that "harde yron" of appearance, as Wallace Stevens once called the quest for reality, is for Emerson the highest function of the imagination.

> Fancy's gift
> Can mountains lift;
> The Muse can knit
> What is past, what is done . . .
> Making free with time and size,
> Dwindles here, there magnifies,
> Swells a rain-drop to a tun.   ("The Poet")

The poetic imagination swallows up the world by turning it into words. When Emerson was preparing the first volume of essays for the press, Rusk tells us, he "dreamed that as he was floating at will in the ether he saw the world not far off, 'diminished to the size of an apple'; and that, in obedience to an angel, he ate it" (Rusk, 283). Mountains are "melted in Promethean alembics and come out men," Emerson says in "Poetry and Imagination," "and then, melted again, come out words, without any abatement, but with an exaltation of power!" (*W,* VIII, 16). Verse itself, according to yet another analogue of Emersonian conversion, undergoes a change whereby the transient and truth-failing expressions disappear, leaving the hardy and essential:

> I hung my verses in the wind,
> Time and tide their faults may find.
> All were winnowed through and through,
> Five lines lasted sound and true;
> Five were smelted in a pot
> Than the South more fierce and hot;
> These the siroc could not melt,
> Fire their fiercer flaming felt,
> And the meaning was more white
> Than July's meridian light.   ("The Test")

In its ambitious sweep, the fact-to-truth process undertakes to transform the nation itself into an idea, indeed, by artistic bravado, into a truth-revealing performance that will, as Emerson said in "The American Scholar," "sing and soar." To his mind, conversion could be an instantaneous act (the eyeball epiphany) or an intricate, deliberate design of the poet. He described the process in "Poetry and Imagination": "the beholding and co-energizing mind sees . . . refining and ascent to the third, the seventh or the tenth power of the daily accidents which the senses report, and which make the raw material of knowledge. It was *sensation;* when memory came, it was *experience;* when mind acted, it was *knowledge;* when mind acted on it as knowledge, it was *thought*" (*W,* VIII, 24, my italics). The idea of graduated ascent to the truth mirrored nature's evolutionary process working through rising spirals of form. At each level, from the paradigmatic example of God's will down through each expression of that will in objective nature, in the human imagination, or in the artifacts of that imagination, the goal is always the conversion of the world itself.

The essential statement is in "The American Scholar": The world "came into [the scholar of the first age] life; it went out from him truth. It came to him short-lived actions; it went out from him immortal thoughts. It came to him business; it went from him poetry. It was dead fact; now, it is quick thought. It can stand, and it can go. It now endures, it now flies, it now inspires" (*W,* I, 87-88). The change unfolds in time or takes place instantaneously, the world altering now in spatial, now in generic character. Transformation piles upon transformation: life to truth; short-lived actions to immortal thoughts (a double change); business to poetry; dead fact to quick thought. Little of human experience seems to evade this encompassing imaginative system of conversion.

In the end the process must make men better. "The supreme value of poetry," says Emerson, "is to educate us to a height beyond itself, or which it rarely reaches; — the subduing mankind to order and virtue" (*W,* VIII, 65-66). When Emerson speaks of the inherent dignity of all intellectual activity, he assumes that the thought into which the world is converted is moral. He was both persistent and conventional in this regard. But we are less concerned with the morality than with the act of conversion, for that is what forms the effective intellectual syntax of his poetry. In "Threnody," conversion of the failed poet is the inward intention of the poem while at its surface it labors to convert Waldo's death to a virtuous order.

So obsessive is this conceptual process in Emerson's work that we may think it unique, but in its general outlines it is not. Keats's "Etherealization," the way material elements are "put into ethereal existence," is at the heart of his scheme of poetic creativity.[5] But its narrowing linear effect in Emerson's poetry is distinctively rigid if we compare it to Coleridge's conception. Emerson, like Coleridge, equated the process of the poetic imagination with nature. He once called the imaginative gesture "a strange process . . . by which experience is converted into thought, as a mulberry leaf is converted into satin. The manufacture goes forward at all hours" (*W,* I, 96). But he posits a fundamental *change* in kind, whereas Coleridge in those famous lines in *Biographia Literaria* about "reconciliation of opposite or discordant qualities" described not a model of irreversible transformation but rather a balancing *poise* wherein are held experiential elements and the relational field between them, the whole activity dramatized without ignoring the process. This texture is recovered by Whitman and Dickinson and in poetry that followed them. But in Emerson's conception it was the payoff of the transformation that really interested him, the destination of the linear path rather than any digressive indulgences in process. When Coleridge reconciled opposites he was not merely undertaking, to use M. H. Abrams' terms, "the common eighteenth-century formula that poetry represents a just mean between extremes."[6] Like Whitman and Dickinson, Coleridge never sacrificed the "lower" elements in the service of the "higher" but rather preserved that living field in which they interacted, reconstituting each other and showing all the while the absorptive range of the poetic imagination. The comparison with Coleridge throws into relief one of the sources of constraint in Emerson's poetry. Both men conceived the function of the artist as the bringing of the whole soul of man into activity. Yet Emerson, even as he theorized about traversing the whole scale of experience, in his poetry reduced possibilities, slackened tension, denied the ambiguities, and thus, as he recognized to his consternation, caricatured reality.

THE CHIEF backdrop to Emerson's conversion principle is the scheme of a dual world which he shared with his contemporaries.[7] He described the coordinates this way: "Every fact is related on one side to sensation, and on the other to morals . . . This head and this tail are called, in the language of philosophy, Infinite and Finite; Relative and Absolute; Apparent and Real; and many fine names beside" (*W,* IV, 149, see also 50-52). Edward Emerson appropriately quoted Pythagoras in his notes on "Merlin": "The world subsists by the rhythmical order of its elements. Everywhere in Nature appear the two elements of the finite and the infinite which give rise to the elementary opposites of the universe, the odd and even, one and many, right and left, male and female, fixed and moved, straight and curved, light and darkness, square and oblong, good and bad" (*W,* IX, 442). A natural Platonism was the common faith of the Romantic mind. Because of the force of its disposition in Emerson's mind and its basic relationship to the conversion principle by which the poet was conceived to realize his genius, Emerson was, as René Wellek has asserted, the epitome of the Romantic temperament.

The duality was not easily bridged. Emerson described the difficulty for the mirroring mind: "The worst feature of our biography is that it is a sort of double consciousness, that the two lives of the Understanding and of the Soul which we lead, really show very little relation to each other, that they never meet and criticize each other, but one prevails now, all buzz and din, and the other prevails then, all infinitude and paradise, and with the progress of life the two discover no greater disposition to reconcile themselves. Yet what is my faith? what is Me? what but now and then a moment of serenity and independence" (*JMN*, VIII, 10-11). Such a polarity has pervaded the American poetic consciousness and, indeed, continues to structure contemporary artists' minds.[8] Yet we must see Emerson's place in this context correctly. "So powerful," says Richard Poirier, "has Emerson been that his works now constitute a compendium of iconographies that have gotten into American writers who may never have liked or even read him."[9] The fact is that Emerson only codified a way of seeing that had long existed in the American literary consciousness, his articulation being the most eloquent registering of that binary view. William Ellery Channing had said in his essay "On the Character and Writings of Milton" (1828), which Emerson praised in his "Historic Notes": "[Poetry's] great tendency and purpose is, to carry the mind beyond and above the beaten, dusty, weary walks of ordinary life; to lift it into a purer element."[10] No one, however, so obsessively as Emerson considered the specific kind of mind by which that passage from the ordinary to the pure was to be made.

The generative instrument that effected conversion from the lower particulars to the higher truth was, according to Emerson, the *imagination*. "The endless passing of one element into new forms, the incessant metamorphosis," Emerson asserted, "explains the rank which the imagination holds in our catalogue of mental powers. The imagination is the reader of these forms" (*W*, VIII, 15).[11] He was careful not to dissociate the imaginative power from mortal possibilities. Though he asserted repeatedly, as he did in the essay "The Poet," that "this insight, which expresses itself by what is called Imagination, is a very high sort of seeing," he conceived it as a natural element in the divine organism of the human mind (*W*, III, 26). Second sight does not necessarily impair the primary or common sense. In the end he drew support from the familiar *dolce e utile* argument: "This union of first and second sight reads Nature to the end of delight and of moral use" (*W*, VIII, 22).

The division of "sight" into lower and higher levels dictated a comparable ordering of the perceived world and thus of the literature that was the imagination's expression. From this division the distinction between poetry and prose took its most decisive terms, however much in his aesthetic speculations Emerson was to blur those distinctions. He said in "Poetry and Imagination" that "the poet affirms the laws, prose busies itself with exceptions, —with the local and individual" (*W,* VIII, 32). Emerson made this distinction emphatic. The poet, guided by thoughts and laws, "is ascending from an interest in visible things to an interest in that which they signify, and from the part of a spectator to the part of a maker" (*W,* VIII, 42). The pairing is highly significant. Emerson conceived this ascent to the role of poet as an elevation from passive observation to the active grasping of the significance of the material world. The movement is analogous to that of Emerson's scholar progressing from passive meditator to active teacher. Emerson regarded the poet as prophetic simply because he makes this conversion instantaneously: "He reads in the word or action of the man its yet untold results. His inspiration is power to carry out and complete the metamorphosis, which, in the imperfect kinds arrested for ages, in the perfecter proceeds rapidly in the same individual" (*W,* VIII, 39).

Poetry as a realm itself was not exempt from bifurcation. Emerson held the Platonic notion of a central man who embodies all aspects of *men,* and he thus carefully distinguished between the individual poet's work and the great language universe of the shared human imagination, the projected totality Wallace Stevens was to call a hundred years later "the supreme fiction." "One man sees a spark or shimmer of the truth and reports it," wrote Emerson, "and his saying becomes a legend or golden proverb for ages, and other men report as much, but none wholly and well. Poems! —we have no poem" (*W,* VIII, 74). For a time, Emmanuel Swedenborg came close to filling the role of the primary seer in Emerson's mind. He "of all men in the recent ages," Emerson declared, "stands eminently for the translator of nature into thought . . . Before him the metamorphosis continually plays" (*W,* III, 35). Considering this central act within Emerson's system of beliefs, we discover little to distinguish the poet from the scholar as *Man Thinking.* The durability of this conception demonstrates the centrality of imaginative metamorphosis in Emerson's idea of the poetic mind. We see it early in *Nature:* "In proportion to the energy of his thought and will, [man] takes up the world into himself" (*W,* I, 20). There are only degrees of facility in individuals: "Every man's condition is a solution in hieroglyphic to those inquiries he would put. He acts it as life, before he apprehends it as truth" (*W,* I, 4).

But the scholar is the paradigmatic figure. Above all men, the world comes into him life, and goes out from him truth. When we recognize how crucial to Emerson's ideas of poetry is this concept of the converting imagination, we see how radical his explorations were as compared, say, to the native assumption Benjamin Spencer has called the "topographical fallacy" in American literary theory of the nineteenth century. Spencer documents that "neoclassic" belief "which Lowell and other critics were to try to expose repeatedly in the nineteenth century: the assumption that grandeur in scenery would issue in sublimity of poetic vision and loftiness of style."[12] Emerson was not so superficial. For him the converting power of the active imagination was primary; the sweeping vistas of the new land simply provided a broader and more accessible language for the poet to read. He was closer to Lowell's practical critical precepts than we may have believed, though his probing for the radicals of form reached far deeper. As Jonathan Bishop has said: " 'The American Scholar' is the classic essay in which to see Emerson arguing for the freedom of mind to do its work in the world."[13]

THE STRUCTURE OF THE IMAGINATION

The casting of experience into ideas, never simple, was a direct ascent up the mental structure. The hierarchy mirrored the dual structure of the world as conceived and the distinct functions of the fancy and the imagination. Although Coleridge's ideas run parallel here, we shall do well to see this model in Emerson's own terms. The Kantian distinction between Reason and Understanding, as Emerson found it in Coleridge and Carlyle, explained the distinction between spirit and matter. This differentiation never decreased in importance for him and seems not to have undergone any substantial evolution.[14]

Emerson claimed the transforming force for every individual. "We too shall know how to take up all this industry and empire, this Western civilization, into thought, as easily as men did when arts were few; but not by holding it high, but by holding it low. The intellect uses and is not used, — uses London and Paris and Berlin, East and West, to its end. The only heart that can help us is one that draws, not from our society, but from itself, a counterpoise to society" (*W*, VIII, 74). The framework of fancy and imagination underlies "The American Scholar," where Emerson speaks of men of mere talent who "set out from accepted dogmas, not from their own sight of principles" (*W*, I, 89). That essay's most inward concern is neither literary nationalism, as most interpretations have it, nor Emerson's own justification of his vocation, though both are present. Basically the essay is concerned with the aesthetic possibilities of the poet-scholar's imagination. The distinction between genius and talent was absolute even though the higher purpose depended for its raw material upon the collective agency of the lower. "The one thing in the world of value," Emerson said, "is the active soul . . . The soul active sees absolute truth; and utters truth, or creates. In this action it is genius." As for talent: "Whatever talents may be, if the man create not, the pure efflux of the Deity is not his; — cinders and smoke there may be, but not yet flame" (*W*, I, 90). The binary model undergoes numerous elaborations in "Poetry and Imagination": the fancy (talent) aspires to amusement while genius loves truth and works to a moral end; fancy provides relief from the passion of thought, while genius is absorbed in the passions of the seeing mind; fancy is Quarles's *Emblems*, genius is Bunyan's *Pilgrim's Progress;* fancy is willed, genius spontaneous in its acts; one is a play, the other a perception; one amuses, the other expands and exalts us; the lower is accidental, the higher a function organic with the universe; fancy aggregates, the imagination (genius — the words are interchangeable) animates; fancy has to do with color, the imagination with forms; the fancy paints while the imagination sculptures (*W*, VIII, 28-29).[15]

We encounter just here the poet's need to retransform idea into language. This faculty Emerson labeled "talent." Genius (*Man Thinking*) carried one from fact to truth, while talent enabled one to clothe that truth in appropriate images. Talent was conceived as the encoder into language, the manifester of the silent reality in the audible. These powers of reification in language were to Emerson's mind nobly practiced by Dante and Shakespeare. Deep sight, on the other hand, he believed to be most powerful in men like Boehme, Swedenborg, and Blake. The ideal poet "is the healthy, the wise, the fundamental, the manly man, seer of the secret; against all the appearances he sees and reports the truth, namely that the soul generates matter. And poetry is the only verity, — the expression of a sound mind speaking after the ideal, and not after the apparent. As a power it is the perception of the symbolic character of things, and the treating them as representative: as a talent it is a magnetic tenaciousness of an image" (*W*, VIII, 26-27).

The metaphor of simultaneous decomposition and connection is basic to the way Emerson sees the structure of the imagination. Moreover, the model organizes a whole range of concerns — moral, geographical, even political. He wrote in *Nature:* "The understanding [the term here means the same as fancy] adds, divides, combines, measures, and finds nutriment and room for its activity in this worthy scene. Meantime, Reason transfers all these lessons into its own world of thought, by perceiving the analogy that marries Matter and Mind" (*W*, I, 36). In the late essay "Montaigne," he said the understanding has "the perception of difference, and is conversant with facts and surfaces, cities and persons, and the bringing [of] certain things to pass; —[this faculty belongs to] men of talent and action. Another class have the perception of identity, and are men of faith and philosophy, men of genius" (*W*, IV, 150).

To an extent unrecognized before, this simulacrum of the poetic mind which exactly reflected a binary Platonic world organized the poetry. Fancy turns up as Cupid in the poem "The Initial Love," the "arch-hypocrite" knowledgeable in the ways of the world:

> Corrupted by the present toy
> He follows joy, and only joy.
> There is no mask but he will wear;
> He invented oaths to swear;
> He paints, he carves, he chants, he prays,
> And holds all stars in his embrace.

The higher constructive power of the imagination (genius) is described in the poem "Wealth," where one encounters again the identification as in Coleridge of the poet with God the creator, both being supreme artists:

> well the primal pioneer
> Knew the strong task to it assigned,
> Patient through Heaven's enormous year
> To build in matter home for mind . . .
> But when the quarried means were piled,
> All is waste and worthless, till
> Arrives the wise selecting will,
> And, out of slime and chaos, Wit
> Draws the threads of fair and fit.

The distinction between the two levels of poetic mind appeared at the very first in Emerson's poetry. In an unpublished poem written in 1827, he derided the "rabble of misguided men" who, "alien born to morals and to mind," have taken to writing poetry. He saw them, like the farmers in "Hamatreya," victims of their own limited sights:

Men of vain hearts but uninstructed souls
Talk out the madness of their midnight bowls. (*JMN*, III, 36)

The etherealizing act of the poetic mind, on the other hand, suggests the science analogues available in the nineteenth century. As Stuart Sperry has said in regard to Keats, "certain fundamental analogies between the laws of physical change and the processes of the imagination were current and readily available in the chemical theory of the day." He quotes from William Nicholson's *First Principles of Chemistry* (1792): "Heat expands solids, then renders them fluid, and afterwards converts them into vapour; and these changes succeed each other as the *intensity* of the heat is rendered greater."[16] Emerson said in *Nature:* "The poet, the painter, the sculptor, the musician, the architect, seek each to concentrate this radiance of the world on one point . . . Thus is Art a nature passed through the alembic of man" (*W*, I, 24). As here, the alembic for Emerson repeatedly resembles the instantaneoulsy transforming lens, which in turn leads to the image of the naked eyeball that so amused his contemporaries.

Inevitably, this disembodied astronomy of the poetic imagination provided the program for the poetry. But Emerson rationalized this disembodiment: "Whilst commonsense looks at things or visible Nature as real and final facts, poetry, or the imagination which dictates it, is a second sight, looking through these, and using them as types or words for thoughts which they signify" (*W*, VIII, 19). Inevitably again, this conception of the poet as seer verges on the mystical. The poet, Emerson says, "can class [divine flowings] so audaciously because he is sensible of the sweep of the celestial stream, from which nothing is exempt. His own body is a fleeing apparition, — his personality as fugitive as the trope he employs. In certain hours we can almost pass our hand through our body" (*W*, VIII, 21). How remote we are at this point from Whitman, relishing every ounce of fat on his body! But it is toward that reality-enhancing opacity on the other side of the divide in American poetry to which Emerson's deepest need pointed. What had to be superseded, as Emerson himself knew better than anyone, was the programmatic ideal that controlled the poetry in its extremity.

Those analogies borrowed from science urged a further impoverishment by justifying the evaporation of personality, the principal element which, in Whitman and Dickinson, endows their poetry with an identity so immediate that it constitutes an authentic poetry voice. Keats wrote in November 1817: "Men of Genius . . . have not any individuality, any determined character."[17] This is the hazardous underside of his doctrine of negative capability. In Shakespeare and Coleridge, that self-negation may be a virtue, as the plenitude of the world is captured by the poet identifying with its variousness. In Emerson, the extinction of individuality resulted in a loss of authority and of the world as resisting and mysterious body. His poet is "the true and only doctor; he knows and tells" (*W*, III, 8). But what he neglects in this high form of knowing is complicated feeling that presses against the density of experience and forces language that conveys a full reality.

"Adam is not so much the Achilles as the Troy of the poem," Jones Very
said of *Paradise Lost,* discussing it as a model of Christian epic. Very justified the attention nineteenth-century poetry was paying to individual and
idiosyncratic concerns: "We cannot sympathize with that spirit of criticism
which censures modern poetry for being the portraiture of individual characteristics and passions, and not the reflection of the general features of
society and the outward man."[18] The turning inward he admired as evidence of a Christian concern with private salvation. But he anticipated a
whole generation of confessional poetry more than a century later. Paradoxically, his sanction of the idiosyncratic sprang directly from the transcendental abstraction of Emerson. We thus see the fundamental irony of
Emerson's position as the man whose aesthetic speculations straddled the
deep discontinuity in American poetry: although his emphasis upon genius
and its ability to see the universal urged a disengagement from particular
reality, at the same time he held to the individual converting experience.
The doctrine of genius led to the poetry of individual revelation and the
private manipulation of experience. As poetry in the twentieth century inevitably turned in its anarchy to the dark side and to the fragmentation of
experience that could not be idealized, it sounded the dissonance of chaos.
Although Emerson's belief led to the terminal purities of abstraction, it
also led in its epistemological anxieties to liberties of language and form
that enabled other poets to see intricacies not tyrannized by ideas. Poe had
anticipated this self-terrifying vision in "The Raven," Dickinson exploited
it intensely, and Whitman, though his faith was everywhere announced,
raised all things to equal rapture and thereby dissolved the hierarchy essential to faith.

EMBLEMS OF THE IMAGINATION

The emblems that hold Emerson's poetics are the same ones that convey
his well-known philosophical beliefs. In the light of his theory of the imagination, however, these figures turn strange and more significant in their
aesthetic meaning as they disclose the bases of his poetic theory. The importance of these icons is most fully apparent as they emerge as the
products of the enormous passion with which Emerson viewed that act of
conversion by the poetic imagination. That crucial emphasis is part of the
essay "The Poet." Emerson quotes Spenser on the Platonic relationship of
body and soul ("For, of the soul, the body form doth take, / For soul is
form, and doth the body make"), then says: "Here we find ourselves suddenly not in a critical speculation but in a holy place, and should go very

warily and reverently. We stand before the secret of the world, there where Being passes into Appearance and Unity into Variety" (*W*, III, 14). That exquisite locus where the many become one, the ephemeral become eternal, and appearance becomes truth—that is the place of revelation. Form becomes idea and Becoming passes into Being. It is Emerson's secular equivalent of the Apocalypse.

Of the icons in which he fixed that supreme moment, none is more significant than the famous transparent eyeball. That naively repellent image reveals in peculiar ways how Emerson conceived the task of the poet as he bridged the "innavigable sea" between himself and the real, and crossed "the whole space between God or pure mind, and the multitude of uneducated men" (*EL*, II, 62). A brief excursion will show how various are the analogues that deepen the meaning of the eyeball emblem. The figure of architecture, for one, is important as the most solid of the metaphors. "Groined vaults" and "frolic architecture" thus become touchstone images of conversion in two of his best-known poems. The identification of making poems with building is explicit in "The House," which begins "There is no architect / Can build as the Muse can." Several other instances demonstrate how the architectural-monumental icon in Emerson anchors a cluster of anxieties over this primary need beneath all the emblems: the necessity of making the flux of experience intelligible. Matthew Arnold shared that concern, and in part it is why he laid great commendation not on Emerson's writing but upon the solid-standing optimism of his guiding principles. For Emerson, the architecture metaphors signified a whole system of beliefs: flux must have a steady principle; facts must have their idea; activity must have its commemoration; life must be understood; and life inwardly organized can be built into visibility by art.

In an early journal note (1837) he equated writing to building, asserting that in making a discourse of "natural rhetoric," "out of the quarry you have erected a temple, soaring in due gradation" (*JMN*, V, 409). The monument figure held quite particular associations for him, suggesting the stabilizing laws of nature beneath various modes of behavior. He speaks, for example, of mutual respect in marriage as constituting its "rock foundation" (*JMN*, V, 208). Such solidity in a more general sense meant to Emerson firm self-possession in the face of popular migrations: "give us the rare merits of impassivity, of marble texture, against which the mob of souls dashing is broken like crockery falling on stone: the endurance which can afford to fail in the popular sense, because it never fails in its own" (*JMN*, IX, 360; *J*, VII, 152-153). His constant aim to find within movement its essential stasis dictated the basic structure and gamut of his poems. It even suggests how the linear design of the poems forms an intellectual equivalent to constructing a building upward to its pinnacle and in what ways the poems had to exclude the unstable materials of life.

Other, more flexible images also make up the group that defined the high function of the imagination. Emerson's organic images have been aptly described by Sherman Paul: "the mind-as-plant transformed matter into its own life (that is, image-forming in a creative memory), and like one of Emerson's favorite images of man—the tree—stood rooted in the earth but aloft in the higher air."[19] There are other metaphors far too numerous to inspect, for the ingenuity was inexhaustible. There is the Noah parable in which the poetic imagination is the ark that joins the species to their noble goal. It traverses that innavigable sea to a new land: "All the creatures by pairs and by tribes pour into [the poet's] mind as into a Noah's ark, to come forth again to people a new world" (*W*, III, 40).

By way of organic, architectural, and many other metaphors, then, we come to the famous eyeball. However grotesque his choice may seem, the image distills Emerson's concept of the poetic imagination. Poems show us how he conceived the converting imagination as existing eyelike in its surrounding world as both the center and the mirror of the world's form. In a fragment of the poem "The Poet," a particularly valuable locus to which I will return, this marvelous juncture of organic and geometric figures refers to the poet:

> He shared the life of the element,
> The tie of blood and home was rent:
> As if in him the welkin walked,
> The winds took flesh, the mountains talked,
> And he the bard, a crystal soul
> Sphered and concentric with the whole.

In this curious conceit of the crystal soul in fleshly air we are a single step from the figure of the eyeball, transparent converter at the center of the round world itself.

In Emerson's iconology, the eyeball is wonderfully innocent, without any of the distortion of experience. "I question not my corporeal eye any more than I would question a window concerning a sight. I look through it, and not with it" (*W*, VIII, 28). It is for us who seek the central Emerson to find the distortions in his eye, however, and all the implications of its selective blindness for, as he says, the assumptions within and the vision outward share the same distortions. "The authority of Reason cannot be separated from its vision," he said. "They are not two acts, but one. The sight commands, and the command sees" (*JMN*, V, 272). Here, now, from *Nature*, is that moment of perfect exhilaration on the wintry common:

> Standing on the bare ground, — my head bathed by the blithe air
> and uplifted into infinite space, — all mean egotism vanishes. I be-
> come a transparent eyeball; I am nothing; I see all; the currents of
> the Universal Being circulate through me.   (*W*, I, 10)

Right at this juncture is Emerson's absolute grasp of his idea of the poetic
imagination. The transparent eyeball *is* the poetic imagination instantaneously and without distortion making that conversion we have been at pains
to understand in the pages up to now. Emerson is *in* the holy place, abso-
lutely pervious to the light of Being, standing at the threshhold between
manifest form and soul, Becoming and Being. Perhaps only this simple description of the moment, many years later in "Poetry and Imagination,"
can add intensity:

> The nature of things is flowing, a metamorphosis. The free spirit
> sympathizes not only with the actual form, but with the power or
> [of?] possible forms; but for obvious municipal or parietal uses
> God has given us a bias or a rest on to-day's forms. Hence the
> shudder of joy with which in each clear moment we recognize the
> metamorphosis, because it is always a conquest, a surprise from
> the heart of things.   (*W*, VIII, 71)

Between epiphanal moments, the self exists. Self-preservation, in fact, is in
the balance. This astonishing paragraph contains the poem "Days,"
neither vision avoiding suggestions of physical passion at touching the eter-
nity that lurks behind the veiled forms of our lives. One of the deep ironies
of this shudder of joy, however, is that the passion stirs at the price of any
sense of individuality. "All mean egotism vanished," Emerson says. The
disappearance of self may make for good revelations, but it enervates poetry. We are at the heart of Emerson's idea of the poetic imagination in its
moment of instant conversion of experience into being. A poem, to Emerson's mind, is itself a "holy place" where the metamorphosis occurs. Such
being the goal of poetry as Emerson saw it, he suffered at the knowledge of
his own failure to induce that exquisite shudder of joy. He rejected miracle
in religion but he required it of poetry.[20]

The eyeball icon enables us to see yet a deeper bias in Emerson's conception of the poetic imagination. At the same time we necessarily speculate
on how the poetic revitalization occurred in Whitman and Dickinson. The
widest possible perspective is needed. Frank Kermode says perceptively of
the figure of the dancer in Yeats that it is one of his "great reconciling images, containing life in death, death in life, movement and stillness, action
and contemplation, body and soul; in fact all that passionate integrity that
was split and destroyed when Descartes, as Yeats puts it, discovered that he
could think better in his bed than out of it."[21] What is the character of the

experience captured by the bodiless eyeball? The question discloses the central issue: we miss a passionate entirety in Emerson's image, and that lack reflects the narrow assumptions gathered in the figure. It is a purely intellectual light that refracts through the eyeball and the poetry. Essentially, Emerson's eyeball is an image of Being purified beyond the capacity for a vision of composite truth, as in Yeats's image. Life is filtered by the eye and therefore limited by it. No delight along the senses contributes to that shudder of joy, only the flash of light. Experience in the poem is restricted to

> Illusions like the tints of pearl,
> Or changing colors of the sky,
> Or ribbons of a dancing girl
> That mend her beauty to the eye.   (Fragment on Nature)

This is a realm surely chaste and disembodied, under the domination of the eye intent upon turning the world to glass. Some of his contemporaries recognized the limitations. In the *Crayon* of 1856, a contributor declared that "the contact of living man with nature does not take place in the eyeball, but in the soul." Like Milton in his time, and Arnold two centuries later, Wallace Stevens speaks for the taste of a post-Emersonian time that is impatient with chaste abstraction: "[Poetry's] function, the need which it meets and which has to be met in some way in every age that is not to become decadent or barbarous, is precisely this contact with reality as it impinges upon us from outside, the sense that we can touch and feel a solid reality which does not wholly dissolve itself into the conceptions of our own minds. It is the individual and particular that does this."[22]

The eyeball is the instantaneous analogue of the more elaborated structure of the poetic imagination with its upward elevations from fancy to imagination, from talent to genius. It is also a spatial converter, reducing experience to the scan of the perceiving lens. Whether temporal or spatial, the process diminishes, distills, and abstracts, disregarding the minutiae of individual events. The character of the poetry is necessarily then identical to the nature of the emblems by which Emerson pictured his idea of the poetic process. The limitations are sharply apparent by contrast, say, to the rich indistinctness and possibilities of Poe's central figure in *Eureka*, the pulsing universe alternately unifying and dispersing in an incessant throbbing that moves even the smallest particulars. Whitman's autochthonic poet grows, warts and all, with each nerve end in the skin possessing its own language. The grass, the railway conductor with coins in his pocket, the tin roofers, all send out a language of sounds that Whitman hears. A similar intricacy is true of Emily Dickinson, who speaks of art trying to be a haunted house. Only Emerson of the four, as his major symbol makes apparent, practiced a poetics that diminished the particular life he could get into a poem and censored the multitude of languages he could actually hear in the world around him.

It was an Emersonian world, formed by a poetics that itself mirrored an extraordinary convergence of cultural assumptions and aspirations. This uncommon intersection of forces in America in the mid-nineteenth century forms the backdrop for the impatient idealism that disciplined the verse, and, by only a shift of emphasis, showed where the roots of a new form had already sprung.

THE CULTURAL MATRIX

Basic cultural predispositions lay at hand to enable Emerson to fashion his simulacrum of the bridging poetic imagination. This fashioning in many ways reflects the larger culture bravely marshaling its political, scientific, and religious assumptions of a moral world.

The fundamental philosophical duality was already in place, conventional, an abyss in the midst of a thoughtful man's life that had to be crossed every day. Emerson's habitual act was to disengage and seek a universe that arched the two sides of the split. His own words for it are familiar: "Our little circles absorb and occupy us as fully as the heavens; we can minimize as infinitely as maximize, and the only way out of it is . . . to kick the pail over, and to accept the horizon instead of the pail . . . instead of worms and mud pies" (*J*, X, 238). The choice between the near ground and the cosmos confronted Emerson even as it did his contemporaries. He needed to go no further than the Harvard of the 1820s to find implanted the poles of divinity and autochthonism between which his own aesthetic ideas were to oscillate. This is the common view of Emerson's polar disposition. Without such disjunctions in the understood world, his conversion system of the imagination had no function.

The main lines of his view go back in Western thought, of course, to Plato. Emerson's formative reading was in the neo-Platonists Plotinus, Proclus, and Iamblichus.[23] In the essay "Montaigne" he sought the balanced flexibility of a center ground: "The abstractionist and the materialist thus mutually exasperating each other, and the scoffer expressing the worst of materialism, there arises a third party to occupy the middle ground between these two, the skeptic, namely . . . This then is the right ground of the skeptic, — this of consideration, of self-containing . . . The philosophy we want is one of fluxions and mobility" (*W*, IV, 154, 159,

160). Here was a dynamic centrism from which a living art form could be devised, but Emerson in his own poetry marched up the straight rational ascent from the lower to the higher. There were strong inducements in the mental set of the time to take that path.

The principal examples were politics and religion. Theodore Parker, in the *Massachusetts Quarterly Review* of 1850, described Emerson with a single impeccable stroke as "the child of Christianity and of American political idealism and yet outside the church and outside the state." In the great democratic experiment to make one society out of many individuals and at the same time to raise the lowly to their proper dignity—goals sought in the full thrust of the assumption that the one political truth of equality would triumph over actual multiplicity and disparity—it seemed natural to make poetry bridge a similar gap. Democratic principles were simply political manifestations of Emerson's principles of art. The argument was an attractive one, and Whitman took it up in the decades that followed. The relationship of the practical concerns of political amalgamation to the aesthetic principles of art was argued most vociferously at the time by the Young America group in New York. The crucial factor was that poetic bridges to noble ends were in no way, as credos have been periodically in English-language art, inimical to democratic ideals.

In religion the labor of reading God's plan in the homely facts of experience only put in moral terms the Platonic duality. Conversion is the basic process of Jonathan Edward's *Images of Divine Things*. It has been argued that a poetics of discovery, of laying open to view, was in effect New England poetics.[24] Whether or not one accepts the generalization about a "New England poetics" (in important ways, it was divergent and contradictory, from Bryant and Longfellow to Dickinson and from Robinson to Frost and after), the bias so described was Emerson's. What came to view most often in that poetics of revelation was man's essential nobility. The idea of Western man's perfectibility in the New Eden thoroughly animated American writing. In Emerson's time, the faith sounded in public debate with great fervor. According to Timothy Dwight's summation, this was the country where men's tragic limitations would finally be overcome. "Here the progress of temporal things toward perfection will undoubtedly be finished. Here human greatness will find a period."[25]

But a special relationship between the world and the individual existed in Emerson's conception, and there lay the potential, even so early as *Nature*, for his radical theoretical insight into a liberating aesthetic form. The relationship held the prospect of a fundamental shift from poetry's pursuit of meaning to its performance of function, poems declaring not *what* existence means, but *how* meaning is possible. The beginnings were in sentences like this one: "There is never a beginning, there is never an end, to the inexplicable continuity of this web of God, but always circular power returning into itself" (*W*, I, 85). In "The American Scholar" Emerson placed his thinking man-poet at the center of the coiled world. He did this in the way Plato centered his just man and refracted the politically stratified system of the republic out from him. In that way Plato projected the kind of society the ideal man would be nurtured in, and the one was not separable from the other. The same correspondence shaped the world Emerson saw. It was not simply phenomenally organic but *morally* organic. The least element worked toward the moral design of the whole. As Emerson wrote in an early journal: "The whole of what we know is a system of Compensations . . . Every suffering is rewarded; every sacrifice is made up; every debt is paid" (*JMN*, II, 341).[26]

It was man's world, a mirror that gave him back his own reflection. Emerson's poetry thereby found its meaning in the revelation of this relationship and in the ramifying truths. But the thought led him always to the problem of form. "Rightly, poetry is organic," he finally wrote. "We cannot know things by words and writing, but only by taking a central position in the universe and living in its forms. We sink to rise: —

> 'None any work can frame,
> Unless himself become the same.'

. . . the fascination of genius for us is this awful nearness to Nature's creations" (*W*, VIII, 42-43). Just here, in a bold assertion, is the theoretical reverse side of Emerson's poetic impoverishment. In such times when Emerson freed himself theoretically from the obligation to make his poetry idealistic and literary, he felt the urgent circuit between art and the life from which art springs. He is beyond the separation of Platonic metaphor here. He is experiencing the central condition of man-in-his-world that came to form the basis of a poetics which called for a radical innovation in idiom.

There were times when this intimate man-world relationship seemed to alter. These were dark moments for the poet, and Emerson had always known them. As early as *Nature* he recognized the doubt. The Orphic poet says there, "We distrust and deny inwardly our sympathy with nature. We own and disown our relation to it, by turns" (*W*, I, 70). When the disowning moments occurred, there stood the irredeemably dual nature of existence.

Yet this divided world was part of the Christian vision, and thus from a doctrinal view a principle also worked to reinforce Emerson's poetics of conversion. In short, without a conversion principle lodged centrally in a convertible world, there was no poetics. He seems never to have looked for long, and only rarely to the point of despair, at the possible question of individual responsibility in a random universe where the atoms blindly run. Rather, his world held, as he called it, "this hidden truth, that the fountains whence all this river of Time and its creatures floweth are intrinsically ideal and beautiful" (*W*, III, 4). In this world of beauty, the poet is "the man of Beauty." Thus the poetics becomes an intrinsic element in the system. The poetics provides the artistic strategy for the revelation of the ultimate unity and beauty of the world. Circular reasoning it is. What Emerson knew despite the times of doubt was that the imagination was a divine revelatory power residing at the center of a world of universally convertible phenomena.

That solipsistic vision merged with the Christian view of existence. Emerson's faith constituted his basic grammar of the converting poetic imagination. Christian belief and natural philosophy combine easily enough in one of his defining metaphors: "The new deed is yet a part of life, — remains for a time immersed in our unconscious life. In some contemplative hour it detaches itself from the life like a ripe fruit, to become a thought of the mind. Instantly it is raised, transfigured; the corruptible has put on incorruption" (*W*, I, 96). "The chain of the old Christian purpose," as Lawrence called it, was strong. The habitual disengagement from experience in favor of the moral scheme was his earliest commitment as he prepared for the ministry. In his Journal of March 25, 1821, he wrote: "I must prepare myself for the great profession I have purposed to undertake. I am to give my soul to God and withdraw from sin and the world the idle or vicious time and thoughts I have sacrificed to them." Years later, writing on the poet's obligation to discover truth in the affairs of the day, he defined this "contemporary insight" as a kind of mental "transsubstantiation": it is the "conversion of daily bread into the holiest symbols; and every man would be a poet if his intellectual digestion were perfect" (*W*, VIII, 35).

Matthew Arnold's judgment of Emerson necessarily comes back: "by his conviction that in the life of the spirit is happiness, and by his hope that this life of the spirit will come more and more to be sanely understood, and to prevail, and to work for happiness, — by this conviction and hope Emerson was great, and he will surely prove in the end to have been right in them."[27]

Modern poetry sundered the identification of art, religion, and nature as a whole system. The combination had forced poetry toward irrelevance. In the service of moral abstractions, it had exchanged its body in a sort of literary paradigm of Christian transsubstantiation. Emerson had said that "men are facts as well as persons, and the involuntary part of their life [that is, the soul, essence] is so much as to fill the mind and leave them no countenance to say aught of what is so trivial as their selfish thinking and doing" (*W*, VIII, 75). No occasion for barefoot indulgence in the abundant world was provided for here. Whatever did not serve high purpose was trivial. In that distinction, which he never abandoned, lay the death of poetry itself. Whatever revolution was to be raised to the aesthetic consciousness by Emerson thus reached the deepest roots imaginable, even to the religious foundations of the culture and the man himself.

THE WORLD AS SEEN

Ideas are a form of perception and particularly so for Emerson, who believed the idea stood always prior to the form of its expression. The same is true of that complex activity called style, for it too discovers a particular kind of world that is neither the complete world nor another man's world. Thus style coincides with idea as an instrument of perception. We are made constantly aware that if we spoke a different language we would perceive a different world. George Steiner wrote of this "linguistic set" towards perception: "Our language is our window on life. It determines for its speaker the dimensions, perspective and horizon of a part of the total landscape of the world. Of *a part*. No speech, however ample its vocabulary, however refined and adventurous its grammar, can organize the entire potential of experience. None, be it ever so sparse and rudimentary, fails to give *some* usable grid. The more we learn about languages, the more are we made aware of the particularity, of the vital idiosyncrasies, of any one language-vision."[28] Historically bound as well, this linguistic perception is what Sartre means by "bad faith," that is, illusions persisting from past acts of perception. The phenomenon is crucial to a broad perspective of the development of any art. Why does art have a history? Ernst Gombrich's insightful answer is that "Art has a history because the illusions of art are not only fruit but the indispensable tools for the artist's analysis of appearances."[29] Reality then is a highly, though not so idiosyncratically as we might suspect, translatable object. Emerson once said reality represented "the horses of thought." Not inhuman and intractably mysterious, reality served him as the conveyance of intellectual activity. In such a reciprocal relationship, the idea is both prior to and formative of the reality it addresses.

Emerson had a steady theoretical grasp of the linked relationship, the radical reciprocity, between language, concept, and percept. In an 1835 journal entry he acknowledged that "the language *thinks* for us as Coleridge said" (*JMN,* V, 9). In that extraordinarily instructive poem "Musketaquid," he asserts quite literally how this can happen when "the order in the field disclose / The order regnant in the yeoman's brain." He said later: "each [lens] shows only what lies in its focus. From the mountain you see the mountain. We animate what we can, and we see only what we animate. Nature and books belong to the eyes that see them. It depends on the mood of the man whether he shall see the sunset or the fine poem" (*W,* III, 50). Even more precisely, he said: "A man's genius, the quality that differences him from every other, the susceptibility to one class of influences, the selection of what is fit for him, the rejection of what is unfit, determines for him the character of the universe. A man is a method, a progressive arrangement; a selecting principle, gathering his like to him wherever he goes" (*W,* II, 143-144).

Part of Emerson's selecting principle involved the dominance he allowed the eye as sensor. Its globular shape and focus integrate what is otherwise a disparate and shapeless world. It is a major metaphor of aesthetic vision and helps to explain the disappearance from view of the mean and trivial. "The eye is the best of artists," Emerson said. "By the mutual action of its structure and of the laws of light, perspective is produced, which integrates every mass of objects, of what character soever, into a well colored and shaded globe, so that where the particular objects are mean and unaffecting, the landscape which they compose is round and symmetrical" (*W,* I, 15). That act of abstracting and generalizing, he was to say later in the Montaigne essay, was a matter of intellectual and moral survival. "The expansive nature of truth comes to our succor, elastic, not to be surrounded. Man helps himself by larger generalizations. The lesson of life is practically to generalize; to believe what the years and the centuries say against the hours; to resist the usurpation of particulars; to penetrate to their catholic sense" (*W,* IV, 185).

Emerson understood the hazards of such a generalizing thrust away from particulars and the distortions of subjective vision. He would have admired Wallace Stevens' crack about how "the squirming facts exceed the squamous mind, / If one may say so." But Bacon had instructed him that poetry "gives some show of satisfaction to the mind, wherein the nature of things doth seem to deny it." Emerson repeated the idea in *Nature*: "The sensual man conforms thoughts to things; the poet conforms things to his thoughts" (*W,* I, 52).

Order, as Emerson knew, is a strategy of the mind. "I know that the world I converse with in the city and in the farms," he said, "is not the world I *think*. I observe that difference, and shall observe it" (*W*, III, 84). But even while he insisted that American writers craved a sense of reality, his habitual movement in the poetry was toward the abstract.[30] In "The Poet" he described the function of the poet's eyes:

> Not lazy gazing on all they saw,
> Each chimney-pot and cottage door,
> Farm-gear and village picket-fence,
> But, feeding on magnificence,
> They bounded to the horizon's edge.

Perhaps the faith of our day in the indissoluble reality of things, of wheel-barrows and chickens in the rain, errs in the other epistemological extreme from feeding on magnificence.

The world Emerson saw through the structure of his ideas and his language was a duplication of his idea of the conversion process. It was a *convertible world* whose each element translated into moral significance. From any angle, it was a lexicon of moral purpose. This selective perception constitutes a form of prior intelligibility. One way to understand the structure of Emerson's perception is to examine his competence among the languages that the world speaks. Which was he capable of understanding? The grammar of Emerson's competence amidst the dialects took its basic structure, of course, from the conversion process of the poetic imagination. "Is the solar system good art and architecture?" Emerson asked; "the same wise achievement is in the human brain also" (*W*, VIII, 39). As for sources for poetic images, he preferred "the advantage which the country-life possesses, for a powerful mind, over the artificial and curtailed life of cities" (*W*, I, 31). But an urban mentality knows how severely restricted is the scope of a "powerful mind" when its language is reduced by the lopping off of a whole lexicon of experience.

Other voices are also quite unheard by Emerson. Usable experiences did not include those that involved ambiguity, chaos, blurred outlines, unbalanced equations—in a word, *eccentricity*. Only convertible experiences presented themselves for moral interpretations: for example, natural activities in which the process of transformation takes place (the honey-making of the bee, the blossoming of a flower, the birth and death of a son) or things placed in the organic system and therefore sharing its ultimate moral meaning (a rhodora, a titmouse) or more substantial "things" that represent levels in the familiar structure of Being and Becoming (a farmer, a sphinx, a snowstorm); things, to sum up, about which it can be said they

are not-this-but-that. The nonconvertible elements included psychic de-
serts of the sort Emily Dickinson inspected; included sex in any of its explicit aspects (though there is strong unconscious sexuality in Emerson's
language); included what Lawrence saw as one of the life elements destroyed by the Puritan consciousness, "the spontaneous passion of social
union." In Emerson's perfect metamorphosis, there was no grappling with
the gross or inarticulate. All those lives whose language Emerson was un-
equipped to read were *the inarticulable elements of existence.*[31]

Emerson had moments, like that in Stevens' "Sunday Morning," when
even the intellectual abstractions of his world provoked no passion in him.
"We are weary," he said in "New England Reformers," "of gliding ghost-
like through the world, which is itself so slight and unreal" (*W*, III, 273).
The world he viewed was seen from a great height, through the intellectual
eye. "The highest minds of the world," Emerson said in "The Poet" essay,
"have never ceased to explore the double meaning, or shall I say the quad-
ruple or the centuple or much more manifold meaning, of every sensuous
fact" (*W*, III, 4). That dutiful reach always for meaning left little in the
grasp of Emerson's poetry that remained mysterious. The poem on the
death of his son is only the most remarkable example. No mystery remains
finally, and consequently no tragedy.

Yet Emerson's journals show us repeatedly that he knew passion that
could not liberate itself into public language. This was the artist's essential
dilemma involving the constrictions upon all men caused by narrow institutions, narrow ways of thinking, and inherited schemas. He lectured his
audiences about the need for men to escape from restrictive forms and to
restore their souls to themselves again. The Divinity School address is the
primary expression. But even as that powerful address urged liberation
and the repossession of authentic passion from outmoded forms, Emerson's
own verse was stifling his poetic imagination.

The irony had desperate proportions because the blockages were of Emerson's own design. But the culture had a critical stake in his dilemma, and
that placed him at the center of a revolutionary situation. The meshing of
individuals and cultures is brilliantly described by Roland Barthes as he
portrays the modern writer similarly caught in the tragic disparity between
what he does and what he sees:

> The writer is forced by his writing into a cleft stick: either the ob-
> ject of the work is naively attuned to the conventions of its form,
> Literature remaining deaf to our present History, and not going
> beyond the literary myth; or else the writer acknowledges the vast
> novelty of the present world, but finds that in order to express it he

has at his disposal only a language which is splendid but lifeless
. . . Before his eyes, the world of society now exists as a veritable
Nature, and this Nature speaks, elaborating living languages from
which the writer is excluded: on the contrary, History puts in his
hands a decorative and compromising instrument, a writing inherited from a previous and different History, for which it is not
responsible and yet which is the only one he can use. Thus is born
a tragic element in writing, since the conscious writer must henceforth fight against ancestral and all-powerful signs which, from
the depths of a past foreign to him, impose literature on him like
some ritual, not like a reconciliation.[32]

Our perspective back from the twentieth century finds in Emerson's insistent theorizing the modern world in the process of creation. In a post-Emersonian age, Wallace Stevens had no trouble choosing between the real
and the abstract: "Kant says that the objects of perception are conditioned
by the nature of the mind as to their form. But the poet says that, whatever
it may be, *la vie est plus belle que les idées.*"[33] Emerson sought in his theoretical excursions a radical discontinuity in poetic form which could again
capture the world's noises and not simply the expectations of the mind.
Sherman Paul very properly says that Emerson's "universe was a universe of
levels and platforms . . . Worldliness and other-worldliness, lower and
higher, material and spiritual—he needed these polarities; they described
the tensions he experienced and that as facts of consciousness his vision reconciled."[34] Emerson's understanding of the corelativity of the world and
the mind is profound: "Poet sees the stars, because he makes them. Perception makes. We can only see what we make, all our desires are procreant.
Perception has a destiny. I notice that all poetry comes, or all becomes poetry, when we look from within and are using all as if the mind made it" (*J*,
VIII, 321). He wanted poetic forms equal to the active soul on which no
experience was to be lost.

The breakthrough sprang from the same aesthetic desiderata as the plea
at the Divinity School for a turning to passionate form-denying belief. The
speech constituted a major dislocation in the sensibility of Emerson's times.
It was no fashionable gesture, but a revolution that Emerson was about,
even as he as a poet sat with the old party. His effort to devise forms that
would carry the new languages of existence was manifest in the address.
His own passage enacts the struggle of new poetic forms to come into existence and, in so doing, to move the American consciousness over the great
divide between the nineteenth century and the twentieth. That struggle
had to do specifically with language.

THE LANGUAGE OF THE IMAGINATION

Language and imagination are both the makers of the world and the world's interpreters. Emerson believed the perceiving mind, the world perceived, and the language of that transaction to be inseparable mirror images. He worked this out in *Nature,* and the equation did not change significantly throughout his life. "The world," he wrote in 1836, "is emblematic. Parts of speech are metaphors, because the whole of nature is a metaphor of the human mind. The laws of moral nature answer to those of matter as face to face in a glass" (*W,* I, 32-33). The world and language are mutually reflexive, as are the structures of matter and the moral figures of the mind. Matter then is the language of the mind, its mirror expression. The structure of language proves this because it is simultaneously the language of nature and the language of mind.

This closed metaphorical system, mirroring itself at all angles, has a cosmic analogue in the divine creation itself. The nature-mind-language system duplicates in small scale the divine power of creation. When Emerson declared to his journal that he would make a lecture on God's architecture, "one of his beautiful works, a Day," he implied that God's language is the direct expression of His will. God, then, is the paradigm of the artist and the seer, that is, Man Thinking. Art in Emerson's purest conception would be spontaneous expression, like God's not written or premeditated. No verbal medium would be necessary finally; will would express itself, like God, directly in action. Thus the ultimate theoretical pull on Emerson's attempt to find a perfectly affective form was a conception of a language identical to action. This was the pure artist thinking.

In practical terms, the process of articulating seemed to Emerson inseparable from the hierarchical structure of the poetic imagination. Expression he saw as the reverse process of rising from fact to thought. Articulation is the passage from thought back down to the "fact" that "clothes" the thought, to use the metaphor of Emerson's time. The world as seen and the language of its articulation replicate the layered structure of the poetic imagination, in which the lower order of talent undertakes to clothe in language the insight of higher-order genius. Fancy gathers discrete parts; the imagination penetrates to their essential idea; talent then takes over to verbalize the idea. Emerson describes the process: "the term 'genius,' when used with emphasis, implies imagination; use of symbols, figurative speech. A deep insight will always, like Nature, ultimate its thought in a thing. As soon as a man masters a principle and sees his facts in relation to it, fields, waters, skies, offer to clothe his thoughts in images" (*W,* VIII,

17). Emerson and his contemporaries called this articulating faculty talent. It was this talent as well as prophetic genius whose lack in his own poetry he periodically lamented: "clothe these hands with power / In just proportion, / Nor plant immense designs / Where equal means are none."

Emerson wrote: "Genius certifies its entire possession of its thought, by translating it into a fact which perfectly represents it" (*W*, VIII, 22). In the verbalization there occurred moral refinement and selection. The essay "The Poet" describes how thought "makes everything fit for use." Even words not quite polite, small and mean things, circumcision (one of Emerson's examples), increase in value as they are drained of specific offensiveness by becoming general symbols. He knew their rhetorical power: "the meaner the type . . . the more pungent it is" (*W*, III, 17).

His own poetic language lacked that pungency despite his recognition that the life of literature declines in ratio to the distance separating reality and the language that structures it. Some writers in every long-civilized nation feed unconsciously on the old language created by their elders, "but wise men pierce this rotten diction and fasten words again to visible things" (*W*, I, 30). In the actual operation of his conceptual model, the visible things had been abstracted to morally convertible elements *before* they became anchors for words. Thus in Emerson's recycling language system, the world and its language were mutually depleting.

"Styles," Richard Ohmann has written, "reflect habits of mind and feeling — conceptual and moral worlds — and . . . this is the main reason for taking a critical interest in style." He elaborates: "style reflects conceptual framework." It is "responsive to the cut of a writer's mind, and that [mind] is only trimmed and decorated by intellectual culture, not created by it."[35] In view of Emerson's use of language as well as his theory, we need to remind ourselves how formative is the language itself in which mind has its very identity. I emphasize this because the hypothesis that language creates attitudes leads to speculation on why the poetry that followed the Emersonian discontinuity somehow lost the possibility of an idealistic outlook. The Emersonian style began to perceive a different world and inevitably altered the attitude with which a later century saw *its* world. Change in language can bring about change in human conduct.

The revolution in poetic mode that defines the great divide in American poetry is a language revolution quite apart from the post-Romantic themes that held sway. No one has plotted the linguistic shifts of that revolution, which still exert pressure on contemporary poetry. Those deep-seated conditions have structures of their own: the conception of the poetic imagination and the set of the language in which that imagination apprehends the world. The two—the concept of mind and the system of language—are inseparable. The world exists in precisely the way the language describes it, and so Emerson's world was his language. The truth of this really sits unnoticed at the center of Carl Strauch's thoughtful description of the purging of dense life by the abstractness of Emerson's language:

> If Emerson . . . did not create an intuitive, musical form, he did this other [in style and form], as I have described it—by indirection, from behind masks, lifting his subjects to the impersonal, the archetypal, the abstract . . . The angle of vision effects a stasis, in which life, experience, a situation, a problem are "upraised above care and fear" . . . In this contemplative mood we are under the sway of the god Apollo, "a cathartic deity and the true saviour of Dionysius," and we submit to the abstracting image that, purging away the circumstantial, holds man's recurring experience in solution under the masks of archetypes. In this catharsis the abstracting image may make a profoundly aesthetic and psychological claim upon the mirroring imagation.[36]

A last note is called for on Emerson's theorizing about the sound of poetry because it too is of a piece with his concept of the poetic mind. The terms are similarly heroic: "the music must rise to a loftier strain, up to Händel, up to Beethoven, up to the thorough-base of the seashore, up to the largeness of astronomy: at last that great heart [of Newton] will hear in the music beats like its own; the waves of melody will wash and float him also, and set him into concert and harmony" (*W*, VIII, 56-57). The "grander harmonies" of such sounds parallel the abstracting thrust of the language. Soaring cadences of necessity leave out the lesser and dissonant sounds of the confused and actual world. Emerson was equating the sound of poetry with moral ends. He intended that equation as a liberating device, an escape from the cave of the world. Simultaneously in his aesthetic theory he desired a noble raising of the sounds of life and a piercing of rotten diction so as to fasten words again to visible things. His philosophical needs warred against his aesthetic instincts. The new authenticity he sought as an artist meant invoking an aesthetic inelegance. That rebarbarization of art sprang in full force from the poems of the amateurs, Whitman and Dickinson.

In theory, then, Emerson held the key: "Poetry will never be a simple means, as when history or philosophy is rhymed, or laureate odes on state occasions are written. Itself must be its own end, or it is nothing" (*W*, VIII, 54). Toward this ideal his theorizing strove. The impatient striding of his verse was the price he paid for the grandest of all American dreams, the conversion of the world.

With understanding now of the highly selective, language-limited, revelation-seeking structure of that converting mind, shall we not say that Emerson's idea of a meter-making argument was a binding doctrine rather than a liberating one? The poetry adopted that converting structure and, because it was thus distracted, it worked a constant violation of reality. The inadvertent corruption of consciousness was opposed to the native aesthetic need that animated the Divinity School address. Out of that freely responsive spirit ("How wide; how rich; what invitation from every property [the world] gives to every faculty of man!") came an altered idea of how a poetry might take up the world.

The energy with which Emerson concerned himself with this artistic dilemma entered the whole body of his poetry. If we look now with a new attention to the structure of the verse we can see it. Poem after poem labors inwardly over an ideal poetics and a vision of artistic power. This concern is the essential activity of his otherwise insubstantial verse, its shadow drama.

CHAPTER 4

The Muse Has a Deeper Secret

THE DEATH OF young Waldo was only the most tragic of all the experiences that were absorbed by Emerson's aesthetic concentration. The poems assimilated experience to the introspective life of his poetic imagination. No matter what the ostensible subject—a walk in the countryside, a snowstorm, a camping trip, a commemorative verse, even the death of a son—the deep determining subject remained constant. But the great writers, as Proust's narrator explains somewhere, have never written more than a single work, expressing rather through diverse transformations the unique ardor by which they are animated. This observation in no way denies the useful groupings of the poems which Emerson scholars have made according to such categories as the domestic poems (say "Threnody"), political ("Ode to W. H. Channing"), descriptive ("May-Day"), or philosophical ("Brahma"). Firkins argued that "the number of *species* in Emerson's verse is large in proportion to the number of poems. He is always doing something not quite like other people and not quite like himself." Others have enumerated the poetic genres at some length.[1] But within the poems exists a structural sameness that organizes the apparent distinctions at the surface.

Detecting Emerson's brooding search for ways to allow the unimpeded outlet of the poetic imagination is quite different from concluding, as readers have, that Emerson's poems are mostly distilled philosophy. They are, in fact, transformings of a persistent inner imperative that lodged below the level of Emerson's conscious aim. Jonathan Bishop's observation on Emerson's preoccupation with the process of the Soul is on the mark exactly: "The metamorphosis of circumstances into consciousness is the consummation of the Soul's great act. The trajectory of that act is sketched in a hundred remarks."[2] The fixation was stronger than that: it was single, intense, distracting. This is why, as Arnold implied when he said the reader of "The Titmouse" never quite arrives at learning what the bird in the poem actually did for the man, many poems are so curiously indecisive. Labeling the poems "philosophical" seems to have been a way of getting at this indeterminate quality that is marked in poems like "The Sphinx" and "The Problem." They are surely not philosophical in the way Wordsworth's poems are, turning identifiable issues in explicit development; they are as inconclusive in statement as they are earnest in tone.

Emerson's poems took their mode from his world of stratified values and of stratified mind. The structure of the mind became the structure of the poems. The basic binarism was mapped out in the poem "Merlin": nature comes in ascending pairs, a kind of moral double helix through which the mind rises, and in this doubled world, "like the dancers' ordered band, thoughts come also hand in hand." Emerson's twoness comprised for him a symmetry that produced balance, replication, and joy, and thus "The animals are sick with love / Lovesick with rhyme." Furthermore, because the doubles reproduce themselves, they are immortal, they repeat truth, keep it "undecayed," triumph over time, and establish the Universal harmony. Like the Platonists, in whose system justice resides in the stable order beneath Truth and Love, Emerson plots that same abstract virtue in the symmetrical structure of nature. "Justice is the rhyme of things," he says in "Merlin."

It was a dynamic order in which the things that rhymed were not nearly so important as the rhyming itself. Emerson's younger contemporary, Matthew Arnold, sought to fix a multitudinous world, to establish for things, as Richard Ohmann has put it, "the fixity of being properly named" and not "to let concepts, actions, properties, or groups of people drift in a limbo of namelessness."[3] Emerson's aim was to keep dissolving those constraining definitions, to break down barriers and life-denying rituals, to rediscover one's manifold being in the universal circuit, and to yield oneself to the perfect whole. It is a powerful vision whose central light was Emerson's conception of the poetic imagination in the act of conversion. This was the enormously beneficent process of savage nature itself. In art, he believed, a comparable radical transforming primitivism was needed. In "The American Scholar," which, together with "Poetry and Imagination," forms the central document in the radical poetics of Emerson, we read this: "Not out of those on whom systems of education have exhausted their culture, comes the helpful giant to destroy the old or to build the new, but out of unhandselled savage nature; out of terrible Druids and Berserkers come at last Alfred and Shakespeare" (*W*, I, 99-100).

That helpful giant is Emerson's wonderfully muscular embodiment of the imagination, filled with power to convert, to liberate, to build the new out of the old, to reject all systems of established religions, able indeed to convert the world. He is the heroic figure of the artist's imagination, and he secretly inhabits almost every poem. Some poems relinquish their own power because they serve the giant and not their particular selves. Others, like "Merlin" and "The Snow-Storm," take on a powerful aesthetic significance.

This covert allegory explains in part why the world has so little reality in Emerson's poems. It is a bright rhyming world a long way from Charles Olson's "In cold hell, in thicket." What the poems lose in worldliness, however, they gain as an artist's concern with the working of creative energy. The discussion that follows is a new look at Emerson's poems as they distractedly circle again and again the three basic aspects of the poet's imagination: how it is structured, how it operates, and what its goal is.

In "Threnody" two levels of mind frame the dialogue of the poem and provide the poles between which the abrupt confrontation takes place. One way to identify these poles is by their Platonic designations of Being and Becoming. The father-mourner is the consciousness directly involved in the experience, actively mourning the death of the son. He confronts the loss and suffers the torments. Yet he fails to see the tragedy in its larger reconciling aspect, which is the function of the "deep Heart." This second consciousness perceives the significance of the death and offers the reconciliation for the mourner. The dramatic basis of the poem and the stage on which the performance takes place come directly from Emerson's idea of the low and high steps of the poetic imagaination. As we have seen, the genetic action of "Threnody" is not the death itself but the negotiation of these levels of the imagination that lead to elevation, understanding, and resolution.

Emerson identified these layers in many ways, always maintaining the distinction that the experiencing stage of the imagination was the lower, the resolving level the higher. In "Poetry and Imagination" he saw them reflected in the separation of science and art. "The solid men," he says, "complain that the idealist leaves out the fundamental facts; the poet complains that the solid men leave out the sky. To every plant there are two powers; one shoots down as rootlet, and one upward as tree. You must have eyes of science to see in the seed its nodes; you must have the vivacity of the poet to perceive in the thought its futurities" (*W,* VIII, 71). In attempting to analyze precisely how contemporary events are transformed to thought,

Emerson had earlier employed a similar vertical division, resorting finally to the orchard metaphor:

> The actions and events of our childhood and youth are now matters of calmest observation. They lie like fair pictures in the air. Not so with our recent actions, — with the business which we now have in hand. On this we are quite unable to speculate. Our affections as yet circulate through it. We no more feel or know it than we feel the feet, or the hand, or the brain of our body. The new deed is yet a part of life, — remains for a time immersed in our unconscious life. In some contemplative hour it detaches itself from the life like a ripe fruit, to become a thought of the mind. Instantly it is raised, transfigured; the corruptible has put on incorruption. Henceforth it is an object of beauty, however base its origin and neighborhood.   (*W,* I, 96)

This process of transformation, both moral and aesthetic as the quotation indicates, habitually informs Emerson's poetry. The separation of functions between the lower experiencing consciousness and the higher perceiving consciousness marks the distinction Emerson defined variously as that between talent and genius, fancy and the imagination, Understanding and Reason. It is the very armature and substance of the poem "The Problem." The speaker's cherished deep truth and creative act rise not from "a vain or shallow thought" but rather issue from fundamental and terrifying sources:

> Out from the heart of nature rolled
> The burdens of the Bible old;
> The litanies of nations came,
> Like the volcano's tongue of flame,
> Up from the burning core below.

Part of the "problem" is that the churchman's cowl signifies a deep consort with primal laws that no one would casually presume to possess. That sort of genius is not acquired simply by choice of the clerical profession. Emerson abhorred that presumption, and the argument of the poem, very much like that in "Threnody" (note the similar humbling rhetorical questions: "Know'st thou what wove yon woodbird's nest / . . . Or how the fish outbuilt her shell[?]"), divides between the lesser powers of mere preaching and the powers of genius, whose love and terror create wonders equal to Nature's.

Ambivalent as the poem is, despite its decisive opening and closing lines, it argues finally the speaker's desire to be an original *maker* and not simply a *transmitter*. It is an artist's poem, for inside its somewhat indeterminate exterior, the poem celebrates beauty and not religion.[4]

"Give All to Love" contains a similar divided structure, based on the same model of the imagination. The poem also proceeds from the lower power to the higher. In the beginning, it cheerfully promotes the human proclivity to give all to love and to the things of the day, ascending in experience with them:

> Obey thy heart;
> Friends, kindred, days,
> Estate, good-fame,
> Plans, credit and the Muse, —
> Nothing refuse.

By its end, abruptly, in that slackening of intention we have seen, the poem urges freedom from those lower claims:

> Keep thee to-day,
> To-morrow, forever,
> Free as an Arab
> Of thy beloved.

The two-staged experience comes directly to the surface in the final lines where the choice between an earthly love and the ideal is made clear:

> Though thou loved her as thyself,
> As a self of purer clay,
> Though her parting dims the day,
> Stealing grace from all alive;
> Heartily know,
> When half-gods go,
> The gods arrive.

Once again Emerson draws the distinction between a half-perception and the full ideal one. The half-gods, corrupted and partial by definition, are kin to those Plato describes in the *Apology* as the demi-gods who are the illegitimate sons of the gods sired on nymphs or mortals. Here they are embodiments of that familiar Emersonian choice between the half-sight focused on means and the full perception open to truth. Of George Herbert's idea of man as microcosm ("Man is one world, and hath / Another to attend him"), Emerson says in *Nature:* "The perception of this class of truths makes the attraction which draws men to science, but the end is lost sight of in attention to the means. In view of this half-sight of science, we accept the sentence of Plato, that 'poetry comes nearer to vital truth than history' " (*W,* I, 69). In Emerson's aesthetic equation, that half-sight of science equals poetic talent as opposed to genius, literary convention as opposed to prophetic content. The hierarchy thus had its personifications not only in the father-mourner as opposed to the deep Heart, but also the work-a-day preacher as opposed to the genius in possession of the word, the sensuous mortal pursuing the half-god of profane love as opposed to the idealist in quest of the gods themselves. The intention of each poem is thus linear, often abruptly so, proceeding from a first state of confusion, ignorance, or paralysis (sometimes all three) to a state of clarity, revelation, and liberation.

This basic structural model provides the armature in almost all of Emerson's poetry. In "Each and All," it is the speaker of simple talent or fancy who "aggregates" experiences, collecting a sparrow and seashells without discerning the plan of "the perfect whole" from which they are organically inseparable. Here again, the speaker starts out misled into thinking he can possess things as he pleases; he soon discovers that removed from their place in the great circuit, they become, like the shells, "poor, unsightly, noisome things." Through a slow, deliberate version of the eyeball experience, the speaker's consciousness finally rises so that he "sees" the larger beauty. Again we confront Emerson's world as it was limited to experiences that could be used to demonstrate the two levels of the imagination. But there was an opening in Emerson's scheme that will be important to us later and is appropriately to be noted here. The philosophical assumption of an organic universe had extremely significant ramifications in Emerson's developing aesthetics of poetic form. He says in a journal entry of May 16, 1834: "I learned that Composition was more important than the beauty of individual forms to effect" (*JMN*, IV, 291). The poem "Each and All" enacts this credo by an allegory of what was essentially an aesthetic tenet of Emerson's, perhaps the most important and most "modern" one, the need for more aggregate and fully receptive forms.

"Brahma" is a late example of his structural obsession. Despite its moebius-loop view of the universe where all things turn on their opposites—it is the insight of genius that Brahma possesses—the poem rests on that familiar ladder of the ascending consciousness. At its conclusion, the half-perception is associated with "heaven" and a partial way of seeing. Brahma in effect says at the end, "Turn your back on single systems of thought exemplified by the idea of heaven and be liberated into the realm of total perceptions with me." The sweep toward revelation and thus at least a theoretical liberation from confinement is both a formal and philosophical paradigm here, as in other Emerson poems. Brahma urges a full and knowing receptiveness to this world below. It is the lower order of mind that thinks it can slay or be slain; the higher order sits where all the contraries converge. We hear in the poem another not so simple version of the deep Heart in "Threnody"; we stand at the burning core in "The Problem"; we face the gods in "Give All to Love."

The overheard Poet in that most inconclusive of all of Emerson's published poems, "The Sphinx," gives us a gloss on the higher sight of Brahma:

> "To vision profounder,
>   Man's spirit must dive;
> His aye-rolling orb
>   At no goal will arrive;
> The heavens that now draw him
>   With sweetness untold,
> Once found, — for new heavens
>   He spurneth the old."

By that marvelous etherializing process of conversion that Emerson never ceased portraying, the drowsy Sphinx finally "melts," "silvers," "spires," "flowers," "flows" into nature's forms. From a stony mystery she becomes the airy spiritual truth of nature, a not unfamiliar progression in the poetry of Emerson. Again he has moved along the trajectory from ignorance to revelation. "The Sphinx" is a paradigm itself of Emerson's conception of the poetic function. For this reason if for no other, Emerson was justified in placing it at the beginning of his first volume of poems in 1846.

But Emerson's contemporaries found the poem impenetrable, as most readers have since. Ambiguous, apparently contradictory in viewpoint, it did not provide a welcome entry to his other poems, and later editors moved it back from the head position. Edward Emerson said it "cut off, in the very portal, readers who would have found good and joyful words for themselves, had not her riddle been beyond their powers" (*W,* IX, 403). The poem's vexing ambiguity comes largely because it is unclear whether or not the Poet solves the Sphinx's riddle. The Poet seems to defeat the Sphinx ("Dull Sphinx, Jove keep thy five wits") and to be defeated (the Sphinx replies: "Thou art the unanswered question . . . And each answer is a lie."). Yet encompassing the two-level structures of the supernatural riddler and the human riddle-solver, joyful nature and melancholy man, is a primary consciousness. This all-seeing maker of the poem contains the dull Sphinx's opacity as well as its protean dynamism, the picture of oafish man as well as the cheerful poet's confident reply. That primary speaker, part Emerson and part an idealization, knows both the Poet's craving for universal principles and the Sphinx's knowledge of infinite forms and transformations. It is this speaker, then, who sees the truth that nature is incessant change and has no single identifiable center such as Love, as the overheard Poet says. And it is this super Emersonian speaker presumably who was intended to preside over the poems in the book. "The Sphinx" was the essential statement and act of all the other poems that accompanied it.

In it, Emerson's speaker is the Central Poet outside his two-tiered system for once, living fully in the world, serene in its flux, beyond grasping after absolutes.[5]

The drama between the grasping but ignorant low mind and the enduring, all-perceiving imagination or high mind is played out later in "Hamatreya" by the farmers on the one hand and the earth on the other. Emerson, we recall, said near the conclusion of "Poetry and Imagination" that "Men are facts as well as persons, and the involuntary part of their life is so much as to fill the mind and leave them no countenance to say aught of what is so trivial as their selfish thinking and doing" (*W,* VIII, 75). In the poem this "trivial doing" is the vain regard of the farmers soon to die. The facticity of their lives is established at the beginning with drumming directness (and no little humor) as their names form a list exactly parallel to the "things" of their toil:

> Bulkeley, Hunt, Willard, Hosmer, Meriam, Flint,
> Possessed the land which rendered to their toil
> Hay, corn, roots, hemp, flax, apples, wool, and wood.

In Emerson's equation men are the facts while the Earth (yet another disembodied voice out of the deep) stands for the larger and finally absorbing truth. In a further parallel, the aggregating lower mind is mirrored in the farmers' vain and possessive beliefs, while the Imagination has knowledge like the enduring Earth's:

> "They called me theirs,
> Who so controlled me;
> Yet every one
> Wished to stay, and is gone,
> How am I theirs,
> If they cannot hold me,
> But I hold them?"

To the extent that Emerson conceived of men as convertible elements in an eternal scheme, they were indeed facts. Both Alcott and Parker remarked that he thought of men as ideas, but Emerson's conception was always a part of a higher humanism. When he saw individual men, like the farmers in "Hamatreya," blinded by their vanity, Emerson's moral wrath could explode. Sampson Reed, his early guide, when he displayed his own kind of vanity in dogmatic narrowness, Emerson condemned in outrage in the poem "S. R.," calling him "Sleek deacon of the New Jerusalem" and "A blind man's blind man" (*VP,* 358). In aesthetic terms, all these men are failed poets, captives of their fancies, unable to liberate themselves from petty vanities and ascend to the higher imagination.

The rural man in nature displayed for Emerson the clear sight of the imagination, while the grasping city man among the money-mad crowd collected wealth but not sane contentedness. The citydweller in "Wood-notes II" does not see beyond his acquisitions. The forester has acquired qualities of the supernatural Sphinx:

> Whoso walks in solitude
> And inhabiteth the wood,
> Choosing light, wave, rock and bird,
> Before the money-loving herd,
> Into that forester shall pass,
> From these companions, power and grace.
> Clean shall he be, without, within,
> From the old adhering sin,
> All ill dissolving in the light
> Of his triumphant piercing sight:
> Not vain, sour, nor frivolous;
> Not mad, athirst, nor garrulous.

The seemingly blessed possessor in "Guy" is another version of factual man mistaking his material abundance for the higher power he lacks. Prosperous but not quite an example of "the balanced soul in harmony with nature," as Edward Emerson describes him in a note on the poem, Guy is rather another vain fact in an allegory of the lower mind. Emerson is careful in the poem to have us distinguish between fancy and genius. Guy's enormous vanity is established at the outset:

> Mortal mixed of middle clay,
> Attempered to the night and day,
> Interchangeable with things,
> Needs no amulets nor rings.
> Guy possessed the talisman
> That all things from him began.

He prospers in all he does, and it appears he has "caught Nature in his snares." In his vanity he supposes, like the farmers of "Hamatreya," that "fortune was his guard and lover." Indeed, he thinks himself (lovely parody of the eyeball) concentric with the universe:

> In strange junctures, felt, with awe,
> His own symmetry with law.

He believes he shares God's genius:

> It seemed his Genius discreet
> Worked on the Maker's own receipt.

But his end, one infers from the repeated overstatements, will be that of Polycrates, who suffered a cruel death despite his unbroken good fortune.

Mere possessiveness and smug satisfaction with the lower virtues are not to be confused with the higher humbling power to see the larger plan. The swelled pride is wonderfully punctured by the Byronic rhyme at the end where Guy's values converge on the single word: "Belonged to wind and world the toil / And venture, and to Guy the oil."

The model of mind was the stage for Emerson's actors, and he directs them in the poems with varying degrees of obviousness. The allegory determined the characters he chose and comprised the shadowy significance of the subjects he presented. The philosophy behind this divided model of the imagination as it perceived a convertible world had more significance for the artist, however, than simply the matters of vain possession and spiritual insight. The two levels of mind were the basis for an aesthetics that was part of the allegory.

Characteristically, the aesthetic suppositions take protean forms, and if we follow his principal ones we will end up seeing in Emerson's cherished snowstorm, of all places, the acting out of a forceful poetics. The way to this disclosure begins with Emerson's idea of the function of a college and his image of a fire. Colleges, he said in "The American Scholar," "only highly serve us when they aim not to drill, but to create; when they gather from far every ray of various genius to their hospitable halls, and by the concentrated fires, set the hearts of their youth on flame" (*W*, I, 93). He describes the ideal college not as a simple aggregating fancy but, like genius, as a distiller and transformer of those aggregated elements to inspiring flame. Only a little leap from this analogy is necessary to see the aesthetic meaning of the famous humble-bee. Emerson calls the bee "rover of the underwoods" and describes him as gatherer of all nature's sweetnesses, who by leaving the chaff and taking the wheat (in the poet's strained metaphor) transforms the gatherings to honey. The bee is his own self-reliant generator of heat ("Thou animated torrid-zone!"), the center of his society ("Joy of thy dominion!"), and perceiver of the ideal ("Yellow-breeched philosopher!"). There is a classical origin of course for these metaphorical associations of the bee, but in Emerson the figure embodies his constant vision of the transforming power of the imagination as it operates on the aggregations of the fancy.

In the aesthetic application of this model, we understand that genius transforms the gathered experiences into art. By way of the bee, we see also the naturalness of this transforming process; its wider analogy is the workings of nature, and these are visible most dramatically in Emerson's snowstorm. That equating of artistic creation with some form of great power appears repeatedly in the prose. In "The American Scholar" Emerson identified "the helpful giant" with the primitive force of the unschooled and natural. Only a transfer of metaphor is needed to make the snow-storm. Or it can be reached by the architecture metaphor with which the snowstorm poem ends. Emerson, in "The Poet," says of the poet that he "does not wait for the hero or the sage, but, as they act and think primarily, so he writes primarily what will and must be spoken, reckoning the others, though primaries also, yet, in respect to him, secondaries and servants; as sitters or models in the studio of a painter, or as assistants who bring building-materials to an architect" (*W*, III, 7-8). Overlapping, merging, the analogues crowd forth—college, bumblebee, giant, painter-artist, and architect. They are the gatherers and transformers, the honey-makers and the builders, all those who make a new construction out of their gathered materials. The fury of this creation and its identification with nature come in a passage of prose on the great poets. All the emblems converge. "Every good poem that I know," says Emerson in "Poetry and Imagination," "I recall by its rhythm also [as well as its rhyme]. Rhyme is a pretty good measure of the latitude and opulence of a writer. If unskilful, he is at once detected by the poverty of his chimes . . . Now try Spenser, Marlowe, Chapman, and see how wide they fly for weapons, and how rich and lavish their profusion. In their rhythm is no manufacture, but a vortex or musical tornado, which, falling on words and the experience of a learned mind, whirls these materials into the same grand order as planets and moons obey, and seasons, and monsoons" (*W*, VIII, 49-50). Here is that habitual movement from flux and chaos to the orderly, from the changeable to the systematic or monumental. That conversion of the mind and the correlative binary view of nature's own processes are ultimately founded in the basic elements that structured Emerson's thought: movement and stasis, chaos and order, the passing and the permanent. The writer, says Emerson in "Poetry and Imagination," "needs a frolic health . . . he must be at the top of his condition. In that prosperity he is sometimes caught up into a perception of . . . funds of power hitherto utterly unknown to him, whereby he can transfer his visions to mortal canvas, or reduce them into iambic or trochaic, into lyric or heroic rhyme. These successes are not less admirable and astonishing to the poet than they are to his audience" (*W*, VIII, 40). We have now in aggregate all of the primary analogies that structure the snowstorm poem, and, whereas earlier we were concerned with discovering the Emersonian linear arrangement and deliverance scheme of the poem, here it stands forth also as a concentrated poetics. While students may search the meteorological records of Concord for the early 1830s in search of an actual snowstorm source, we can satisfy ourselves that the much more demanding subject was Emerson the Artist's, and that was the idealized storm of poetic creation to which he yearned to submit. The poem is about a snowstorm and it is a program for poetry. It is worth quoting in its entirety:

> Announced by all the trumpets of the sky,
> Arrives the snow, and, driving o'er the fields,
> Seems nowhere to alight: the whited air
> Hides hills and woods, the river, and the heaven,
> And veils the farm-house at the garden's end.
> The sled and traveller stopped, the courier's feet
> Delayed, all friends shut out, the housemates sit
> Around the radiant fireplace, enclosed
> In a tumultuous privacy of storm.
>
>   Come see the north wind's masonry.
> Out of an unseen quarry evermore
> Furnished with tile, the fierce artificer
> Curves his white bastions with projected roof
> Round every windward stake, or tree, or door.
> Speeding, the myriad-handed, his wild work
> So fanciful, so savage, nought cares he
> For number or proportion. Mockingly,
> On coop or kennel he hangs Parian wreaths;
> A swan-like form invests the hidden thorn;
> Fills up the farmer's lane from wall to wall,
> Maugre the farmer's sighs; and at the gate
> A tapering turret overtops the work.
> And when his hours are numbered, and the world
> Is all his own, retiring, as he were not,
> Leaves, when the sun appears, astonished Art
> To mimic in slow structures, stone by stone,
> Built in an age, the mad wind's night-work,
> The frolic architecture of the snow.

Emerson's superb oxymorons—"tumultuous privacy," "fierce artificer," "so fanciful, so savage," "astonished Art," "slow structures," and "frolic architecture"—combine in a severely compacted way his idealized contraries of free imagination and ordered art. What seems chaotic, the storm, in the final perception is ordered, still, graceful, a part of nature itself in the way the Pyramids, St. Peter's, and the Parthenon are in the poem "The Problem." There is more: those freely formed contours of the snow sculpture rest upon but at the same time *obliterate* the rigid supporting forms beneath:

> So fanciful, so savage, nought cares he
> For number or proportion. Mockingly,
> On coop or kennel he hangs Parian wreaths;

A swan-like form invests the hidden thorn;
Fills up the farmer's lane from wall to wall.

The aesthetic principle behind the metaphor of the storm is central to Emerson's move toward more open compositional forms. He admonished writers not so much to await inspiration (this is a superficial view of Emerson's hardheaded methods) as to allow language strings, like snow, to fall into mimetic shapes: "Shun manufacture or the introducing an artificial arrangement in your thoughts, it will surely crack and come to nothing, but let alone tinkering and wait for the natural arrangement of your treasures." In the light of the poetics within the poem, we see as much an *aesthetic* sense in the famous thorn passage as a moral one. Emerson's moral stance was one with his aesthetics: poetry rightly shows the beautiful and ideal, and they in turn are moral because the humdrum and base are raised to the spiritual level. The moral and the aesthetic were to Emerson inseparable, as were the forces both of nature and human genius. As in "The Problem," it was an artist's philosophical system that had at its center not a moral point but the sensuous ideal of Beauty.

One final association and I shall be done with this line of exposition. When Emerson says in the essay "The Poet" that he sees nowhere among his contemporaries the poet of America, that is, the *genius* of the country, we understand now that he is calling for that great converting consciousness figured in the poetic snowstorm and in the great creative act of the helpful giant. The poet is to transform, like the bee, like the architect, like the storm itself, the vast and varied materials of the country into an aesthetic and visionary whole. That deep impulse to transform America to its noblest essence — at the same time to see it as an aesthetic whole — is Emerson's meaning when he says "America is a poem in our eyes." "We have yet had," he said, "no genius in America, with tyrannous eye, which knew the value of our incomparable materials" (*W*, III, 37). What Emerson missed in the poets of past ages, as he contemplated the kind of ideal imagination needed to convert the diverse nation to *its* ideal, were the basic qualities that emerge in "The Snow-Storm": the epic-sized transforming imagination with language equal to the task. "If I have not found that excellent combination of gifts in my countrymen which I seek," Emerson said, "neither could I aid myself to fix the idea of the poet by reading now and then in Chalmer's collection of five centuries of English poets. These are wits more than poets, though there have been poets among them. But when we adhere to the ideal of the poet, we have our difficulties even with Milton and Homer. Milton is too literary, and Homer too literal and historical" (*W*, III, 38). Emerson glimpsed that ideal poet in himself, animated as he was by a vision of what was possible. He had already freed himself from the literal by his constant process of transforming to the essence; he sought in theory a way to free himself also from the literary past that had no voice for his age. In the poems is the tirelessly worked ground of that theme.

THE SEER-GENIUS stage of the imagination found expression in Emerson's structural drama through a dissociated voice, in a curious but habitual separation from his poet-speaker. We took account earlier of the admonitory voice of the deep Heart in "Threnody" which catechizes the mourning father and argues the way to consolation for the death of the son. That strategy of the wise counter-voice has deep roots in Emerson's poetry. In his journal for 1845 he saw his own poetic role as that of a reporter of this voice of natural wisdom: "I will sing aloud and free / From the heart of the world" (*JMN,* IX, 168). Much earlier, in "The American Scholar," he considered this transmitting of the heart's voice to be one of the principal functions of the scholar: "Whatsoever oracles the human heart, in all emergencies, in all solemn hours, has uttered as its commentary on the world of actions, — these he [Man Thinking] shall receive and impart" (*W,* I, 102). The schema of the separated poetic consciousness appears almost everywhere in the poetry. The dissociated voice, which is the expression of that schema, sounds conspicuously in "Hamatreya" (fancy speaks in the person of the farmers, the earth is the imagination), "Monadnoc" (the mountain speaks), "Woodnotes II" (the pinetree speaks), "To Ellen at the South" (flowers), "Hermione" (the dying Arab and Nature), "Celestial Love III" (God), "Saadi" (fakirs and the muse), "Dirge" (the bird), "May-Day" (old man), "Freedom" (spirit), "Boston Hymn" (God), "Voluntaries" (Destiny), "Boston" (the mountain, Boston, King George), "Solution" (the muse), "The Titmouse" (bird), "Seashore" (the sea), "Song of Nature" (nature), "Terminus" (the god Terminus), "The Poet" (the mighty). Even so selective a list indicates the fixity of Emerson's preoccupation.

Confronting a voice out of the heart of things was not uncommon in the work of Emerson's contemporaries, but it was less programmatic. The enchanting paradigm of the encounter occurs in the "Spring" section of *Walden,* where Thoreau finds himself present at Creation. The railroad bank thaws, flows into primal forms, and thereby speaks to Thoreau the language of the earth's original plan. "No wonder that the earth expresses itself outwardly in leaves, it so labors with the idea inwardly." Inwardly the earth speaks liquid words; outwardly they are leaves and wing feathers. Wet *love* becomes dry *leaf.* Thoreau's literal-mindedness was, characteristically, total. There are comparable meetings in Emily Dickinson, the essential text being "Further in Summer than the Birds," where the voice is the cricket nation's in a canticle of death. A similar encounter takes place in Frederick Tuckerman's great poem "The Cricket." In a rapt moment, the poet feels himself on the verge of conversing in the secret language of nature, drawn toward its mystery, and tempted finally to die into it (the dissolution that Yvor Winters called moral failure). In a later day, it is this direct encounter, as we have seen, that Robert Frost's solitary characters seek in the woods, even cry out for as in "The Most of It" but, with the exception of the mower in "The Tuft of Flowers," never accomplish. Because revelation, the eyeball experience, does not really come, Frost's is a poetry of aborted communion. A contemporary version of the instinctual heart-actor — predatory, brooding, bereft of light, yet stubborn, unkillable, wily, surviving — is Ted Hughes's crow.

Merlin is the lately-at-court figure in whom Emerson's own emblematic deep Heart, the technique of the separated voice, and his idea of the poet come together. The identification is most fully apparent if the poem "Merlin" is held alongside Emerson's extended remarks in "Poetry and Imagination." Emerson quotes in the essay as a high and memorable experience the section in *Morte d'Arthur* when Merlin speaks for the last time to Gawain from his enchanted prison in the forest. "Whilst I served King Arthur, I was well known by you and by other barons, but because I have left the court, I am known no longer, and put in forgetfulness, which I ought not to be if faith reigned in the world." The similarity to Emerson's leaving the ministry and his later ostracism because of the lecture to the divinity students is striking. Merlin continues: "you will never see me more, and that grieves me, but I cannot remedy it, and when you shall have departed from this place, I shall nevermore speak to you nor to any other person, save only my mistress; for never other person will be able to discover this place for anything which may befall; neither shall I ever go out from hence, for in the world there is no such strong tower as this wherein I am confined; and it is neither of wood, nor of iron, nor of stone, but of air" (*W,* VIII, 61). This voice literally imprisoned in the heart of nature is Emerson's exemplary voice. He described that particular passage from *Morte d'Arthur* as the "height which attracts more than other parts, and is best remembered" (*W,* VIII, 60). It is concerned with the voice Emerson believed poets should strive to hear and to transmit. Aspects of it rise again and again from other poems, most fervently in "Threnody," very pointedly in "The Problem," where the seer inside nature is the very figure the speaker cannot presume to be, even though he might wear the cowl that signifies it.

The humbling voice issues from the center of all the circles: "Out from the heart of nature rolled / The burdens of the Bible old." But it also sounds in the forest, like Merlin's, to the lover's ear:

> The word by seers or sibyls told,
> In groves of oak, or fanes of gold,
> Still floats upon the morning wind,
> Still whispers to the willing mind.

Emerson sought that willing mind in the poem and in himself and elaborately projected it as Man Thinking. The poet of willing mind will earn his freedom and learn his craft from that voice of knowing nature. Merlin, then, is the exemplary poet, and in the Merlin poem Emerson stresses liberation from constraints of form, calls for artful thunder, and specifies the goal: "Great is the art, / Great be the manners, of the bard." Merlin is the authentic voice, Guy's is delusive, for despite all his pride of nature's cooperation, Guy gets only the oil. Merlin's

> blows are strokes of fate,
> Chiming with the forest tone,
> When boughs buffet boughs in the wood;
> Chiming with the gasp and moan
> Of the ice-imprisoned flood.

No simple meddling wit can stand with the angels, but rather only the propitious mind.

> There are open hours
> When the God's will sallies free,
> And the dull idiot might see
> The flowing fortunes of a thousand years.

Emerson also knew the blind moments. He experienced the failure of nature's language and the blockage of the poetic imagination when communication is shut down. The ambivalence cuts into the lines of "Merlin" which follow immediately and end the positive first section:

> Sudden, at unawares,
> Self-moved, fly-to the doors,
> Nor sword of angels could reveal
> What they conceal.

Edward Emerson accurately described Merlin as typifying for Emerson "the haughty, free and liberating poet, working the magic of thought through the charm of Art" (*W*, IX, 440). Merlin says the primal word because he is unencumbered by the courtly restraints of artifice. In Emerson's early journal version of the poem, the poet is admonished to reject the devices of the merely talented poets—"gentle touches," the tinklings of a guitar, telling "a pretty tale" only to "pretty people in a nice saloon," all false creations "borrowed from their expectation" (*JMN*, IX, 167-168). There are, instead, qualities of the self-reliant, manly figure in Emerson's poet. He described that unfettered myth-phallic figure in the powerful essay "Experience": "The great and crescive self, rooted in absolute nature, supplants all relative existence and ruins the kingdom of mortal friendship and love" (*W*, III, 77).

Among Emerson's constructs of the poetic imagination, the central one is Merlin. All those dissociated voices speaking out of his poems are versions of that central poet.

THE FIGURES crowd Emerson's verse. In "Threnody" alone, as we saw, there are three: young Waldo as the budding poet dead before his time, the desperate father as the failed poet-seer, and the deep Heart as the thunder-poet out of the volcano.

The variety of forms this allegory takes attests to the obsessiveness of the poet's role in Emerson's thought. He could be quite literal-minded in pointing out likenesses. Some of the psychological faddists of his time—people he believed capable of controlling other individuals because they possessed an absolute "natural" power—share, perhaps debased a bit, the ways of the poet. Among examples of "the action of man upon nature with his entire force,—with reason as well as understanding" Emerson includes "Animal Magnetism" and "the miracles of enthusiasm" as reported by Swedenborg, Hohenloke, and the Shakers. These, says Emerson, are examples of "Reason's momentary grasp of the sceptre; the exertions of a power which exists not in time or space, but an instantaneous in-streaming causing power" (*W*, I, 73).

Emerson's literal-mindedness in this respect is unique. It was his attempt to make his insights available to the common man, *to make the poet's revelation a democratic enterprise.* This distinguishes him in a fundamental way from the willfully alienated poet-seers of the Romantic temper. The convention of isolation was a concomitant of the higher vision with its sight of revelation. Frank Kermode defines the direct correlation between "these two beliefs—in the Image as a radiant truth out of space and time, and in the necessary isolation or estrangement of men who can perceive it."[6] Not so with Emerson. He refused to promote the fanciful isolation of the seer-poet but rather, as he says in "Merlin," strove to open the doors, making the vision available to all who would attempt it. In so doing, he staked out the fundamental American variant to the central Romantic myth.

Carl Strauch calls Emerson's poet figures masks: "Uriel, Merlin, Saadi, these are poetic masks for the attributes and functions of the poet as Emerson saw them. Uriel is an archetypal emblem of the rebellious intellect, Merlin typifies power, and Saadi represents the cheerful acceptance of isolation until the propitious moment has arrived for the poet to deliver his message."[7] Beyond these, however, and enclosing them all is the basic figure of the perceiving imagination. The variety of versions indicates how obsessive this theoretical subject was for Emerson. Uriel, for example, who possessed a "look that solved the sphere" and who is able to declare "Line in nature is not found" and "Evil will bless, and ice will burn," acts as much the role of a conscious eyeball as a resigned minister or the rebellious deliverer of the Divinity School address.[8] Each role contributes to his conception of the liberated and liberating poet, which is to say that while the free and imaginative man took many forms in Emerson, he was never distinct from the poet, whether Man Thinking or angel rebelling.

One inevitably sees "Brahma" as a version of the poet. Here again is Emerson on the eye: "The eye is the best of artists. By the mutual action of its structure and of the laws of light, perspective is produced, which integrates every mass of objects, of what character soever, into a well colored and shaded globe, so that where the particular objects are mean and unaffecting, the landscape which they compose is round and symmetrical" (*W*, I, 15). Condensed here is every basic element of Emerson's structural poetics: the converting imagination as the eyeball, its structure integral with nature, its highly selective and transforming power over reality, the consequent reduction of reality to a symmetrical moral equation. The prose contains the aesthetic and the moral geometry of the poem "Brahma," with the Oriental consciousness as the transforming center of the poem. It is Emerson's basic model of the world as seen through a shaping eyeball that merges the moral and aesthetic imagination and inevitably abstracts reality to a scheme inseparable from that vision. Brahma is one of Emerson's ultimate poets and, not surprisingly, the poem for all its economy and control presents the moral and aesthetic problem of his poetry. The final line, in that habitual Emersonian movement, dismisses the half-god of a human belief ("turn thy back on heaven") for the whole but abstract purity of the ideal vision.

There are yet other poet figures. The poet in "The Sphinx," overheard by the yet more complete mind of the poet's maker, literally converts the beast from ugliness to beauty, from mystery to intelligibility, liberating mankind as befits the poet Emerson described as a liberating god. The Sphinx is ponderous fact; the poet transforms it into bright Truth. In a

similar plot, though less dramatic, the protagonists in "The Rhodora" and
"Each and All" who are failed poets as the poems begin, come, through the
auspices of nature, to their own revelation of the natural symmetry of the
world's beauty and the imagination ("Rhodora": "The self-same Power
that brought me there brought you"), and a fresh recognition that the
higher unity includes man ("Each and All": "Beauty through my senses
stole; / I yielded myself to the perfect whole.")

Nonhuman actors embody types of the artist, as we saw in "The Snow-
Storm." Another actor is the humble-bee. As he transforms the materials
of his foraging, he plays the part of the imagination. The same qualities of
intellectual nomadism, in characteristic Emerson fashion, circulate in all
his actors. The "forest seer" in "Woodnotes I," while justifiably identified
as Thoreau in literal readings of the poem (see Edward Emerson's note, *W*,
IX, 420), is very much the poet as a personified bee! The terms are identical:

> It seemed that Nature could not raise
> A plant in any secret place . . .
> But he would come in the very hour
> It opened in its virgin bower . . .
> It seemed as if the breezes brought him,
> It seemed as if the sparrows taught him;
> As if by secret sight he knew
> Where, in far fields, the orchis grew . . .
> What others did at distance hear,
> And guessed within the thicket's gloom,
> Was shown to this philosopher,
> And at his bidding seemed to come.

"In poetry," Emerson says, "we say we require the miracle. The bee flies
among the flowers, and gets mint and marjoram, and generates a new
product, which is not mint and marjoram, but honey . . . and the poet lis-
tens to conversation and beholds all objects in Nature, to give back, not
them, but a new and transcendent whole" (*W*, VIII, 16-17). There is a further loop in this skein of concern with the poet and the imagination. Emerson says in the essay "The Poet" that the Ancients remind us that poets
speak "not with intellect alone but with the intellect inebriated by nectar"
(*W*, III, 27). In the Emersonian aesthetic, the nectar is visionary. Having
come round by way of snowstorm, Brahma, and bee, we recognize how
deep-drawing is the concern in the poem "Bacchus" with the poetic enterprise. A colossal ballast of aesthetic rumination feeds the urgent imperatives of the poet-speaker:

> Give me of the true . . .
> Wine of wine,
> Blood of the world,
> Form of forms, and mould of statures,
> That I intoxicated,
> And by the draught assimilated,
> May float at pleasure through all natures;
> The bird-language rightly spell,
> And that which roses say so well.

A circuit closes between this poem and the Sphinx poem that Emerson had placed at the head of the 1846 edition:

> I thank the joyful juice
> For all I know, —
> Winds of remembering
> Of the ancient being blow,
> And seeming-solid walls of use
> Open and flow.

"Imagination intoxicates the poet," Emerson tells us (*W,* III, 30), and the poet in turn, by his clarifying symbols, intoxicates and therefore liberates men. The poetic act centers in the plenitude of the single imagination, self-intoxicating. This is the aesthetic equivalent in his poetics of what Emerson called in social and moral contexts the self-reliant man.

We are not done with versions of the poet. The pinetree in "Woodnotes II" admonishes the poet-listener in a long discourse marked by some of Emerson's most egregious rhymes and meters:

> "Come learn with me the fatal song
> Which knits the world in music strong, —
> Come lift thine eyes to lofty rhymes . . .
> I, that to-day am a pine,
> Yesterday was a bundle of grass.
> He [God, the eternal Pan] is free and libertine,
> Pouring of his power the wine
> To every age, to every race;
> Unto every race and age
> He emptieth the beverage;
> Unto each, and unto all,
> Maker and original."

God, Bacchus, humble-bee, forest seer, Uriel, Brahma, pinetree: all are versions of the poet and types of the imagination just as Bulkeley, Hunt, and Willard, Guy, the mourning father, the hiker in the snowy woods (and many more both early and late) are figures of the merely acquisitive or perceiving sense. Ideas of the aesthetic transaction were so crucial to Emerson's imagination that even the rifles that fire the shot in "Concord Hymn," as we shall discover, inescapably figure as yet another version of the imagination. We shall reach that disclosure by leaving off now the examples of structures of the imagination in the poems to see how Emerson's conception of the *process* of the poetic alembic lies equally deep and formative in the poetry.

WORDSWORTH SAID that objects should be reported not as they are but as they seem, and it is the seeming that is literally reported. In Emerson's poetry, the process of conversion is reported, the apparent subjects being thus quite interchangeable. The poems, no matter what objects occupy their vision, enact the process of the beholding and coenergizing mind as it transforms reality on the way from the nerve ends to the mind in that now familiar train of conversion from sensation to experience to thought.

This transfer of energy inevitably rests on the pairs that stand behind the spirals that Emerson's figurative thought favored. These different structural metaphors are related. His circles and spirals are the connecting motions of the mind as it plays over the fundamental dialectic, which takes the form of horizontal and vertical dualities. The horizontal doubleness embraces the reassuring paired structure of nature that everywhere manifests the universal symmetry. Emerson located himself pleasurably in that cosmic rhyme. As he put it in a marvelous lexical playback: "The animals are sick with love, / Lovesick with rhyme." The vertical duality consists in the Platonic division of experience into lower shadows of Becoming and the higher light of Being. Across this grid of two dimensions Emerson conceived the imagination playing its constant act of conversion. In the poems, the conversion arcs again and again.

The more complicated motions of conversion I traced in several poems: facts transformed to principle in "The Snow-Storm," "Humble-bee," "Each and All," "Rhodora." Its outline rationalizes the otherwise awkward and even fractured progress of "Threnody," a major display of the powerful structural set of Emerson's aesthetic beliefs. A revealing occasion occurs in "Each and All," where the conversion seems made with little conviction, almost as a gratuitous assertion. It is in fact the structure of Emerson's poetics right on the surface, with no shadowing allegory. Instead, in a kind of eyeball instance, there is an abrupt transfer of fact into thought at the end of the poem. The revelation arrives out of the blue with no explanation of how the "facts" fly together in the viewer's mind to make the instructive principle.

> I said, "I covet truth;
> Beauty is unripe childhood's cheat;
> I leave it behind with the games of youth:" —
> As I spoke, beneath my feet
> The ground-pine curled its pretty wreath,
> Running over the club-moss burrs;
> I inhaled the violet's breath;
> Around me stood the oaks and firs;
> Pine-cones and acorns lay on the ground;
> Over me soared the eternal sky,
> Full of light and of deity;
> Again I saw, again I heard,
> The rolling river, the morning bird; —
> Beauty through my senses stole;
> I yielded myself to the perfect whole.

We can see in this apparently random list of natural things the familiar Platonic structure of the high and low: the ground-pine beneath the towering trees; the fallen acorns beneath the soaring and eternal sky. In what seems a casual but is surely a deliberate symmetry are what Emerson called the visual rhymes of nature. Out of the details of this picture, the cosmic coherence is more or less taken on trust. The viewer in the poem, at the outset a poet lacking imagination and possessing a fragmenting scientific mind, wins through despite himself to a final ideal vision. Because the process is so mechanically delivered here, "Each and All" discloses the assumptions in the deeper part of Emerson's consciousness. There is almost no surface enactment of the process of conversion. In a revealing prose passage, Emerson came no closer to explaining that buried transfer: "It is easier to read Sanscrit, to decipher the arrow-head character, than to interpret . . . familiar sights. It is even much to name them. Thus Thomson's 'Seasons' and the best parts of many old and many new poets are simply enumerations by a person who felt the beauty of the common sights and sounds, without any attempt to draw a moral or affix a meaning" (*W*, VIII, 22-23).

The most fully drawn conversion unfolds in "The Snow-Storm." It is a process that reaches back to the mythopoeic confrontation in "The Sphinx," the individual deciphering the code of his existence. Poem after poem, as it enacts the conversion, points to the centrality of this movement in Emerson's mind. In "Berrying" the occasion is virtually identical to that in "Each and All," revealing now as well its links to other poems, like "The Titmouse":

> "May be true what I had heard, —
> Earth's a howling wilderness,

Truculent with fraud and force,"
Said I, strolling through the pastures,
And along the river-side.
Caught among the blackberry vines,
Feeding on the Ethiops sweet,
Pleasant fancies overtook me.
I said, "What influence me preferred,
Elect, to dreams thus beautiful?"
The vines replied, "And didst thou deem
No wisdom from our berries went?

The poem "Étienne de la Boéce," based on a friendship of Montaigne's, is a rare and stunning example where the process obsessive to Emerson the artist dominated even the treatment of this historical relationship. Once again the goal of the poem is to disclose the essential value of the experience, which for the Montaigne-Emerson figure is the divine spark that makes a "resistant" manhood, not simply a shadow of Boéce but his equal in inspiration. We recognize how much like Brahma is that miraculously transforming soul Emerson ascribes to Montaigne:

if I could,
In severe or cordial mood,
Lead you rightly to my altar,
Where the wisest Muses falter,
And worship that world-warming spark
Which dazzles me in midnight dark,
Equalizing small and large,
While the soul it doth surcharge,
Till the poor is wealthy grown,
And the hermit never alone, —
The traveller and the road seem one
With the errand to be done, —
That were a man's and lover's part,
That were Freedom's whitest chart.

The same converting process exists as a plaintive fixation of the artist who speaks in "Blight." The poem begins with what is now familiar to us as the act of drawing the visionary out of the factual. Again, the syntax is demanding because completion is deliberately suspended:

Give me truths;
For I am weary of the surfaces,
And die of inanition. If I knew
Only the herbs and simples of the wood,
Rue, cinquefoil, gill, vervain and agrimony,
Blue-vetch and trillium, hawkweed, sassafras,
Milkweeds and murky brakes, quaint pipes and sundew,

> And rare and virtuous roots, which in these woods
> Draw untold juices from the common earth,
> Untold, unknown, and I could surely spell
> Their fragrance, and their chemistry apply
> By sweet affinities to human flesh,
> Driving the foe and stablishing the friend, —
> O, that were much, and I could be a part
> Of the round day, related to the sun
> And planted world, and full executor
> Of their imperfect functions.

Here is the characteristic recognition once more of the deep forces that generate the green outer world's language. It was the way Emerson sought the significance of the life around him, and it was the way of his poems.

The conversion act is imminent in "Days." He described the scholar as "watching days and months sometimes for a few facts" (*W,* I, 101). His speaker in "May-Day" saw hidden in the spring days the gods themselves:

> I saw them mask their awful glance
> Sidewise meek in gossamer lids . . .
> It was as if the eternal gods,
> Tired of their starry periods,
> Hid their majesty in cloth
> Woven of tulips and painted moth.

The man in his pleached garden is one more Emersonian poet waiting for the revelation. The association is suggested by an 1843 journal entry: "Somebody . . . saw in a dream a host of angels descending with salvers of glory in their hands. On asking one of them for whom those were intended, he answered, 'for Shaikh Saadi of Shiraz, who has written a stanza of poetry that has met the approbation of God Almighty' " (*W,* IX, 447-448). The same archetypal visitation constitutes the central metaphor in the early poem "The Day's Ration." As in "Days," the awaiting consciousness, the mind's chalice, cannot take the inflow:

> To-day, when friends approach, and every hour
> Brings book, or starbright scroll of genius,
> The little cup will hold not a bead more,
> And all the costly liquor runs to waste.

A specific emphasis in "Days" is worth noting: the imagination confronts not only visionary moments but actual days. Emerson, as his journals show, was acutely aware of the facts of his own days, from political and economic to intellectual, and he searched them with the poet's transfiguring imagination for their essential truth. He urged the same on every poet. The pleached garden of his poem was already implicit in a passage from the essay "The Poet" seven years earlier: "I look in vain for the poet whom I describe. We do not with sufficient plainness or sufficient profoundness address ourselves to life, nor dare we chaunt our own times and social circumstance. If we filled the day with bravery, we should not shrink from celebrating it. Time and nature yield us many gifts" (*W*, III, 37). I shall have more to say about Emerson's occasional depiction of the poet as a reluctant converter, for this passivity is one of the crucial aspects of the deeply idealistic structure of the imagination. For the present, we can see that "Days" provides the quintessential converting situation undisguised. The poem has no diversionary subject — a walk, a bereavement, a characterization — but like "The Sphinx" deals directly with a conspicuous allegory of the imagination confronting reality. The conversion fails, and we are surprised by Emerson's explicit depiction of the defeat:

> I, in my pleached garden, watched the pomp,
> Forgot my morning wishes, hastily
> Took a few herbs and apples, and the Day
> Turned and departed silent. I, too late,
> Under her solemn fillet saw the scorn.

"Days" takes account of untranslatable realities rarely brought into Emerson's poetry. Here is an occasion when experience presents itself but is not taken up, as if it were unintelligible to the poet-viewer. This is a lurking nightmare in Emerson that readers often miss. The balletic imagery of "Days" does not penetrate to the depth we glimpsed in "Threnody," but the desperation over a whole reality that goes unperceived and unconverted is as genuine.

SUCCESSFUL CONVERSION takes place almost everywhere else in Emerson's poetry. The opening of second sight into the compensatory plan of nature manages to occur. As each poem makes its drama out of that process, each then is a variation of the transparent-eyeball experience at the visionary heart of *Nature*. The eyeball conversion is the accelerated ideal. The others in the individual poems, though they may be extended out in time for dramatic purposes, are in fact deliberately slackened examples of that one ecstatic act of the poetic imagination.

Seen in its full coherence, the eyeball process defines the aesthetics of Emerson's moral beliefs by establishing the emblematic equation between the physical eye and the poetic imagination. It is the single, homely metaphor in which the Platonic terms Emerson adopted for himself converge in an instant dependence of form upon soul. Once we see the centrality of this crucial image, we recognize how it ramifies into other analogies. The

pleached garden of "Days," in which the poet stands passively and enclosed, is itself a sort of enlarged eyeball and the two figures in turn make a
metaphor for the receiving consciousness. In the allegory of "Days," that
consciousness confronts reality in the form of maidens. Exotic, their appearance distracts the fancy of the waiting man, and the encounter fails of
revelation. What did *not* happen is the poem's subject, and we find it described in "Poetry and Imagination": "The test of the poet is the power to
take the passing day, with its news, its cares, its fears, as he shares them,
and hold it up to a divine reason, till he sees it to have a purpose and
beauty, and to be related to astronomy and history and the eternal order of
the world" (*W*, VIII, 35).

There are inescapable consequences, both for Emerson's view of reality
and for his perception of contemporary culture, in this idea of the poetic
imagination and its relation to reality. He called the eye the best of artists,
integrating groups of things so that where particular objects are mean and
unaffecting, the landscape they compose is round and symmetrical. That
vision of balanced wholeness composes the "each" and the "all"; the individual reality, of whatever form or moral state, is part of the whole, being
swept up in a final aesthetic incorporation. Particulars are sacrificed to the
demands of the symmetrical, dramatic, and moral whole. The perceiving
eye registers a world whose moral and cultural disparities, whose tragic
possibilities, and whose grey ambiguities and indefiniteness disappear in
the aesthetic compass and balance. The overviewing eye has no vision
capable of rendering the finer lines of reality. If the world we live in is the
words we use, then the world Emerson's poetry saw is the poetry that Emerson wrote. The vision sacrificed the possible subjective life of individual
poems to the underlying structure of a harmonizing aesthetic theory.

Emerson returned again and again in the poems to the image of monumentality. It seems a repudiation of the dynamism in the essay "Circles,"
for instance, and in the circular poems "Brahma" and "Uriel," where perceptual motion pushes out from concentrated centers of self-knowledge to
the edges of dispersal. That yielding to the perfect whole is the plot of
many familiar outward-flowing passages from the poems, but the little-
noticed monument image, briefly noted earlier, came out of the poetics
and determined the focus of some of the poems. The monument stands
against the flux, providing stasis amid the onwardness and outwardness of
Emerson's contrary images. It is an integral part of the mind's converting
process even though it seems a compromise of Emerson's concept of natural
organicism. It most certainly is a departure from the biological figure upon
which Coleridge depended in discussing art. There is a strong sense of de-

liberate craftsmanship in Emerson's view of the artist. A monument stands at the end of "Threnody," an objective parallel to the consolation of the deep Heart as it unfolds the larger purpose in which the boy's death is made intelligible as well as blessed.

The snowstorm poem follows the metaphor of architecture, the graceful forms taking shape by the savage and chaotic labors of the storm. The oxymoron "frolic architecture" captures that instantaneous creation of stasis from movement, order from chaos, and beauty from savagery. The contradictory joining of "fierce" and "artificer" holds the paradox of wild genius issuing in graceful form. In "The Problem" the most noble expression of genius takes the form of buildings: the Parthenon, the Pyramids, St. Peter's, and England's abbeys. "Out of Thought's interior sphere / These wonders rose to upper air." Buildings, then, are emblems of inspired genius. In Emerson's ordering system, as in Pythagoras', the fixed is associated with the preferred (bright, straight, male) and with eternal values (the good, the one). The realm of shifting values and Becoming (many, female, moving) is associated with flux. But Emerson, like Swedenborg, could sit without terror in the midst of flux, among the "hated waves." The poem "Illusions" speaks of "the endless imbroglio" of this universe where "no anchorage is." But the vision leads Emerson not to existential terror, but rather to the durable confidence that Arnold admired.

> first shalt thou know,
> That in the wild turmoil,
> Horsed on the Proteus,
> Thou ridest to power,
> And to endurance.

Monumentality has two principal associations for Emerson, and they merge in the figure of the poet. The first association is philosophical, that monumentality is a way of standing in the world. The second association is aesthetic, that monumentality is a way of conceiving art in its relationship to that world. Philosophically, the monumental is principled firmness. In "Ode: Inscribed to W. H. Channing," for example, whoever does not stand fast to principle is on the side of ignorance, slavery, and chaos. In Emerson's bitter closing parable, the Muse is the solid mooring point when the victors divide and "Half for freedom strike and stand." The positive philosophical association is emphatic in "Monadnoc" where the poet-speaker proclaims the virtues of the mountain:

> Man in these crags a fastness find
> To fight pollution of the mind;

> In the wide thaw and ooze of wrong,
> Adhere like this foundation strong,
> The insanity of towns to stem
> With simpleness for strategem.

This is a virtuous monumentality to set beside Robert Frost's definition of poetry as a momentary stay against confusion. It is Platonic Being set against Becoming. The man who sees the immutable and can make the permanent symbol of it is the poet. Emerson says in the essay "The Poet": "He is the poet and shall draw us with love and terror, who sees through the flowing vest the firm nature, and can declare it" (*W*, III, 37). Swedenborg, as I noted earlier, was one of Emerson's early heroes who fulfilled that role: "Swedenborg, of all men in the recent ages, stands eminently for the translator of nature into thought . . . Before him the metamorphosis continually plays" (*W*, III, 35).

To Emerson, the thought that is taken from the flowing metamorphosis was the artifact itself, and that is the aesthetics of his monumentality. Thought put into language—poem, essay, lecture—was a fixed entity, a verbal monument. There was no doubt the biblical association: "The word unto the prophet spoken / Was writ on tables yet unbroken." In "Uriel," with spirited humor, Emerson parodied the lesser documents of order, the "Laws of form, and metre first," even the calendar of months and days, which the vain young gods discuss. It is Uriel who "solves the sphere" with his higher knowledge ("Line in nature is not found"), and immediately Fate's balance beam gives way and heaven slides to confusion.

In the poem "To Ellen," the lives of the two lovers are intelligible only as they are recorded on a page:

> And Ellen, when the graybeard years
> Have brought us to life's evening hour,
> And all the crowded Past appears
> A tiny scene of sun and shower,
> Then, if I read the page aright
> Where Hope, the soothsayer, reads our lot,
> Thyself shalt own the page was bright,
> Well that we loved, woe had we not.

Emerson's neoclassical predilection for attaching general values to monuments, seeing life over the shoulder as exemplum, strait-jacketed his poetry. The fixity at the end of "The Snow-Storm," despite the summoning of savage genius and colossal artistic energy, makes the closing exclusionary, cold, and inanimate. Whitman managed a more difficult unity by inclusion. His reality was not abstracted into monuments but, by a new linguistic drift and sweep, caught up not only the contradictions but the wayward drama of experience taking form.

EMERSON'S IMPULSE toward liberation in his philosophy, in his life, and in his art equaled his need for monuments. Structure and constraint, the "virtue of self-trust," appear in the middle essays "Montaigne" and "Experience" as necessary modes for life, just as the young Emerson acknowledged the utility of custom, as here in the early poem "Grace":

> How much, preventing God, how much I owe
> To the defences thou has round me set;
> Example, custom, fear, occasion slow.

But Emerson's compulsion toward liberation in the name of imaginative exploration and deep-diving moral and aesthetic discovery, the discovery of self, was the dynamo of his existence. It sounded in his poems at times with exultant tones. More often it was a plaintive undertheme in which the artist considered the ideal ability to feel fully and to give fully in his art.

Liberation paired in Emerson's mind with power, as if the imagination, once freed from material vanities, could possess the resources of nature itself. The circulation of nature's forces concentrated and replenished the sources of imaginative energy. The poet, Emerson wrote, "is capable of a new energy . . . by abandonment to the nature of things" (*W*, III, 26). In "The American Scholar," he saw no dissipation of this energy once tapped: "There is never a beginning, there is never an end, to the inexplicable continuity of this web of God, but always circular power returning into itself" (*W*, I, 85). Once gathered by the poetic imagination, ideally transformed into poetry, this concentrated power liberates mankind. Readers of poetry, he said, are like persons who come out of a cave or cellar into the open air. It was a new way of seeing that comes when men are freed, as Gertrude Stein was to say about Picasso's revolution, from the habit of knowing what they are looking at. Emerson's dilemma, then, was not in the theory of goals, but in the creation of a language that could grasp the energies of liberation.

In the geology of his poems this liberation from closed forms recurs as the principal but sometimes buried meaning. In "Brahma," as I pointed out earlier, the admonition "turn thy back on heaven" is less a rejection of Christian doctrine than a summons to the higher imagination to turn away from single forms of seeing. "Form is imprisonment and heaven itself a decoy," he wrote in his journal a decade earlier (*JMN*, IX, 322). And before that, in the essay "The Poet," he said: "Every thought is also a prison; every heaven is also a prison (*W*, III, 33). The admonition in "Brahma" is echoed earlier still in "The Sphinx" as the Poet describes man's instinctual restlessness:

> The heavens that now draw him
> With sweetness untold
> Once found, — for new heavens
> He spurneth the old.

"The Sphinx" was a bold credo of the poet's liberating crusade. By a parable, because to be explicit about the poet as the converter of the world was absurdly heady, the poem set out the goal of the poet, the goal of Emerson's book of poems, the goal of Emerson the artist. Other poems, extending out to the limits of Emerson's poetic canon, by one plot or another follow the same impulse. In "Bacchus" it takes the form of intoxication; in "Give All to Love" it is transacted in the exchange of half-gods for the gods. Each was a reenactment of the archetypal release from the cave into the sun. As in "Threnody" and all the others, that linear arrangement of dramatic action led in the same direction. With such assumptions so dominant in Emerson's vision, it is not surprising that in poems like "Rhodora" and "Each and All" the revelation arrives presumptuously. The archetype is more integral in the structure of "Uriel" and "The Snow-Storm." Rarely, however, was that mental chain that leads to revelation broken or distorted.

Emerson, to our great relief, took account of the contrary workings of fate and the preposterous optimism of his poet's credo. In "Nemesis," following the rhetorical question "Will a woman's fan the oceans smooth?" we find the counterclaim:

> In spite of Virtue and the Muse,
> Nemesis will have her dues,
> And all our struggles and our toils
> Tighter wind the giant coils.

This dire aspect Harold Bloom emphasizes in plotting the dark-bright dialectic in Emerson's world. But though Emerson came to grips with the negation of his idealist philosophy, the set of his deepest beliefs assumed a powerful converting imagination whose function in turn necessarily assumed the free state into which art was to liberate all men.

Emerson's poetic theory was so powerful a generator of his poems that it molded to its own shape even the geographical and historical facts of the Concord battle that opened the Revolutionary War. The landscape, the action, and the actors he selected for the ceremonial poem "Concord

Hymn" were an artist's choice. It was an unlikely vehicle for a theory of poetry, but there was no material that could withstand alteration in the deep set of Emerson's mind.

MOST FAMOUS of all American works of the artistic mind, "Concord Hymn" took its shape and hidden concerns from the poetics. Emerson wrote the poem in 1837 when he was thirty-four for the dedication of the Revolutionary battle monument raised at Concord on July Fourth of that year. The citizens of Concord sang the poem's sixteen lines to the tune of the familiar hymn "Old Hundred." There were prayers and an address by a congressman. The local paper said the hymn spoke for itself, exciting "ideas of originality" and "poetic genius." Emerson himself was absent from the ceremony, visiting his in-laws in Plymouth and trying to get over a cold.

This year was the watershed of Emerson's life. On April 21, 1837, he wrote in his journal his own declaration of independence from guilt over his choice of writing as a profession. Like the Massachusetts industrialists, Emerson surmised, the writer did not depend on the weather. He could stop his own "morbid sympathy" for the farmers every time New England temperatures fell. "Climate touches not my own work," he concluded. "Where they have the sun, let them plant; we who have it not, will drive our pens." He declared with elation, "I am gay as a canary bird with this new knowledge." And then he announced: "I will write and so teach my countrymen their office" (*JMN,* V, 301).

While Emerson prepared his hymn, his great address "The American Scholar" was also taking form in his journal. He had been invited on June 22, at short notice, to be a substitute speaker and deliver the Phi Beta Kappa address at Harvard College on August 31. That speech, as Holmes said, was America's intellectual Declaration of Independence. The audacity of it still shocks us if we look at the proposition Emerson makes. The work of the native scholar was to be nothing less than "the conversion of the world." Emerson's purpose, he announced at the beginning, was to awaken "the sluggard intellect of this continent," and to free it from subservience to the Old World. "We will walk on our own feet; we will work with our own hands," he declared. "It is for you," he charged the young men at Cambridge, "to dare all."

At this high-running time of his life, Emerson's journal is filled with the urgent language from which he eventually extracted passages for more than three dozen essays and lectures. His personal life was equally crowded. Among his many activities, he finished delivering a series of lectures in Boston on the philosophy of history, planted thirty-one fruittrees near his house, corresponded with Thomas Carlyle in London, took lessons in German pronunciation from the formidable Margaret Fuller, and resisted his brother's entreaties to put some of the inheritance from his deceased first wife into a real-estate venture on Staten Island.

He records his alarm at the condition of the country. The times are bleak with fear of economic collapse. Men are breaking, and there is a run on banks in Boston and New York. The Exchange in New Orleans is burned. Emerson grieves for "the desponding hearts of the people in these black times." Yet "Concord Hymn" with its soaring affirmation never swerved from Emerson's first concern, freedom from stifling conventions. Here is the complete poem:

> By the rude bridge that arched the flood,
>   Their flag to April's breeze unfurled,
> Here once the embattled farmers stood
>   And fired the shot heard round the world.
>
> The foe long since in silence slept;
>   Alike the conqueror silent sleeps;
> And Time the ruined bridge has swept
>   Down the dark stream which seaward creeps.
>
> On this green bank, by this soft stream,
>   We set to-day a votive stone;
> That memory may their deed redeem,
>   When, like our sires, our sons are gone.
>
> Spirit, that made those heroes dare
>   To die, and leave their children free,
> Bid Time and Nature gently spare
>   The shaft we raise to them and thee.

"Concord Hymn" is an Emersonian conversion poem. The several binary pairings mirror the same pattern in his other poems. "Justice is the rhyme of things" he said in "Merlin," which keeps "truth undecayed." Those paired elements — in setting, actors, action, and time — are visible in "Concord Hymn": the river and the land, the soft stream and the stone shaft, the conqueror and the foe, the deed and the memory, sires and their sons, the battlefield and the wide round world, the stream and the sea, the heroes and their children, Time and Nature (the *rude* bridge becomes in line seven a *ruined* bridge), then and now. The close interior rhyme of bridge *swept* and votive stone *set* focuses, perhaps without Emerson's conscious design, his basic opposition of what is in motion and what holds fast. Symbolically, every pair divides in Pythagorean fashion along Emerson's line between the transient and the permanent.

The conversion process goes on everywhere. The flux of battle becomes the stasis of the monument, the fact becomes the ideal of freedom, matter becomes spirit, the stream finds its way to the world-coiling sea, and Concord's battle becomes the world's battlecry. The arching conversion is the death and transsubstantiation of the original actors who, like Bulkeley, Hunt, and Willard of "Hamatreya," pass into dust and are held by the abiding earth. Foe and conqueror alike have become one. The high truth has been revealed in the Concord fight. Every element participates in the elaborate process.

Because it is under the dictate of that deep structure, the shot heard round the world sets up a veritable hum of resonances from other poems. The shot is an audible variant of "that world-warming spark / Which dazzles me in midnight dark, / Equalizing small and large" from the poem "Étienne de la Boéce." Twenty years to the day after the monument ceremony, Emerson picked up the analogy in the recently laid Atlantic cable, commemorated in his "Ode: Sung in the Town Hall, Concord, July 4, 1857." Cannons boom from town to town in that poem, but the cable is to carry the earth-circling song:

> henceforth there shall be no chain,
> Save underneath the sea
> The wires shall murmur through the main
> Sweet songs of liberty.

Emerson himself got word of the cable hook-up to America while he was on the camping trip to the Adirondacks in 1858. He reports in his poetic account that two campers return with news of

> the wire-cable laid beneath the sea,
> And landed on our coast, and pulsating
> With ductile fire.

"We have few moments in the longest life," he then declares, "Of such delight and wonder as there grew." Electricity was now schooled to spell "with guided tongue man's messages / Shot through the weltering pit of the salt sea." These echoing lines transmit a single idea and share visual forms and symbolic associations, for the trajectory of the bullet and the path of the cable make actual arcs that become conceptual circles that travel around the world.

Uriel, a poet figure, sees a world whose apparently straight lines bend into the closing arcs that structure the universe. His voice has the effect of a shot, and the result parallels the Emersonian revelatory "shudder of joy":

>   As Uriel spoke with piercing eye,
>   A shudder ran around the sky.

Stephen Whicher suggested the relationship of this shooting figure to Emerson's poetics. Referring to the essay "Circles" and to "Uriel" he wrote: "Both speak for Emerson's pride in the explosive properties of his thought, and his ill-concealed delight at the thought of the havoc he could wreak — if people were once to listen to him."[9]

Emerson's prose repeatedly links poets and soldiers. He conceived his self-reliant man as an embattled defender at the parapets. He says in the lecture series he began in Boston in 1836, entitled "The Philosophy of History," "Society must come again under the yoke of the base and selfish, but the individual heart faithful to itself is fenced with a sacred palisado not to be traversed or approached unto, and is free forevermore" (*EL*, II, 186). To his mind the thundering affectiveness of the poet was a manly virtue to be preferred to the character of Bryant's poems, Greenough's sculpture, and Dr. Channing's preaching. Of these he said: "They are all *feminine* or receptive and not masculine or creative" (*JMN*, V, 195). He idealized the devastating power possible in public address, whose form he described in his journal as "a panharmonicon, — every note on the longest gamut, from the explosion of cannon to the tinkle of a guitar. Let us try if Folly, Custom, Convention and Phlegm cannot hear our sharp artillery" (*JMN*, VII, 265). The orator feels the discharge the same as the soldier: "The least effect of the oration is on the orator. Yet it is something; a faint recoil; a kicking of the gun" (*JMN*, V, 362). To re-establish Adam in the garden, to recover our power and mission as divine beings, he says elsewhere, we "must fire . . . the artillery of sympathy and emotion" against "the mechanical powers and the mechanical philosophy of this time" (*JMN*, VII, 271).

The poets are liberating gods. The Concord minutemen are liberating poets. At the heart of the identification is the chief element in Emerson's concept of the poetic imagination: power and the ability to convert the present act into the ideal vision it contains. Emerson's passage in "Poetry and Imagination" now rings with added resonance: the poet "reads in the word or action of the man its yet untold results. His inspiration is power to carry out and complete the metamorphosis" (*W*, VIII, 39). The crucial passage describing conversion in "The American Scholar" reveals how he identified Man Thinking, poet in action, and soldier with his musket: the world "came into him life; it went out from him truth. It came to him short-lived actions; it went out from him immortal thoughts. It came to him business; it went from him poetry. It was dead fact; now, it is quick thought" (*W,* I, 87). The shot at Concord is like a poem of freedom, the riflemen are figures of the imagination. What came to them as lead musketballs went from them as the force that would convert the world. It was a marvelous allegory of the brave belief in "Poetry and the Imagination," that poetry could trigger the conversion of the world: "Is not poetry the little chamber in the brain where is generated the explosive force which, by gentle shocks, sets in action the intellectual world?" (*W,* VIII, 64).

New power is the good which the soul seeks, Emerson announced. It was the gigantic duty of his poet. As Emerson inevitably associated the farmer-rifleman with the American poets, he called upon them to overthrow the foes of literary freedom. In the Concord battle poem not only are Minutemen firing on British Redcoats, but, I unabashedly propose, rebel American poets are shooting down the stiff, ornamented troops of poetic tradition.

That breakthrough into freedom is the principal quality by which we know the open-form poetry we call modern. William Carlos Williams carried the rebellion forward. In the mid-twentieth century he is the great hater of blockages. *Paterson* (1946-1958), his splendid, sprawling poem of release, sings of

> — a dark flame,
> a wind, a flood — counter to all staleness.

Two marvelously subversive lines in *Paterson* sum up the American aesthetic that began with the revolutionary ferment in Emerson's stirring hymn:

> beauty is
> a defiance of authority.

Oliver Wendell Holmes said that the poem's "one conspicuous line — 'And fired the shot heard round the world' — must not take to itself all the praise deserved by this perfect little poem."[10] The syntax of that most famous American line, however, holds emblematically the trajectory of the poetics. So powerful is the conversion structure of Emerson's poetic forms that inevitably his syntax duplicates that structure. In "Threnody," the paradox at the end of the poem sets out a compact linguistic model of the conversion toward which the poem works. "Lost in God, in Godhead found" holds syntactically the movement from material dissolution to spiritual fulfillment and from the mistaken idea of "loss" to the spiritual revelation of discovery. In "Concord Hymn," the famous line compacts the Emersonian conversion process, its syntax acting out the basic movement of the conversion. The "plot" of this crucial line proceeds precisely from the fact to the truth. The actual line, with the one preceding it, has undergone fairly complicated transformations to achieve this. The deep content structure would look something like this: (Someone) embattle(d) the farmers. The farmers (stood) here once. The farmers fire(d) the shot. (Someone) (heard) round the world the shot.[11] But because Emerson conceived the process of conversion always as from fact to truth, from the act to its significance, he wrote what he did. Its order is exact as the flowing of the stream to the sea, another linear and transmutive image in the poem. As the shot becomes the idea of freedom, the syntax manifests the movement from act to idea, from the farmers to the world, from the smaller to the larger, from the small musket ball to the great globe itself.

The poem's larger transaction (from adversity to triumph, from the embattled to the redemptive) parallels in an extraordinarily close way the structure of "The Snow-Storm." Both poems move from frantic activity to stasis and from confusion and paralysis to liberation. The monument of "Concord Hymn" is a model for that aspect of Emerson's poetics in which the poet extracts the lasting from the transient, making art the votive stone of experience. The poet "sees through the flowing vest the firm nature, and can declare it" (*W*, III, 37). The shaft fills the now familiar objective of Emerson's poetics by its upward idealizing sign toward the Platonic realm. The activity in "Concord Hymn" is quintessentially Emersonian, as the generalized citizen-speaker gathers his crucial elements from the horizontal landscape for the purpose of building the vertical shaft of significance. It is the literal setting-up of the moral coordinates from a journal entry of the same year: "Pride, and Thrift, and Expediency, who jeered and chirped and were so well pleased with themselves, and made merry with the dream, as they termed it, of Philosophy and Love, —behold they are all flat, and here is the Soul erect and unconquered still" (*JMN*, V, 332). Sherman Paul discerned the basic structural alignments in Emerson's moral space: "The paradoxes and polarity of his thought reflect [the] struggle to inform the life of the horizontal with the quality of the vertical, and by means of the horizontal to raise himself into the erect position."[12] Whereas Whitman's poems pushed out to preserve the full process of experience, Emerson's monument poems carved closely to preserve the meaning. In the hymn, the shaft is the artifact, literally the truth of the matter.

The poem, with all its associations, is an intricate model of the poetics. The two Emersonian forces, one outward toward fluid dissipation and the other inward toward concentration and fixity, work simultaneously. The obsessive design of the poem, its surface faultlessly crafted as a communal

tribute for a public ceremony, is fundamentally that of a poet commemo-
rating the poetic enterprise. Ralph Rusk said of "Concord Hymn" that
"Though it was to become a part of the American tradition and deserved
immortality," the poem "offered Emerson no pattern for his future verse"
(Rusk, 274). Quite to the contrary, the poem reflects in every element—its
structure, players, images, syntax, its *idea*—the poetics that presided over
Emerson's craft. The poem's deepest springs, as we have seen, fed his other
aesthetic pronouncements. It would be remarkable, in fact, if this were not
so, for the poem was composed at a highly charged time when Emerson's
theoretical energies and sense of mission were beaming out in every direction. Within a year and a few days he was to deliver both "The American
Scholar" address, his credo on the artist's imagination, and the Divinity
School address, his explosive call to liberation from the old forms. When
those Concord worthies sang the hymn for their dead heroes, they were also
singing of Emerson's hopes for a new poetry. A remarkable occasion indeed. But knowing that Emerson's poetics was the dynamo that energized
all he did, we also know it could not have been otherwise.

CHAPTER 5

Crisis

EMERSON'S SENSE OF failure as a poet courses far more widely through the
poetry than we have realized. At the dark center of his doubt as an artist
was the specter of the collapse of the miraculous energizing imagination.
Given the godly power he ascribed to that faculty, the pervasiveness of that
ideal in his poetic theorizing, and the recognition that the power is, after
all, a *human* faculty, it is not surprising that Emerson conceived of its
intermittent paralysis, if not its breakdown. Emerson faced those moments
when the poet is bereft of imagination. He wrote his own odes to dejection,
explicit in many instances and implicit in submerged analogies. The specter of this breakdown of the essential imagination was a crucial aspect of
Emerson's own wrestling with the angel of creation. It was his *agon,* the
deep fear at the core of his artistic being.

This figure of the dejected Emerson is not wholly unfamiliar. It is the
Emerson of "the noble doubt" facing the epistemological dilemma described in *Nature* over whether exterior reality exists. He sidestepped the
issue by his characteristic syntactical disguising of an assumption as a fact.
The theory that denies the existence of matter, he wrote, "makes nature
foreign to me, and does not account for that consanguinity which we acknowledge to it" (*W,* I, 63). It is the Emerson who wrote in his journal in
1845: "I go discontented thro' the world / Because I cannot strike / The
harp to please my tyrannous ear" (*JMN,* IX, 167). It is Emerson struggling
in 1838 to find his voice in the poem "The Poet." And it is the Emerson
who agonized privately over the failure of his lectures to work miracles.
"These lectures give me little pleasure," he confided in his journal. "I have
not done what I hoped when I said, I will try it once more. I have not once
transcended the coldest selfpossession. I said I will agitate others, being
agitated myself. I dared to hope for extacy and eloquence. A new theatre,

a new art, I said, is mine . . . Alas! alas! I have not the recollection of one strong moment . . . fine things, pretty things, wise things, — but no arrows, no axes, no nectar, no growling, no transpiercing, no loving, no enchantment" (*JMN,* VII, 338-339). Emerson craved a thaumaturgical flashpoint, but, as in the Romantic parable, imaginative inhibitions were the seer's antagonists.

Emerson's twin struggles were to maintain the shadow-piercing imagination and to bring into being fresh and dynamic forms of expression. His resignation from the Boston pastorate and his subversive plea at the Divinity School were stunning paradigms in his public life. His aesthetic activism was, if anything, more vigorously sustained and contradicts the accepted view of Emerson as having preferred to be the Romantic and perplexed student instead of a social reformer. But his triumph rose from the aesthetics through which he sought the way to new art, suffered his defeats, and did not, like the student he sometimes admired, repine impassively.

Emerson's view of the unsteady course of the poetic imagination has already come out in my earlier remarks on the poem "Merlin." He described there the moments when a man is blessed with imagination and the moments when inexplicably the gates of insight are sealed. The seemingly inconstant intelligibility of nature proceeded in direct accord with the operation of the receiving imagination. Emerson gave notice that he knew men's limitations even as he lyricized about their transcendent faculties. In the passage that is prescient with regard to his own problems as a poet hobbled by conventional theories of art, he asserts that total correlation: "We animate what we can, and we see only what we animate. Nature and books belong to the eyes that see them. It depends on the mood of the man whether he shall see the sunset or the fine poem" (*W,* III, 50).

Emerson troubled over expressive form on the one hand and the more grave problem, on the other, of the blind periods in the life of the imagination. It was one thing to struggle to articulate the insights, turning them into liberating language, but it was a terrifying dilemma to misread or not to read at all the language of nature. Both would be basic failures of competence in facing nature's signs, a withering of power at the heart of the conversion process. Emerson understood the failure of the man who can articulate but in whom the vision has died.

The anxieties over both poetic form and the insightful imagination grew out of the structural characteristics and hierarchy of the poet's consciousness as Emerson conceived it. He knew the specters of failure in the lower order of fancy and talent — the aggregating, articulating, image-making power — and blindness in the higher order of the prophetic imagination, that final alembic of the converting mind. The one was the seer's "music music-born," the other was the sayer's "untaught strain that sheds beauty on the rose." Let us look first at the crisis in the lower order.

THE FAILURE OF FORM

Emerson's difficulty with form was also a problem of his contemporaries in freeing themselves from the strictures of eighteenth-century artifice, but his was the more severe because in his moments of exhilaration, as on the frozen commons, he knew he possessed the transforming power of the poetic imagination. To possess this but not the ideal talent to say it was a failure of extreme painfulness. The deprivation engaged Emerson all his active years. In 1832 he took account of the energy dissipated through borrowed forms: "if the whole man acted always, how powerful would be every act and every word. Well then or ill then how much power he sacrifices by conforming himself to say and do in other folks' time instead of in his own!" (*JMN*, III, 318). Seven years later, he entered this in his journal: "At church today I felt how unequal is this match of words against things. Cease, O thou unauthorized talker, to prate of consolation, and resignation, and spiritual joys, in neat and balanced sentences" (*JMN*, VII, 196-197). In 1871 he still had the visionary theory of a complete reconciliation between a subject and its articulate form. Emerson had been reading some "experimental verse" and noted in his journal: " 'The newness.' Every day must be a new morn. Clothe the new object with a coat that fits it alone of all things in the world. I can see in many poems that the coat is second hand. Emphasis betrays poverty of thought" (*J*, X, 360).

The question of "mere talent," as he called it in that same journal, was of far greater importance to him than the stock concern over whether the poet was adequately appreciated. Emerson settled this himself, for in an act of principle similar to Arnold's striking "Empedocles on Etna" from his 1853 volume of poems, Emerson excised from the printed version of "Woodnotes I" the self-indulgent passages on the poor unrecognized poet ("what he knows nobody wants"). The failure of expressive talent haunts the curiously ambivalent poem "Terminus," even though its final tone is resoundingly positive. The poem is complicated by its indecision, and this indefiniteness is compounded for readers who are aware that the poem is not, as is generally thought, of late, that is 1866, composition entirely, but has parts begun as early as 1850 or 1851 when Emerson was in his forties.[1] The poem seems at the outset a lament for the loss of the artistic fancy that was half of Emerson's plan of the poetic mind. Terminus, the god of bounds, enters as a beamed-in voice at line six and seems to urge resignation to age:

> "No farther shoot
> Thy broad ambitious branches, and thy root.
> Fancy departs: no more invent."

Emerson's personal cry of frustration is audible when the god echoes Emerson's own feelings of artistic failure. They are illogically and pathetically tied to the fact of his earlier feebleness of constitution. Curse if you will your sires who, says the god, when they gave you breath,

> "Failed to bequeath
> The needful sinew stark as once,
> The Baresark marrow to thy bones,
> But left a legacy of ebbing veins,
> Inconstant heat and nerveless reins, —
> Amid the Muses, left thee deaf and dumb,
> Amid the gladiators, halt and numb."

Against this withering diagnosis, however, stand the metaphors of focused strength, the first of *pruning:*

> No farther shoot
> Thy broad ambitious branches, and thy root . . .
> Contract thy firmament
> To compass of a tent.

The god urges *economy* and selective concentration: "Economize the failing river . . . / Leave the many and hold the few." Fleetingly, the god talks of fruition, admonishing the speaker to "Mature the unfallen fruit," to make *completion* his objective before undertaking further elaboration or exploration. Finally, against the negative cast of the poem cuts the metaphor of sinews tightened against the storm:

> As the bird trims her to the gale,
> I trim myself to the storm of time.

For Emerson there was important aesthetic significance attached to this trim-and-arrange metaphor. It meant power and penetration, the ability to reach the *goal:* similar lines turn up in "The Poet," where he speaks at the first of the ideal poet, whose strong, fresh words are like water-haunting birds, divers and dippers, which, when the "noisy scorn" of the anomalous clowns along the bank is past, appear as a "new vision." Then

> Emerge the wingèd words in haste.
> New-bathed, new-trimmed, on healthy wing,
> Right to the heaven they steer and sing.

Awkwardly, Emerson turns to a sailing metaphor in "Terminus" to make the man more believably birdlike:

> I man the rudder, reef the sail,
> Obey the voice at eve obeyed at prime.

This second beamed-in voice, the spiritual one, obeyed at prime of life, counters most forcefully the desperation in the poem and the facing of boundaries. It counsels the poet-speaker in the same way other Emerson voices counsel strength and demand insight and purpose:

> "Lowly faithful, banish fear,
> Right onward drive unharmed;
> The port, well worth the cruise, is near,
> And every wave is charmed."

The two Emersonian forces of the poetic consciousness meet in this poem: the understanding that counsels limits and taking-in; the other, genius, whose urge is to *drive*. Their convergence makes of this poem, like "The Problem," an ambiguous work. The speaker presumably holds in his mind, like the father in "Threnody," the two disparate concerns. What just misses accomplishment in the poem is a fusion of these concerns in a single figure of force to suggest the ideal concentration of the poet's power. Had that occurred, the trimmed bird and the pruned tree might have become a version of the musket ball of the Concord rebels. The crisis of being halt and numb among the gladiators pierces the poem. The elements of the liberation are all there but, typically, the grasp of them in a single artful gesture lay outside the poem.

His vexing knowledge of crisis comes out repeatedly in his journals. The plaint over the spirit-muse's withdrawal is registered in the journal of 1840: "The moon keeps its appointment — will not the good Spirit? Wherefore have we labored and fasted, say we, and thou takest no note? Let him not take note, if he please to hide, — then it were sublime beyond a poet's dreams still to labor and abstain and obey, and, if thou canst, *to put the good Spirit in the wrong*. That were a feat to sing in Elysium" (*JMN,* VII, 529). This was Emerson's "On His Blindness," his perseverance to the point of defiance in the face of the failure of the fancy to articulate the deep vision he was confident he possessed.

Inevitably, the pain over the failure of craft takes up a large part of the poem "The Poet," never completed by Emerson and entitled significantly in its early form "The Discontented Poet, A Masque." The poem rises out of a powerful disappointment. It is another working of Emerson's "Lycidas" but secular and oblique, for it does not seriously question faith in the value of poetry in an annihilating universe — or the proposition of sporting with Amaryllis in the shade — but the justice of a plan that endows a creature with the genius of insight without "equal means" to express it. Comparable to "Threnody" but more explicit, the poem is Emerson's consideration of the existential inequities of artistic creation that lay unresolved in his encompassing meditation on aesthetics, responsive life, and cosmic order. The formal impoverishment of the poetry, its rigid monumentality, the stolidity of the language, the predictable gestures that failed of passion — the elements I have been at pains to point out — Emerson's recognition of these failures is latent everywhere in this plaintive poem and explicit in the couplet on the poet who "Seeks how he may fitly tell / The heart o'erlading miracle." The poem is the lament of the poet without talent at the same time that it bears witness to his possession of the higher order of poetic sight. "Constrained by impotence," the poet-speaker summons his familiar metaphors of incompleteness and fire to the point of the dilemma:

> Discrowned and timid, thoughtless, worn,
> The child of genius sits forlorn . . .
> A cripple of God, half true, half formed,
> And by great sparks Promethean warmed.

The analogy is searingly appropriate. Emerson in his unhappiness over his lifeless stanzas saw himself as Prometheus, bound to the rigid conventions of a poetry which, unlike those other ritual forms in the Boston church, he could not so simply repudiate. Aesthetic freedom provided no promise that other more resonant forms would replace the old ones. He could not, like the Minutemen, rout the oppressors.

There is no deeper lament for the lack of actualizing talent than his poet's plea for skill commensurate with a spirit that has access to the stars:

> "clothe these hands with power
> In just proportion,
> Nor plant immense designs
> Where equal means are none."

Images of this impasse recur in fragments related to the poem. An example: the encounter of Saadi with the self-righteous Dervish (Emerson's Eastern figure of the vain Concord farmers, of Guy, and others) whose head holds ritual but no living forms by which to retrieve the spiritual energy of the universe. It is an angry rehearsal of the issue in "The Problem." Saadi says to the Dervish, in words that invert but all the same underscore Brahma's admonition:

"I cannot sell my heaven again
For all that rattles in thy brain."

The other half of Emerson's distress was the structural twin of this concern with form: it was his apprehension over the failure of the imagination. Here we see the darkest recess of the cave from which he liberated himself, in a removal that enacts for us the appearance of the modern poetic mind. Several of his poems play out the allegory. The poem "The Poet," we shall see, is the crisis work that might stand as the first modern American poem.

THE FAILURE OF THE IMAGINATION

Within Emerson's poetic consciousness lay a terror over the cessation of the converting process. Stephen Whicher referred to something of the sort when he wrote of Emerson's "radical difficulties" and "the inconsecutiveness of his own moods, the impossibility of preserving the moments in which he felt his unity with the power within him."[2] His system of perception was metaphoric, and its basis was the fusing of an aesthetic and moral figuration. When Emerson said in "Merlin" that "We are sick with rhyme," he meant that rightly seen the universe and man exist in metaphoric equation. Thus when the equating faculty stalled or paled away, the world became terrifying. Such periods were Emerson's times of dejection, when the shaping spirit of the imagination halted. The signs of his recognition of the contingency of the imaginative power appear in various ways. His habitual separation of the speaker in his poems from the voice of the deep Heart of nature seems evidence of apprehension. Certainly Emerson avoided, except arguably in "The Sphinx" and "The Problem," identifying that voice with his mortal poets. The dichotomy is the surface mark of a deep but perhaps not always consciously faced recognition of the separability of the language-making function and the divining function. When the latter failed, the poetic and philosophic enterprise ceased, and that was aesthetic and moral death for Emerson. The cessation of the liberating function of the imagination he sometimes traced to the machinations of fate. In dark moments that ability to convert the solid world seemed a futile dream in the face of the overwhelming power of the impersonal universe. In "Nemesis," as we saw, he declared: "In spite of Virtue and the Muse, / Nemesis will have her dues." These poles of Emerson's conception of the creative power may first appear dialectical in pattern, but the metaphor of health and sickness as alternate states in time is more appropriate. Emerson saw imaginative power and the lack of it not as poles of a productive tension but rather as linear, a periodic cessation of a power that in times of imaginative health operated with exhilarating capacity. That relationship is consistent with Emerson's structures of thought. Indeed, fate in Emerson's view most often seemed a passive force contingent upon the abdication of the imaginative ego. "As long as I am weak," he wrote in his journal in 1842, "I shall talk of Fate; whenever the God fills me with his fulness, I shall see the disappearance of Fate" (*JMN,* VIII, 228).

There was more than philosophical idealism at stake, however, in the periodic loss of the imaginative power. In those periods the impassable sea, as he called it, opened its vastness between the poet, other men, and the world about them. Only the man of active genius could cross the space between pure mind and the multitude of men. The poem "Days," set symbolically in a garden, is about that state when the gulf yawns between the mind and the convertible world. Emerson, committed to the idea of the power of the converting imagination upon which no less than the entire world depended, wrote his own dejection odes. They avoid the very darkest passion in the wilderness, but they are of a piece with Coleridge's dejection ode ("this wan and heartless mood") and with the lines of Wallace Stevens which describe the man without imagination as

> the listener, who listens in the snow,
> And, nothing himself, beholds
> Nothing that is not there and the nothing that is.

Dejection is a gray outcropping across the landscape of Emerson's prose. It is in the uncharitable passage he copied out of *The Vishñu Puráña* into his journal of 1845 that parallels the more sympathetic picture of earth's "boastful boys" in "Hamatreya." The sovereigns of earth, wrote Emerson, "and other kings who with perishable frames have possessed this ever-during world, and who, blinded with deceptive notions of individual occupation, have indulged the feeling that suggests 'this earth is mine' . . . have all passed away" (*JMN,* IX, 321).

"Threnody," in its inner allegory about the death of the imagination, enacts the same desolation Emerson confessed as he led up to the chilling passage in the essay "Experience" about the evanescence of his grief for his dead son, that "most unhandsome part of our condition": "Was it Boscovich who found out that bodies never come in contact? Well, souls never touch their objects. An innavigable sea washes with silent waves between us and the things we aim at and converse with" (*W,* III, 48). Scene painting, the counterfeit and shallow, the intellect that plays about the surface reality — these are Emerson's terms of dejection. But when we read his closing cry about paying the costly price of sons and lovers, we hear the measure of the desperation. The essay "Experience" is Emerson's prose ode to dejection, saved only, as Arnold saw, by the invocation of patience and self-trust. As one reader has said, the elegiac tone reverses his usual earnestness. Achilles no longer rallies his legions.[3]

THE POETRY shows as clearly as the prose the sharp breaks in Emerson's idealistic structure. His treatment varies in individual poems from passing observation to defeat so dark that the failed imagination and the absence of a resolution provide, as in "Threnody," the dramatic structure. The crisis is obsessive in the poem "The Poet," the unfinished work that entered the discussion in connection with Emerson's knowledge of his failures of talent. Partly composed by Emerson in verse-book *P* as "The Discontented Poet," mixed in tone, discontinuous, with abrupt shifts and apparent breaks, this painful meditation touches the nerve of Emerson's anxieties as an artist.[4]

It opens in the voice of Emerson's supreme poet and with the same encompassing vision that contains "The Sphinx." In striding, confident tones, the voice describes the Orphic figure who was Emerson's Platonic model of the central poet:

> Right upward on the road of fame
> With sounding steps the poet came;
> Born and nourished in miracles,
> His feet were shod with golden bells,
> Or where he stepped the soil did peal
> As if the dust were glass and steel.

This mythic picture continues through Part I and for eighteen lines into Part II. At this point, where Emerson inserted forty-three lines composed separately, perhaps in 1843, a new speaker enters the poem — mortal, subjective, seemingly an outsetting poet, and ambiguously characterized as a poet speaking to himself but also, it seems, addressing the first poet of the omniscient voice. The doubt begins. Vaguely part of a metaphor of dawn and incomplete but coming light, the outsetting bard speaks of patience, incomplete beginnings, and unrealized possibility:

> Not yet I sing: but I must wait,
> My hand upon the silent string . . .
> These are but seeds of days,
> Not yet a steadfast morn,
> An intermittent blaze,
> An Embryo god unborn.

Abruptly, the true poet is born:

> How all things sparkle,
> The dust is alive,
> To the birth they arrive:
> I snuff the breath of my morning afar,
> I see the pale lustres condense to a star.

Immediately upon the emergence of the poet, with obvious links to the eye-ball instance in *Nature,* the poem ascends in one of Emerson's most sustained moments of revelation in his poetry. The dust is alive, the pale lights form a star, and the vision unfolds:

> The vanishing are seen,
> And the world that shall be
> Twins the world that has been.

Concurrently, disconcertingly in the midst of the transport, a beamed-in voice of "The Mighty" commands dutiful resignation to whatever time holds:

> "attend the enriching Fate
> Which none can stay, and none accelerate."

But the revelation floods in, time ceases, and the poet finds himself at the sun-filled convergence point:

> I am neither faint nor weary,
> Fill thy will, O faultless heart!
> Here from youth to age I tarry, —
> Count it flight of bird or dart.
> My heart at the heart of things
> Heeds no longer lapse of time,
> Rushing ages moult their wings,
> Bathing in thy day sublime.

Sustained but peculiarly compromised by the drifting metaphors, the revelation goes on for thirty-one more lines. Then, jarringly again, anxiety intrudes, the vision is suspended, and the poet seeks a middle state where he can stand against changing fortune:

> Ah, happy if a sun or star
> Could chain the wheel of Fortune's car,
> And give to hold an even state,
> Neither dejected nor elate,
> That haply man upraised might keep
> The height of Fancy's far-eyed steep.
> In vain: the stars are glowing wheels,
> Giddy with motion Nature reels.

Morning comes but with it "thrice-piled clouds," and the poem grates with Emerson's terms of failure—half-formedness, impotence, "brittle health," withdrawal, and the condition of being hemmed-in by stale convention, "false usage," from which there seems to be no escape. The passage, mostly from his draft of "The Discontented Poet," ends with a plea for extinction or vision. Emotions pull against each other, mortality and ill health haunt the lines, and, inconsistently, the poet glances at stars that Emerson forgot were still hidden in clouds. The crisis is profound.

> Discrowned and timid, thoughtless, worn,
> The child of genius sits forlorn:
> Between two sleeps a short day's stealth,
> 'Mid many ails a brittle health,
> A cripple of God, half true, half formed,
> And by great sparks Promethean warmed,
> Constrained by impotence to adjourn
> To infinite time his eager turn,
> His lot of action at the urn.
> He by false usage pinned about
> No breath therein, no passage out,
> Cast wishful glances at the stars
> And wishful saw the Ocean stream: —
> "Merge me in the brute universe,
> Or lift to a diviner dream!"

The dejection does not lift despite encouragement by loved ones. The poet indulges in his senses, indiscriminate in his enthusiasms, and, like Prufrock who knows the mermaids will not sing to him, lives on the surface of things:

> He, foolish child,
> A facile, reckless, wandering will,
> Eager for good, not hating ill,
> Thanked Nature for each stroke she dealt;
> On his tense chords all strokes were felt,
> The good, the bad with equal zeal,
> He asked, he only asked, to feel.
> Timid, self-pleasing, sensitive,
> With Gods, with fools, content to live;
> Bended to fops who bent to him;
> Surface with surfaces did swim.

Manly composure is urged on this weak poet by inserted voices of "Angels," and another break in the poem occurs. Night has descended, and the poet in Emerson's sketchy narrative walks by the seashore and on the old sea-walls as first a star and then a constellation break through the clouds. This gives the poet the occasion to meditate on how the stars exist in the vision of

the poet, answer the "light-asking life" in him, and die if he is sightless.
This thought of blindness moves the poet to another climactic cry:

> "I to whom your light has spoken,
> I, pining to be one of you,
> I fall, my faith is broken,
> Ye scorn me from your deeps of blue."

And then comes the pleading from the heart:

> "clothe these hands with power
> In just proportion,
> Nor plant immense designs
> Where equal means are none."

Now as in "Threnody," a dialogue sets in between the plaintive poet and a
"Chorus of Spirits." The Chorus, in the imperious voice we know from
other poems, says the soul's desire is means enough and, lacking the talent
for outward expression, one must be content to be his "own theatre."
Moved by this argument in a quiet way, the poet is momentarily consoled,
but now in another onset of fear and anxiety, he pleads for the Spirits to
stay with him. When they reply in Brahman tones that they will, that in
fact they are innate ("From thyself thou canst not flee, — / From thyself no
more can we"), the poet, unhearing, goes on with his doubt in the metaphors of changeful tides and abandonment:

> Is there warrant that the waves
> Of thought in their mysterious caves
> Will heap in me their highest tide,
> In me therewith beatified?
> Unsure the ebb and flood of thought,
> The moon comes back, — the Spirit not.

The last seven lines in the poem, written perhaps as early as 1831, six or
seven years before the body of the work, are a serious falling-off of engagement. Cliché-ridden, they assert a simple moralistic lesson on man's divinity. But just before these lines, in what is surely the strong dramatic close of
"The Poet," the Spirits tell the poet, despite all his wretchedness and dis-
couragement, to serve. It is a hollow summons, but it bares the stark anxiety of the artist's crisis:

> Serve thou it not for daily bread, —
> Serve it for pain and fear and need.
> Love it, though it hide its light;
> By love behold the sun at night.
> If the Law should thee forget,

> More enamoured serve it yet;
> Though it hate thee, suffer long;
> Put the Spirit in the wrong.

The tones anticipate a host of defeatist poet-figures from Whitman's in "As I Ebb'd with the Ocean of Life" to Eliot's and Hart Crane's and on to Robert Lowell's in "Skunk Hour." Emerson was in rats' alley, and the wavering tone and irresolute form of the poem hold the fragments that the twentieth century was to shore against its ruins. "The Poet" is a self-conscious monologue on latter-day themes: the defeat of the poet, the loss of the dream, the blinding of the vision. Emerson's failure to complete the poem is of a piece with his failure to compose the dilemma in the poem. Its fragmentation is the beginning of what came to be an aesthetics of pieces. The poem dealt with Emerson's passage in the waste land and its subject, tone, and form, particularly its failure to close and resolve, mirror the crisis. For these reasons, though it lurks in the trailing shadows of the "appendix" to the Centenary Edition, it can stand by itself as the first modern American poem.

THE CRISIS obliquely enters poems like "The Problem" and "Destiny," where alluring alternatives to the powerful imagination are posed and then rejected. In the two-value structure of "The Problem," the speaker chooses against "a vain or shallow thought," in fact against conscious thought or cunning. Instead, he celebrates instinct, "thought's interior sphere." Similarly in "Destiny," he chooses against the world's imagined virtues the natural power of creation beyond mere decoration. At the beginning, the poem addresses minds of lower talent and the self-deluded:

> That you are fair or wise is vain,
> Or strong, or rich, or generous;
> You must add the untaught strain
> That sheds beauty on the rose.

And then, in choices similar to the ones implicit in "The Problem," the poem's imperious voice chooses against mere toil, art, or wit. The terms of poetic genius are Orphic:

> There's a melody born of melody,
> Which melts the world into a sea.
> Toil could never compass it;
> Art its height could never hit;
> It came never out of wit;
> But a music music-born
> Well may Jove and Juno scorn.

There follows immediately yet another instance of the aesthetics of power Emerson articulated in "The Problem" and elsewhere:

> Thy beauty, if it lack the fire
> Which drives me mad with sweet desire,
> What boots it?

Now we are distracted, given the idealistic concern of the poem, by two more of the most egregious lines in Emerson's poetic works:

> What all the goods thy pride which lift,
> If thou pine for another's gift?

Fortunately, there are less solemn treatments of the possibility of the corruption of the imagination. Emerson turned the apprehension over and over in a variety of moods. In "Alphonso of Castile," for example, he moves very close to a parody of his ideal poet. The poem begins soberly, the king describing how things "deteriorate" as Nature goes "astern":

> Lemons run to leaves and rind;
> Meagre crop of figs and limes;
> Shorter days and harder times.

The catalogue of depletion — the declining season and declining fruitfulness — presents an exact counterpart to the description of surging life and power we see in the poem "May-Day." Here the debility is comically endemic and the tormented cry in "The Poet" — "merge me in the brute universe, / Or lift to a diviner dream!" — is echoed with fine satirical bite as Alphonso advises the gods:

> Eyes of gods! ye must have seen,
> O'er your ramparts as ye lean,
> The general debility;
> Of genius the sterility;
> Mighty projects countermanded;
> Rash ambition, brokenhanded;
> Puny man and scentless rose
> Tormenting Pan to double the dose.
> Rebuild or ruin; either fill
> Of vital force the wasted rill,
> Or tumble all again in heap
> To weltering Chaos and to sleep.

The tone lifts even more as the Spaniard gets overly familiar with the gods: "Say, Seignors, are the old Niles dry?" The lines parody what elsewhere Emerson sees ideally as the meeting of the poet face to face with the eternal beings, "they alone with him alone" (*W*, VI, 325). Alphonso treats the gods as clients:

Masters, I'm in pain with you;
Masters, I'll be plain with you;
In my palace of Castile,
I, a king, for kings can feel.
There my thoughts the matter roll,
And solve and oft resolve the whole.
And, for I'm styled Alphonse the Wise,
Ye shall not fail for sound advice.

He demands a kind of cosmic stock-split from the gods ("For one sun supply us twenty"); failing that, he counsels the gods to "condense" the population that has to be served. In his ill-concealed greed, Alphonso is a caricature of Emerson's central man, urging the gods to stuff more brains into one hat. There are wry reflections of the poet's plea to the Soul-Muse not to "plant immense designs / Where equal means are none."

Earth, crowded, cries, "Too many men!"
My counsel is, kill nine in ten,
And bestow the shares of all
On the remnant decimal.
Add their nine lives to this cat;
Stuff their nine brains in one hat;
Make his frame and forces square
With the labors he must dare . . .
So shall ye have a man of the sphere
Fit to grace the solar year.

The poem "Mithridates" parodies the theme of the humble-bee poem so vigorously that a reader familiar with Emerson's doctrine of the wide-ranging and converting imagination is struck by the debasement of the noble idea. Fanatic, self-serving to the point of absurdity, Mithridates in his nomadic accumulation is said to have taken even poison so as to become immune to it.

Every thing is kin of mine.

Give me agates for my meat;
Give me cantharids to eat;
From air and ocean bring me foods,
From all zones and altitudes; —

From all natures, sharp and slimy,
Salt and basalt, wild and tame:
Tree and lichen, ape, sea-lion,
Bird, and reptile, be my game . .

Hither! take me, use me, fill me,
Vein and artery, though ye kill me!

The foraging man of imagination, the philosophical and poetical humble-bee, and other versions of the central man are figures of the poet. Some are parodies and some are somber depictions of the corruption of the poetic mind. They reveal Emerson coming to grips by various strategies with the problem of the poet of inadequate or failed imagination.

Poem after poem turns dark in the contemplation of the failure of the imagination and the consequent darkening of the outside world. "Blight" begins with a plea comparable in tone to that of the imagination-bereft father in "Threnody": "Give me truths; / For I am weary of the surfaces, / And die of inanition." A solemn monologue in Emerson's infrequent but comfortably solid blank verse follows, concerned with the spiritual sterility of the young scholars who invade the hills and love not the flower though they catalogue it by Latin name. Armed with science, they are strangers to the stars. Nature withholds its meaning:

> in the midst of spoils and slaves, we thieves
> And pirates of the universe, shut out
> Daily to a more thin and outward rind,
> Turn pale and starve.

The soul bereft of imagination, a spiritual orphan, reappears in "Wood-notes II," addressed by Nature through the pinetree's voice:

> poor child! unbound, unrhymed,
> Whence camest thou, misplaced, mistimed,
> Whence, O thou orphan and defrauded?
> Is thy land peeled, thy realm marauded?
> Who thee divorced, deceived and left?
> Thee of thy faith who hath bereft,
> And torn the ensigns from thy brow,
> And sunk the immortal eye so low?

In the light of this passage, we might reconsider the implication of the term orphan applied to Ishmael at the end of *Moby-Dick*. Ishmael, far from being the spokesman for Melville or even the practical compromiser many readers choose to see, is rather a character much like the narrators in "Bartleby" and "Benito Cereno," moral and imaginative orphans, unable to dive deep, content to live in moral self-delusion on the surface of life.

Emerson's snowman vision of nothingness is explicit in lines that counterpoint the confident vision of infinite flux at the end of "The Sphinx." The pine continues its monologue in "Woodnotes II":

> Hark! in thy ear I will tell the sign
> By which thy hurt thou may'st divine.
> When thou shalt climb the mountain cliff,

> Or see the wide shore from thy skiff,
> To thee the horizon shall express
> But emptiness on emptiness.

His tone in "Monadnoc," Emerson's consummate monument poem, shifts momentarily to bitterness as he parades the "spruce clerk" (shade of Eliot's carbuncular clerk, shade of Prufrock) as the poet without imagination. The mountain awaits the bard and sage. But a clerk from the despised city ascends Monadnoc instead, and he sees not in ever-growing circles of perception but only inward at the terror in himself and the infinite mindlessness without. This is as sustained and uncompromising a passage as Emerson ever wrote about the root fear that lay at the center of his agony over the loss of the imagination. The mountain speaks:

> "Oft as morning wreathes my scarf,
> Fled the last plumule of the Dark,
> Pants up hither the spruce clerk
> From South Cove and City Wharf.
> I take him up my rugged sides,
> Half-repentant, scant of breath, —
> Bead-eyes my granite chaos show,
> And my midsummer snow:
> Open the daunting map beneath, —
> All his county, sea and land,
> Dwarfed to measure of his hand;
> His day's ride is a furlong space,
> His city-tops a glimmering haze.
> I plant his eyes on the sky-hoop bounding;
> 'See there the grim gray rounding
> Of the bullet of the earth
> Whereon ye sail,
> Tumbling steep
> In the uncontinented deep.'
> He looks on that, and he turns pale.
> 'T is even so, this treacherous kite,
> Farm-furrowed, town-incrusted sphere,
> Thoughtless of its anxious freight,
> Plunges eyeless on forever;
> And he, poor parasite,
> Cooped in a ship he cannot steer, —
> Who is the captain he knows not,
> Port of pilot trows not, —
> Risk or ruin he must share.
> I scowl on him with my cloud,
> With my north wind chill his blood;
> I lame him, clattering down the rocks;

> And to live he is in fear.
> Then, at last, I let him down
> Once more into his dapper town,
> To chatter, frightened, to his clan
> And forget me if he can."

AGAINST THIS background of crisis moments in Emerson's poems, the poem "Days" emerges as an important enactment of the time when the imagination fails. It can be seen as the most explicit actualization of the agony from which Emerson sought to liberate himself. "Days" is his decorous dejection ode, his understated and, significantly, unresolved ode to the west wind. By a relatively simple symbolic reading, one makes out this pale figure of the stunted poet masked by the figures gesturing at the surface of Emerson's poems. The prospect of power against impotence and exhilaration over dejection determined in numerous poems the actors and settings.

"Days" presents a situation where experience fails of conversion because of the imaginative lassitude of the gardener-poet. He settles for a few body nutriments within arm's reach while the spirit lacks fulfillment of "morning wishes." The poem is about absent essences that, through a failure of the insightful imagination, are not brought into being. Unlike Emerson's other poems concerned with the failed imagination, however, there is no attempt at consolation in "Days" or any winning admonition at the close. The poem ends with the poet unredeemed, with scorn.

The subject was a persistent one for Emerson. Twenty-four years earlier, in 1827, he had undertaken essentially the same poem, but he lacked then the skill he was to develop in concision and imagery. So thoroughly conventional were his metaphors that, by comparison, his later lyrics of crisis seem outspoken in personal anguish.

> My days roll by me like a train of dreams;
> A host of joyless, undistinguished forms,
> Cloud after cloud, my firmament deforms.
> While the sweet Eye of Heaven his purple gleams
> Pours in rich rivers of Promethean beams
> On all his ample family beside,
> On me, on me the day forgets to dawn;
> Encountering darkness clasps me like a bride,
> Tombs rise around, and from each cell forlorn
> Starts with an ominous cry some ghastly child
> Of death and darkness, summoning me to mourn.
> Companion of the clod, brother of worms —
> The future has no hope, and memory mild
> Gives not the blessed light that once my woes beguiled.
>
> (*JMN,* III, 36)

The subject endured to the end. Its counterbalancing positive also endured, as in "Poetry and Imagination": "The impressions on the imagination make the great days of life: the book, the landscape, or the personality which . . . penetrated to the inward sense . . . is not forgotten" (*W*, VIII, 15-16). The metaphor of penetration was common in Emerson's work; in "Days" the figure is ambiguously employed, for the pleached garden is a bower accessible through its interwoven branches but also capable of preventing traffic with the outside world. When the traffic failed, the spiritual benefits also failed. D. H. Lawrence recognized in Emerson the possibility that ideal communication could be mistaken out of sheer enthusiasm or ignorance. "When Emerson says: 'I am surrounded by messengers of God who send me credentials day by day,' then all right for him. But he cozily forgot that there are many messengers."[5] It is quite clear that Emerson never forgot.

The characteristic latent sexuality in Emerson's writing appears in "Days" in the female figure, inevitably suggesting the analogy of impotence to convey a sense of passion missed, intimacy fumbled, and insight failed. A similar equating of powers occurs in his sober and dutiful early poem "The Summons":

> I've learned the sum of that sad history
> All woman-born do know, that hoped-for days,
> Days that come dancing on fraught with delights,
> Dash our blown hopes as they limp heavily by.

There was much other preparation for the poem that would become his best-known treatment of the failed poet. A similar situation presented itself in "The World Soul" where in solemn preachment the speaker tells us that, despite the corruptions around us, the days present noble opportunities:

> We plot and corrupt each other,
> And we despoil the unborn.
>
> Yet there in the parlor sits
> Some figure of noble guise, —
> Our angel, in a stranger's form,
> Or woman's pleading eyes;
> Or only a flashing sunbeam
> In at the window-pane.

In "Days" the passive man in the bower is the failed poet. William Gilman succinctly described Emerson's idea of the interdependence of the power to respond and the power to convert: "The soul was an organic composite of powers in the person, a hypersensitive power of response, like a spontaneous reflex, to all forms of experience, the power of creating something out of the response, emotional power, moral power, and the power of mind" (*SW*, xii). By his failure to convert the moment, the poet loses the world itself, for when its unifying principle goes ungrasped the world disintegrates into fragments. It is then no more than the discrete things Emerson methodically mixes up and enumerates in the poem: diadems, fagots, bread, kingdoms, stars, the sky itself, herbs and apples. The implications of the failed imagination in "Days" reach well beyond simply the moment of passiveness and lost opportunity, to a glimpse of aesthetic damnation. For Emerson, that was a fragmented vision and the moral breakdown of the world. The situation depicted in "Days" had for him the profoundest ramifications for an attitude toward the world, and thus for the structure of the world itself. In such a view lay a tragic anarchy that Emerson knew was a consequence of the collapsing imagination. "If the mind live only in particulars," he said, "and see only differences (wanting the power to see the whole—all in each), then the world addresses to this mind a question it cannot answer, and each new fact tears it in pieces, and it is vanquished by the distracting variety" (*W*, IX, 412).

This carefully measured statement in the fullness of his maturity in 1859 looks directly into the heart of the void. Without the sense of the whole, the disabled poet sees from his pleached garden not a divine design but rather the world's "poor, unsightly, noisome things." This world is far different from the convertible one refracted through Emerson's higher optics. Just at this point is the *nadir* of his vigorous meditations on the artist, and just here is the crisis of imagination which in allegory after allegory entered the design of his poetry. From this recurring low point, Emerson devised his own liberation as an artist.

THE WAY OUT of the crisis was also enacted in the poetry. Allegories of the strong resurgence of the imaginative function become visible to readers familiar with Emerson's figures of the failed poet. Such poems counterbalance his odes to dejection, and none more insistently concentrates Emerson's vision of surging artistic power than the long poem "May-Day," the title poem of the 1867 volume of poetry. It is as much a paradigm as "The Sphinx." "May-Day" is one of Emerson's closest studies of nature, but simultaneously it gathers up every one of his aesthetic themes. Its seasonal schema provides the familiar linear movement from confinement ("All was stiff and stark; / Knee-deep snows choked all the ways") to free movement:

> Up and away! where haughty woods
> Front the liberated floods:
> We will climb the broad-backed hills,

> Hear the uproar of their joy;
> We will mark the leaps and gleams
> Of the new-delivered streams,
> And the murmuring rivers of sap
> Mount in the pipes of trees,
> Giddy with day, to the topmost spire.

It celebrates the Emersonian shibboleths: spring as the abundantly talented artist, as the supreme converter making "life out of death, new out of old," and as the liberating god. It is a chant of fullness, of "a hid unruly appetite," of the "potent blood" of May, the "fiery force the earth renews," the "wealth of forms," and the "flush of hues" (169). Emerson labors at the emblems of surging power returning. The poem is equal to the spring section of *Walden* as a lyric to the return of inspiration, of deep understanding, of a vision of beauty and the world's plenitude.

Like the titmouse allegory and others, spring shows the powers of nature as it converts, rebuilding the ruin, mending defect. This transforming power is the main attribute of the imagination. The poet-speaker at the opening of "May-Day," as in so many of Emerson's poems, is a man without imagination "struggling through the drifted roads":

> The whited desert knew me not . . .
> All the sweet secrets therein hid
> By Fancy, ghastly spells undid . . .
> The piny hosts were sheeted ghosts
> In the star-lit minster aisled.
> I found no joy: the icy wind
> Might rule the forest to his mind.

But if one of God's days could be creative and instructive, as in "The Snow-Storm," the onset of spring is a manifold and extravagant display of this. Beginning in other ways much the same as "The Snow-Storm," with "sudden passion," "whistlings," "vagrant booming of the air," a "cannonade," a "tumult" and "rush of wings," "May-Day" interests itself in nature's sculpting and painting. The poem works out minutely the rebirth of the earth's beauty. There is movement, color, fragrance, sound—the transmutations are lovingly accumulated. The deep instinctual associations of mind and nature are allegorized:

> The old wine darkling in the cask
> Feels the bloom on the living vine,
> And bursts the hoops at hint of Spring:
> And so, perchance, in Adam's race,
> Of Eden's bower some dream-like trace
> Survived the Flight and swam the Flood,

> And wakes the wish in youngest blood
> To tread the forfeit Paradise.

Nature demonstrates on a mighty scale the workings of the imagination. The genius of Nature converts the world quite literally from dead winter to summer vitality, uncovering the hidden essence: "the grass beneath the rime / Has hints of the propitious time" (167). Nature works as the poet does. It is the "helpful giant" rebuilding the ruins and repairing the defects. Ostensibly a nature poem, "May-Day" has an important place in the poetics as Emerson's great lyric celebration of the health of the imagination.

Nature also represents in "May-Day" the poet with the other essential element of the poet's make-up, talent. Nature not only converts the world but at the same time speaks its multiform language through flowers, birds, flowing streams, sky and clouds, fragrances and sounds. Spring is the artist of power and prophesy,

> Soothsayer of the eldest gods,
> Repairer of what harms betide,
> Revealer of the inmost powers
> Prometheus proffered, Jove denied;
> Disclosing treasures more than true,
> Or in what far to-morrow due;
> Speaking by the tongues of flowers,
> By the ten-tongued laurel speaking,
> Singing by the oriole songs,
> Heart of bird the man's heart seeking.

Spring is both orator ("There is no orator prevails / To beckon or persuade / Like thee") and, as Nature was in "The Snow-Storm," visual artist:

> The million-handed sculptor moulds
> Quaintest bud and blossom folds,
> The million-handed painter pours
> Opal hues and purple dye.

The artist-air selects from nature's wild sounds the "godlike words" that are strange and pure, savage and musical, pantherlike and convent-chanted. Emerson distilled his poetics of expression in eleven lines of "May-Day":

> The artful Air will separate
> Note by note all sounds that grate,
> Smothering in her ample breast
> All but godlike words,
> Reporting to the happy ear

Only purified accords.
Strangely wrought from barking waves,
Soft music daunts the Indian braves, —
Convent-chanting which the child
Hears pealing from the panther's cave
And the impenetrable wild.

Nature here is the very model of Emerson's poet, possessing on a grand scale the attributes we have seen Emerson accumulating in his theory and his allegories. Finally pictured is the poetic act that could exist only in his ideal poetics: the poet who would not talk in words but in wonders. Nature would gladly give them place, he said in "The Problem," and Earth wear them with pride.

Crises may be a necessary precondition for the emergence of new theories. Having witnessed Emerson's most fearful anxieties as an artist in the poem just discussed, we can now trace how, with brilliant concentration, he made the theoretical breakthrough to a new literary consciousness. The radical poetics that supported that passage enabled the essential artist in him to surmount the crisis of the imagination. At the same time, his poetics became an *ars poetica* that did what a revolutionary creed must do: it justified the prosaic, seemingly casual art form into which his language was flowing with a power immeasurably greater than in his poems.

CHAPTER 6

A Breakthrough into Spaciousness

AT THE END of *Six Epistles to Eva Hesse*, his biting, affectionate verses on experimentation in American poetry, Donald Davie supplies the phrase with which I have titled this discussion of Emerson's theoretical liberation:

> A breakthrough into spaciousness,
> New reaches charted for the mind,
> Is solid service to mankind.

Emerson's reality-denying verse showed the tyranny of his conceptual model of the imagination. The crucial conversion process at the center of the concept and the verse, continually pressuring reality into ideal forms, making natural law rhyme with moral law, could not but dissipate poetic power. The same begetting concept, as we saw in the previous chapter, induced the terror of stasis and sterility in the poet bereft of imagination and frozen in dejection.

But even as he represented in conventional respects the master current of the literature of his epoch, Emerson brought about a revolution in the articulation of his own consciousness. This emergence of a new mathematics of expressive form is a case study, in effect, of how a swerve occurs in the history of art, for the Emersonian shift was latent in the tenets of his poetic beliefs that had to do not with moral correspondence but with the plenitude of human and natural creation. This generative faith was rooted in some of the familiar ideas of the literary consciousness of his time. Like Dante, he created new permutations of the old forms.

We watch a consciousness of enormous energy and aesthetic commitment openly spinning loose of constraint, away from closed linguistic schema, and intent upon transferring by a new integrity its own and the world's complex energies. Emerson talked a great deal about the poet seeing moral meaning in experience but, as the artist, what he wanted was a language to grasp the abundance of sensation that filled his days.

It is an unusually explicit struggle out of an aesthetic crisis to draw up a new poetry contract in which the old conventions and associations would be broken and a new commitment made to veracity. This is not a matter of progressive chronology, as I have been careful to point out, but of concurrent genres in which Emerson worked: verse form, on the one hand, with its restraint and imposed perception and, on the other, the spoken essay that was both yielding and potent, and still not at the limit of its capacity, where Emerson could insert his freedom and therefore his identity as an artist.

Emerson set out a part of the libertarian credo in homely terms in *The Dial* of 1840:

> The philosophy of the day has long since broached a more liberal doctrine of the poetic faculty than our fathers held . . . This new taste for a certain private and household poetry, for somewhat less pretending than the festal and solemn verses which are written for the nations, really indicates, we suppose, that a new style of poetry exists . . . We have fancied that we drew greater pleasure from some manuscript verses than from printed ones of equal talent. For there was herein the charm of character; they were confessions; and the faults, the imperfect parts, the fragmentary verses, the halting rhymes, had *a worth beyond that of a high finish.*[1]

A quarter-century later Emerson did not doubt the triumph of the revolution: "The plasticity of the tough old planet is wonderful," he wrote in 1866. "Everything has grown ductile . . . Things once not possible are probable now" (*SW,* 179). His goal was the devising of poetic forms of full sweep and resonance, appropriate to his definition of poetry in an 1848 journal: "The excursions of poetry into lower nature, into the winds, waters, beast, bird, fish, insect, plant-tribes, are Man taking possession of the world" (*JMN,* VII, 83). He thereby envisioned a direct, conjugal engagement with life.

The contingent forces that produce in a single artist's mind this intense new coupling of life and art are manifold. As Leo Bersani acutely observed, "Those *given* forms which limit us can obviously come from an individual history (can perhaps even be born and nurtured in an individual work of art), as well as from the cultural myths we are steeped in or the language we more or less helplessly inherit . . . writers we admire have experimented with ways of breaking away from such self-limiting and even self-denying structures."[2] In the case of Emerson, Jonathan Bishop distilled in passing but more accurately than anyone else the belief in whose service Emerson set about devaluing the old forms: "Emerson's work consists essentially of doctrines and demonstrations intended to show the ways we can best experience our experiences."[3]

Emerson was remarkably consistent in his writing and actions in the pursuit of an aesthetic liberation. The phenomenon is threaded with irony, for the release into new configurations of expression and experience which Emerson envisioned was but the other side of the conceptual model of the imagination that impoverished his verse. Assertions of moral correspondence prevented his poems from expressing the consciousness of a new age, but correspondence simultaneously implied the full exchange of sensations, and this is one of the elements that determined the new reconciliation. That engagement through form was to involve a de-composing and a prosaicizing of the poetic imagination.

Emerson's small success as a poet is thus closely related to his role as a liberating god, to his cultural importance as a figure at the juncture of a literary revolution, the visible actor of the epochal consciousness reviving itself. The process was not without personal distress. In him an imagination possessed of a giant's vision of renewal and metaphysical power existed alongside anxieties and frustration over his capacity for open feeling and savage eloquence. In a real sense he was a prisoner of the theory he opposed, for all the while Emerson preached the organic fullness of life and art, his own verse was cramped in the strictures of the rationalist-idealist mind. Though in theory he was to call for a full sensuousness, the poetry remained formulaic, plotted along binary tracks toward a presupposed revelation. His rationalist idealism was rooted in the eighteenth century while his vision of a sensual language sprang from the contemporary Romantic faith in organicism. Out of the paradox grew Emerson's intense consciousness of the change in articulation, the new threshholds and new anatomies, that were to take shape in his time.

Emerson's periodically stated impatience with any artistic representation as compared with direct unmediated contact is apparent in fragments on nature, such as this one where he considers form simply as a *medium* and not an indispensable scheme for the deepening of experience:

> when I would recall the scenes I dreamed
> On Adirondac steeps, I know
> Small need have I of Turner or Daguerre.

At other times, he harbored mixed feelings about the constriction and security of forms. In verse fragments on the poet, he follows a catalogue of homely images of rural simplicity, of ring of ax and of huts and tents, with these lines on Said:

> nor loved he less
> Stately lords in palaces,
> Princely women hard to please,
> Fenced by form and ceremony,
> Decked by courtly rites and dress
> And etiquette of gentilesse.
> But when the mate of the snow and wind,
> He left each civil scale behind.

In his frustration over the lack of a poetics to give full performance to his imagination, he considered the abandonment of the literary enterprise itself: "A great soul will be strong to live, as well as strong to think. Does he lack organ or medium to impart his truths? He can still fall back on this elemental force of living them. This is a total act. Thinking is a partial act" (*W*, I, 99).

The familiar view of the gap in Emerson's poetic enterprise is that his poetic practice was never as liberal or as modern as his poetic theory and that the theory contrasted sharply with traditional ideas, especially those of the eighteenth century. The contrary actually seems to be true. Not only did Emerson's "modernist" revolution derive conspicuously from inherent contradictions in "traditional" theory, but his practice, if we will see it in its totality, bore out in a remarkably consistent way the theory he proposed. In this view there is no discrepancy between theory and practice, but rather an exhilarating consummation of the imaginative thrust. In fact, we can now see clearly for the first time the intimate and vivifying connection between the concept and the practice, see in fact quite the contrary of the familiar view that "his practice never achieved the poetic freedom which his theory proclaimed."[4] Emerson achieved an astonishingly eloquent power himself while promoting so successfully the liberated consciousness that was emerging in his age.

We must reconsider familiar assertions that Emerson as well as his contemporaries were blinded by their abstract libertarian enthusiasms to the practical consideration of form.[5] I want to show that quite the reverse occurred, that Emerson not only was concerned theoretically with form, but that he was intimately engaged with the minute elements as each contributed to the poetics developing out of his frustration.

This is a new view of Emerson, showing that the totality of his work — theory and practice — was a consistent and self-generating passage toward a new calculation of the way language might grip experience without tyrannizing it. Perry Miller said of the heady years of *The Dial,* "There was a breath of new air, much vague expectation, a consciousness of power not yet finding its determinate aim."[6] That presentiment of power in Emerson was exploited with fresh genius, fulfilling a need perfectly consistent with the larger developmental progress of Emerson the thinker. His turning from a concern with moral *meaning* to a concern for experiential *function* in art, from formula to sensation, as I have perceived it, Stephen Whicher described in other terms: "His transcendentalism is steadily giving way to a basic empiricism—one which, though it includes and stresses man's peculiar experience of the Soul, nevertheless pragmatically recognizes the priority of experience over 'Reality.' "[7] Forced by the vectors at work in Emerson's aesthetics, something had to burst out. There was an essential contradiction in his imaginative makeup: the inclusiveness of his organic conception of existence was everywhere thwarted by the closed space of his poetic expression. Out of this dilemma in the active consciousness of the artist, the theoretical lines of the modernist mind had to erupt.

The personal need existed in concert with a cultural awareness of enormous power and the challenge to harness it. In the artists' terms, it was a matter of joining language and experience. The mid-century consciousness sought two things: to grasp power and purpose together, including what Emerson called "the stupendous riches of man's nature" that lay outside the inherited forms of perception. It called for the devising of new forms of perception and articulation that would make those worlds of experience available. No one defined the need more urgently than Emerson: "Power, new power, is the good which the soul seeks." He saw the issue, in the essay "Experience," in its absolute simplicity: "Human life is made up of the two elements, power and form, and the proportion must be invariably kept if we would have it sweet and sound" (*W,* III, 65).

If the fundaments of Emerson's aesthetic program are anywhere compacted in three or four sentences, it is in the essay "Art." The three poles of moral truth, affective form, and intellectual liberation stand together as the solid underpinning: "There is but one Reason. The mind that made the world is not one mind, but *the* mind. And every work of art is a more or less pure manifestation of the same . . . It differs from the works of Nature in this, that they are organically reproductive. This [work of art] is not, but spiritually it is prolific by its powerful action on the intellects of men" (*W,* VII, 50-51). The search for the power of new forms was shared by others. Orestes Brownson, in an essay of 1840 entitled "American Literature," spoke of the "new spirit lately breathed into our publications." The spirit he referred to was codified in the Emerson-Fuller preface to the first issue of *The Dial,* the editors admittedly obeying the "strong current of thought and feeling, which, for a few years past, has led many sincere persons in New England to make new demands on literature, and to reprobate that rigor of our conventions of religions and education which is turning us to stone, which renounces hope, which looks only backward, which asks only such a future as the past, which suspects improvement, and holds nothing so much in horror as new views and the dreams of youth."[8]

The spirit had a voice, though vague in its purpose, in the poetic clichés of the younger Channing. His intense but confused poem "A Poet's Hope" contains these lines:

> Would I could summon from the deep, deep mine,
> Glutted with shapely jewels, glittering bright,
> One echo of that splendor, call it thine,
> And weave it in the strands of living light.

The new spirit could be made indistinguishable from a general diffuse Romantic aspiration by clichés such as these. But Emerson put everything on the quest, and his purpose was clear. In the later essay on Montaigne, he said again that only the artist's greatest powers would find the new reconciliation with the age. "Talent makes counterfeit ties; genius finds the real ones" (*W,* IV, 170). The search involved a new mode to manifest new-found relationships and stores of power, and not simply an attempt to emphasize a new and timely public theme.

Essentially an aesthetic pursuit and thus a search for new eyes, it is generally ignored in studies of American literature in favor of attention to synthesizing themes. Roy Harvey Pearce suggested that egocentricity was forced upon the nineteenth-century American poet by the antipoetic attitudes of the culture, and this made for "the basic style." But by basic style he necessarily means a theme: "the Adamic poem."[9] When we discriminate between themes—of which there is a small durable cluster in American poetry—and forms, we begin to approach the basic matter of signifying in poetry. To make the discrimination is to see the radical prize of Emerson's search. He saw that it was in the anatomy of articulation that new reaches of perception were possible. This was how his world was to be converted to a new one.

The search, then, was for power and for the forms that could perceive it, contain it, and transfer it. We best understand Emerson when we see that this goal was central and made inevitable by his recognition that the language forms available to his poetry could not bear the search. The vast novelty of the world, to use Barthes' term, lay out of reach of the modes of perception. Emerson's need was to feel the world exactly as it is. Visionary needs are a different order from what Emerson called the "abandonment to the nature of things" (*W,* III, 26). Emerson sought to penetrate the intellectual order that controlled the surface of his poems, concealing the factual world. His was a search for the dance of language that Charles Olson was to speak of a hundred years later. Olson's comparable need was for the "simplicities that a man learns, if he works in OPEN, or what can also be called COMPOSITION BY FIELD, as opposed to inherited line, stanza, over-all form, what is the 'old' base of the non-projective." He meant to attend to

> the *kinetics* of the thing. A poem is energy transferred from where the poet got it (he will have some several causations), by way of the poem itself to, all the way over to, the reader. Okay. Then the poem itself must, at all points, be a high energy-construct and, at all points, an energy-discharge. So: how is the poet to accomplish same energy, how is he, what is the process by which a poet gets in, at all points energy at least the equivalent of the energy which propelled him in the first place . . .
>
> This is the problem which any poet who departs from closed form is specially confronted by. And it involves a whole series of new recognitions. [10]

Olson and Emerson a century apart called for a new reconciliation of the world and the language in which it is to be experienced. Here is one of the ways Emerson described poetry capable of the modernist reconciliation: "In contrast with their writing [poets of the lowly — Burns, Wordsworth, and others], the style of Pope, of Johnson, of Gibbon, looks cold and pedantic. This writing is blood-warm. Man is surprised to find that things near are not less beautiful and wondrous than things remote" (*W,* I, 112).

A tenacious, nearly lifelong, and complicated consideration of a new relationship of the imagination, language, and reality lies beneath the iceberg tip of Emerson's assertion that the experience of each new age requires a new confession. The new ordering demanded simultaneously a new perception and a new voice. Conventions and thus irrelevance are the inheritances he worked to eliminate. "Poems," he says in the essay "The Poet," careful to distinguish individual poems from the supreme poem, "are a corrupt version of some text in nature *with which they ought to be made to tally"* (*W,* III, 25; my italics). This was the philosophical ideal; he had already in *Nature* called for the practical craft, for wise men to pierce the rotten diction of habit and fasten words again to visible things. How deeply and how long and in how many ways Emerson saw the problem of the poet and his language has been obscured by the variety of his manifest subjects. Yet no question was more central to his life. The briefest sort of extractions from his journals over forty-five years indicate how his private thoughts circled and recircled the artist's concern with his experience and medium. As early as 1820, not yet seventeen years old, he recorded a careful enthusiasm for full Sensation: "Mixing with the thousand pursuits and passions and objects of the world as personified by Imagination is profitable and entertaining" (*JMN*, I, 3). Just as early, he recognized how form had to be faithful to the reality it sought to convey. Writing in his journal of 1823 after hearing Channing, he said approvingly: "The language was a transparent medium, conveying with the utmost distinctness the pictures in his mind to the mind of the hearers" (*JMN*, II, 160-161). In his essay on Shakespeare, much later in *Representative Men,* he described the ideal poet as "a heart in unison with his time and country." Of Shakespeare's form, he said, still employing the criterion of fidelity, "Things were mirrored in his poetry without loss or blur" (*W,* IV, 189, 213).

That faithful mimetic form accomplished an openness to experience and absorptive power commensurate with what Emerson in 1836 described passionately as the ideal self in relation to "the deeps of spiritual nature." It was yet another metaphor for the eyeball moment: "The walls are taken away; we lie open . . . But I am nothing else than a capacity for justice, truth, love, freedom, power" (*JMN*, V, 230). He could see in Carlyle, with an urban awareness in 1837 that is prophetically modern, the practical accomplishment of registering equally great but prosaic landscapes of experience: "his genius is the redolence of London 'the Great Metropolis.' So vast, enormous, with endless details, and so related to all the world, is he. It would seem as if no baker's shop, no mutton stall, no Academy, no church, no placard, no coronation, but he saw and sympathized with all, and took all up into his omnivorous fancy, and hence his panoramic style, and this encyclopediacal allusion to all knowables" (*JMN*, V, 291).

Yet again the idea of an expressive form that could turn the rush of experience into power made Emerson see similar possibilities in the lecture form. In an 1839 journal entry labeled simply "Eloquence" and "Lyceum," he laid out breathlessly (it seems) a program for an art form:

> Here is all the true orator will ask, for here is a convertible audience and here are no stiff conventions that prescribe a method, a style, a limited quotation of books, and an exact respect to certain books, persons, or opinions. No, here everything is admissible, philosophy, ethics, divinity, criticism, poetry, humor, fun, mimicry, anecdotes, jokes, ventriloquism. All the breadth and versatility of the most liberal conversation, the highest, the lowest, the most personal, the most local topics, all are permitted, and all

> may be combined in one speech; it is a panharmonicon, — every
> note on the longest gamut, from the explosion of cannon, to the
> tinkle of a guitar. Let us try if Folly, Custom, Convention and
> Phlegm cannot hear our sharp artillery. Here is a pulpit that
> makes other pulpits tame and ineffectual — [Here] with their cold
> mechanical preparation for a delivery the most decorous, — fine
> things, pretty things, wise things, but no arrows, no axes, no nec-
> tar, no growling, no transpiercing, no loving, no enchantment.
> Here he may lay himself out utterly, large, enormous, prodigal,
> on the subject of the hour. Here he may dare to hope for ecstasy
> and eloquence. (*JMN,* VII, 265)

An artist's credo of spaciousness was gathering over the years. Because it
occupied Emerson's thought and ranged through endless analogues in his
journals, this credo has a cumulative brilliance that his more rationalized
essay on the poet lacks. The operative concepts come out again and again
in one context or another: deformalization of the language genres, flexibility, leveling, plainness, earthiness. We see him turn repeatedly to his
own Concord landscape for images of the qualities he sought, including the
"elastic principle." Dante is described with telling simplicity as throwing
the weight of his body into his art. And Emerson's use of the lowly dog as
an emblem of the poet makes him William Carlos Williams' contemporary.
Here collected for the first time is the artist's primer, a Preface to *Lyrical
Ballads,* from twenty-five years of the journals. My italics highlight each
element we have been observing.

> [October 19, 1839] In the country the lover of nature dreaming
> through the wood would never awake to thought if the scream of
> an eagle, the cries of a crow or a curlew near his head did not
> *break the continuity.* Nay if the truth must out the finest lyrics of
> the poet come of this *coarse parentage;* the imps of matter beget
> such child on the Soul, fair daughter of God.

> [November 14, 1839] At last I discovered that my curve was a
> parabola whose arcs would never meet, and came to acquiesce in
> the perception that although no diligence can rebuild the Uni-
> verse in a model by the best accumulation or disposition of details,
> yet does the World reproduce itself in miniature in every event
> that transpires, so that all the laws of nature may be read in the
> smallest fact. So that the truth speaker may *dismiss all solicitude
> as to the proportion and congruency* of the aggregate of his
> thoughts so long as he is a *faithful reporter of particular impres-
> sions.*

> [December 22 (?), 1839] A judge and a banker must drive their
> craft poetically as well as a dancer or a scribe. That is, they must

exert that higher vision which causes the object to become *fluid and plastic*. Then they are inventive, *they detect its capabilities*. If they do not this they have nothing that can be called success, but the work and the workman become blockfish and near the point of everlasting congelation. All human affairs need *the perpetual intervention of this elastic principle* to preserve them supple and alive as the earth needs the presence of caloric through its pores to *resist the tendency to absolute solidity*.

[April 24 (?), 1841] I frequently find the best part of my ride in the Concord coach from my house to Winthrop Place to be in Prince Street, Charter Street, Ann Street and the like places at the North End of Boston. The *dishabille* of both men and women, their *unrestrained attitudes and manners* make pictures greatly more interesting than the clean shaved and silk robed procession in Washington and Tremont Streets . . . I feel the painter in me: these are the traits which make us feel *the force and eloquence of form* and the *sting of color*.

[November-December 1841] All writing is by the grace of God. People do not deserve to have good writing, they are so pleased with bad. In these sentences that you show me I can find no beauty, for I see death in every clause and every word. There is a fossil or a mummy character which pervades this book. The best sepulchres, the vastest catacombs, Thebes and Cairo pyramids are sepulchres to me. I like gardens and nurseries. Give me *initiative, spermatic, prophesying, man-making words*.

[June-July 1846] Do they stand immoveable there, — the sots, and laugh at your so-called poetry? They may well laugh; it does not touch them yet. Try a deeper strain. There is no makebelieve about these fellows; they are good tests for your skill; therefore, a louder yet, and yet a louder strain. There is not one of them, but will spin fast enough when the music reaches him, but he is very deaf, try a sharper string. Angels in satinette and calico, — *angels in hunting knives, and rifles, — swearing angels, roarers with liquor; — O poet, you have much to learn*.

[July-August 1849] I think if I were professor of Rhetoric, — teacher of the art of writing well, to young men, I should use Dante for my textbook. Come hither, youth, and learn how the brook that flows at the bottom of your garden, or the farmer who ploughs the adjacent field, — your father and mother, your debts and credits, and your web of habits are the very best basis of poetry . . . *Dante knew how to throw the weight of his body into each act* . . . Yet is not Dante reason or illumination and that essence we were looking for, but only *a new exhibition of the possibilities*

*of genius. Here is an imagination that rivals in closeness and pre-
cision the senses.*

[June 7, 1852] We had a good walk, W. E. C. [Channing] and I
. . . C.'s young dog scampered and dived and swam at such a
prodigal rate, that one could not help grudging the youth of the
Universe (the animals) their Heaven. They must think us poor
sedants in petticoats, as poet Cowper is painted in the Westall
Editions. *How much more the dog knows of nature than his master,* though his master were an Indian. The dog tastes, snuffs,
rubs, feels, tries, every thing, everywhere, through miles of bush,
brush, grass, water, mud, lilies, mountain and sky.

The urgency with which Emerson conceived an instinctive, impulsive form
with the capacity for manifold power and reality rings in a last quotation,
from the 1865 journals. Here is Emerson, at sixty-two, still facing the central aesthetic need of his life:

[August-November 1865] The conduct of intellect must respect
nothing so much as *preserving the sensibility.* That mind is best
which is most *impressionable.* There are times when the cawing of
crows, a flowering weed, a snowflake, a boy's willow whistle or a
porter's wheelbarrow is more suggestive to the mind than the
Yosemite Gorge or the Vatican would be in another hour. In like
mood, an old verse, or particular words gleam with rare significance. *How to keep, how, how, to recover at will this sensibility?*

Form is the inescapable problem of the original artist. Reconciliation
with reality constitutes his search, and his successes, as is true from Chaucer to Wordsworth and Williams, not only stand as milestones in any history one might make of poetics but, more significantly, account for the fact
that the poetic art has any history at all. Barthes has written most penetrat-
ingly on the relationship between form and perception. I have quoted him
earlier in another regard, and my term "reconciliation" is derived from
him. Of the writer he says: "History puts in his hands a decorative and
compromising instrument, a writing inherited from a previous and different History, for which he is not responsible and yet which is the only one
he can use. Thus is born a tragic element in writing, since the conscious
writer must henceforth fight against ancestral and all-powerful signs
which, from the depths of a past foreign to him, impose Literature on him
like some ritual, not like a reconciliation."[11] In that reconciliation a vast
and varied reality becomes visible again. Emerson's achievement was just
such a renewed contract that embodied profound ramifications not only
for the forms but for the attitudes of the modernist poetic consciousness.

He did not confuse ingenuity with art. Nor was he tempted to turn inward on his ego as an alternative to the more difficult creation of an adequate art form. He was surer-footed, more consistent, and deeper-diving in the aesthetic quest than most other theoreticians among American poets. "By rejecting tradition," a colleague of mine has observed, "the American artist has dared his defeat; by turning his back on the past he has often engaged in a futile search for new forms, confusing ingenuity with art; by naming himself as the subject of his art the American writer has . . . 'no means of getting a foothold except personal ones' . . . The absence of a tradition and an awareness of the responsibility this imposes has been *the* tradition in American letters."[12] Emerson aspired to more than eccentricity, however, and so he was forced to the roots of artistic form where epochal innovation begins. The shift set in motion in his thought was fundamental, and the tradition in America of rejecting tradition highlights Emerson's primacy. He theorized deeply enough so that, if he did not invent single-handed one of the long-lived modernist traditions, he at least found it on its way to the twentieth century to be born.

Thoreau's search for a new reconciliation of consciousness, language, and reality was important in an emblematic way. Tony Tanner's view of Emerson's contribution to this is the common one: "Where Emerson prescribed, Thoreau ventured forth and made a real effort to insert himself into the physical world, to become its intimate undemanding acquaintance."[13] But Emerson, again to distinguish him, was aesthetically sophisticated and aesthetically radical in a way Thoreau was not. Camping out at Walden was a manner of coupling life with things, but the deliberate translation into artistic principles was Emerson's particular contribution. He sought not a social arrangement but a glossary for possessing the whole scale of experience. His terms, as Hart Crane's were to be, are remarkable for their scope: "The poet cannot spare any grief or pain or terror in his experience; he wants every rude stroke that has been dealt on his irritable texture. I need my fear and my superstition as much as my purity and courage, to construct the glossary which opens the Sanscrit of the world" (*JMN*, VII, 390).

"One of the outstanding qualities of American literature," D. H. Lawrence wrote, is how "the deliberate ideas of the man veil, conceal, obscure that which the artist has to reveal."[14] Emerson contained this full drama of artistic renewal in himself. His calculated aesthetics took form in the strictly tiered model of the imagination and in the cold icon of the transparent eyeball. Counter to that controlling set of mind, instinctive and therefore irrepressible, ran what Lawrence called "art-language" and the "truth" of the artist. In Emerson its release signaled the renewal of the integrity of the imagination. It was the surfacing, to use other terms, of the latent imperatives from within the strictures of a manifest dream. The overlooked sentence that follows Emerson's famous dictum about poets being liberating gods deserves attention. The poets take men out of their cellars into the open air, where "Men have really got a new sense, and found within their world another world, or nest of worlds." This is the artist's imagination opening into a new self-definition, and moving toward the acquisition of a new voice. It is, in effect, a definition of the phenomenon of radical literary innovation.

Ultimately he was to evolve in his prose the techniques of composing according to forms of Becoming — he called it "inward skill" — that marked a departure from the conventions of his poetry, opening up mental room and allowing a freedom of voice that we recognize today as modern. "Inward skill" represented a new principle of improvisational artistic structure, making way for the flowing imagination, providing a new stage for the performance of a voice meshed in a full way with the new age. It also provided a structure that in turn revealed a new world that Emerson had not counted on. The conceptual and cultural movement toward this liberation of the imagination and the development of a new voice is the subject of the next paragraphs.

THE CULTURAL moment that supported Emerson's break from self-limiting forms seems to have had a single dominant theme that was partly rooted in the libertarian and egalitarian politics of the American Revolution. Emerson was the translator of that history into a long-lived aesthetic ferment. Derived also from latent necessities in his philosophy and from the culture about him, this descendentalism reached toward a wider common audience, a wider sweep of experience, a new candor, and new specifics of existence. In the end it produced a sort of anti-literature.

Philosophically, the inevitable direction for Emerson was toward greater scope and a closer apprehension of the phenomenal plane of existence. This is a central irony, for though Emerson's willing conversion of the material world to a moral clarity led always in the poetry to the strict scheme of revelation and consequent qualities of abstraction, the doctrinal inclusiveness of the philosophy also held a potential for the prosaicizing and de-idealization of art. The reasons were plain enough: if every fact embodied its metaphysical possibility, then the whole scale of the world to its minutest phenomenon had to be taken into account. "What is it to be a poet?" he asked in his journal in 1840. With a lateral attentiveness that anticipates Whitman and Williams, he goes on: "What but a sensibility so keen that the scent of an elderblow or timberyard and corporation works of a nest of ants is event enough for him" (*JMN*, VIII, 468). If the full world was charged with convertible energy, then a form and a voice and a perspective had to be found to discover that dispersed power, to hold it in suspension, and to transfer it through language. While the moral impulse of the philosophy impelled Emerson upward toward the abstract, its universal implications thrust him repeatedly back, in theory at least, to the particular world. "There is a correspondence," he summarized, "between the human soul and everything that exists in the world, more properly everything that is known to man" (*JMN*, IV, 84). The poem "Rhodora" is an early instance of this belief, and it confirms the accuracy of Sherman Paul's description of Emerson's doctrine: "The faculties were the seeds planted in man in anticipation of the nutrition they were to find ready for them in a universe designed to call them forth."[15] Full commerce between the consciousness and reality, the ideal by which Emerson was to measure his aesthetic forms, was the idea near the heart of his work. Jonathan Bishop sees this clearly: "The Soul in Entire Action is the central drama of all Emerson's work . . . We cannot understand what Emerson is getting at until we have made the connection between the particular piece of wit we appreciate and an ideal of complete human activity."[16]

In that central document of Emerson's conception of the imagination, "The American Scholar," he measured the scope of the perception necessary to capture the specific world: there is "no fact, no event, in our private history, which shall not, sooner or later, lose its adhesive, inert form, and astonish us by soaring from our body into the empyrean" (*W*, I, 96-97). The metaphysical transfer reflects the philosophical Emerson, but the totality of the grasp demands from the artist new capacities in literary form and imagination. Emerson's aesthetic salvation lay in the inclusive corollary of the organic doctrine: all experience was morally instructive and consequently had to be accommodated. To employ some of R. P. Blackmur's words on Dante's allegory, Emerson's belief in the basic moral task of poetry became an instrument of inclusive freedom rather than exclusive bondage. It called for an aesthetics of difficult unity through inclusion of the previously disdained.

The organic model of nature as ultimately a single construct also urged an aesthetic impulse toward a more direct reconciliation with reality and a more responsive form by which to view that reality. The moral implication of organicism was properly Christian, that each part helped every other part. This being so, all experience was fit material for poetry. Moral revelation being the purpose, *any* literary form that revealed the unity of the specific world was the equal of poetry. He wrote to an acquaintance in 1869: "Natural Science *is* the point of interest now, and, I think, is dimming and extinguishing a good deal that was called poetry. These sublime and all-reconciling revelations of nature will exact of poetry a corrrespondent height and scope, or put an end to it" (*L,* VI, 63). In such a context, it is not surprising that Emerson could label as "poetry" the prose aphorisms of Richard Owen the paleontologist, Augustine, Sir Thomas Browne, and others (*W,* VIII, 50-51). Emerson saw that an increased mental field was directly related to the spatial possibilities of the literary form. In "Poetry and Imagination," he dealt with the restraints of prosodic convention: "The senses imprison us, and we help them with metres as limitary, — with a pair of scales and a foot-rule and a clock" (*W,* VIII, 23). In an unpublished verse entitled "Woods" and appropriately subtitled "A Prose Sonnet," he again drew the parallel between nature and aesthetic means:

> This I would ask of you, O sacred woods, when ye shall next give me somewhat to say, give me also the tune wherein to say it. Give me a tune of your own, like your winds or rains or brooks or birds; for the songs of men grow old when they have been often repeated, but yours, though a man have heard them for seventy years, are never the same, but always new, like time itself, or like love.
>
> (*JMN,* VII, 248)

Emerson's philosophy of universally available revelation contributed theoretically to the opening of his literary forms. One of the signs of the "coming days," he wrote in "The American Scholar," is that "instead of the sublime and beautiful, the near, the low, the common was explored and poetized." Instead of foreign subjects, the "literature of the poor," the child, the street, the household, and topics of the times were to be taken up. "It is a great stride," he concluded, and as men of genius who descend to confront vulgar reality he cited Goldsmith, Burns, Cowper, Goethe, Wordsworth, and Carlyle. Metzger's conclusion confirms my view: "his approach to beauty through the forms of nature required him to contrive esthetic principles which covered vastly greater numbers of specific instances."[17]

The impulse toward the new and spacious was even more broadly based in the culture. Perry Miller describes the age as one "of severance, of dissociation, of freedom, of analysis, of detachment." The new race, he says, was heady and rebellious.[18] This emphasis dictated a great leveling in literary values and a new tolerance in accord with democratic inclusiveness. The attitude of this modernism was not cliquish difference but rather a reconciliation of art with the belief in the common man. Democratic thought was alive in religion, politics, and science, and the democratic obligation seemed clear to Emerson. In the leveling process the old discriminations among poetic powers began to dissolve. "Who loves nature?" Emerson asks in "The Poet." "Is it only poets, and men of leisure and cultivation, who live with her? No; but also hunters, farmers, grooms, and butchers, though they express their affection in their choice of life and not in their choice of words" (*W,* III, 15).

Emerson saw the connection between the political doctrine of each man's worth and the art of the age: "the same movement which effected the elevation of what was called the lowest class in the state assumed in literature a very marked and as benign an aspect" (*W,* I, 67). He catalogued the homely topics newly available to poetry, and presumed the existence of the poetic imagination in all men as a natural possession. He urged the poet to draw out "that *dream*-power which every night shows thee is thine own" (*W,* III, 40). To Emerson, dream-power proved how all men share the art of the poet by creating characters and settings and plots in their dreams (*W,* VIII, 44-45).

Literary leveling was virtually Emerson's invention, because he was the eloquent translator of the new consciousness coming into being around him at many levels of life. The style of art about which he theorized so energetically sought to convey the new temper.[19] He was scholar and confessor for the age but, more significant by far for the course of poetry in America, he was a poet whose conscious aims came into conflict with his intuitive needs as an artist, forcing the breakdown of the conventions and evoking a brilliant body of theory to justify the assault.

Even as he declared the moral purpose of the poet, his unsuppressible artistic needs were shifting the criteria of artistic judgment away from moral and philosophical content to the adequacy of the means to take hold of a dense and even nonmoral world that his own poetry persisted in excluding. With consistent transcendental emphasis he viewed poetry as the supreme form of expression, philosophical insight, and moral example, but in more effective ways he was bringing about the dissolution of that clerical idea. His need for a language adequate to the dynamic activity of his own poetic imagination — under the pressure of converging cultural and personal vectors — created the opening. Notes he made on English poetry in 1853 show the need for imaginative flexibility and for a new voice capable of engaging, if only in bits and patches, a much larger world: "I find or fancy more true poetry, the love of the Vast, in the Welsh and Bardic fragments of Taliessin and his school, than in a good many volumes of British classics" (*W,* IX, 440).

Everywhere in Emerson's theoretical poetics, though belied by his poetry
with its crabbed awkwardness and narrow movements, he insisted on the
primacy of the senses. He understood in a crucial way that fidelity to sense
was the difference between the formulaic blockage of the poetic imagination and its liberation. Science contributed peripherally to this liberation,
for it was scientific principle as Emerson conceived it which engaged life
rather than categories, and which insisted that intellectual forms and discriminations correspond to life. The scientific approach accorded with
Emerson's need to align his expansive poetic imagination with the voice he
was seeking to develop. This is his meaning when he says with more than
ordinary conviction in the essay "The Poet" that the poet "uses forms according to the life and not according to the form. This is true science" (*W*,
III, 21). He acted on this principle when he rejected the pulpit, where he
felt spiritual life was sacrificed to the outworn forms of worship.

ORATORY, prominent in the rise of the Lyceum movement of the 1830s as a
means of popular education, also contributed importantly in this convergence of personal and cultural elements. Oratory served Emerson as a
model of means that accommodated widely varied purposes and had sufficient flexibility to convey an individual's unique powers. The shift toward
oral address and away from written modes of expression represented the
onset of an anti-literary personalism. The importance of oratory in styles of
American literature is, of course, a familiar observation.[20] It shows with
extraordinary clarity in the case of Emerson, in whose thinking we can plot
the basic outline of its contribution to the phenomenon of radical literary
innovation. The marks of its influence on Emerson are scattered abundantly throughout his work.

The two inestimable advantages of Christianity, Emerson declared at
the end of his Divinity School address, are the Sabbath and the institution
of preaching. The virtues of preaching for Emerson were its directness of
communication and its availability to all sorts of expression. He called
preaching "the speech of man to men, — essentially the most flexible of all
organs, of all forms" (*W*, I, 92). It was not then eccentric for Emerson, and
certainly not inconsistent with the esteem in which orators were held in this
flourishing time of the Lyceum, to begin to identify the orator with the
poet and to do this by removing distinctions between them. He suggested in
a passage from "The Poet" that the orator provides a distinct image for the
audience in a direct confrontation the more powerful for being unob-
structed by the conventions of literary forms. "The poet," Emerson wrote,
"in utter solitude remembering his spontaneous thoughts and recording

them, is found to have recorded that which men in crowded cities find true for them also. The orator distrusts at first the fitness of his frank confessions, his want of knowledge of the persons he addresses, until he finds that he is the complement of his hearers; — that they drink his words because he fulfils for them their own nature" (*W*, I, 103). Emerson's identification of the poet in solitude in his study and the orator in the public hall was a step in his breakdown of the discriminations between the two crafts. Indeed, to Emerson's mind, the function of the orator was superior, for he confronts his fellow men in person and helps them to see and fulfill themselves. The orator is at once, that is, the type of a more democratic and a timelier form for Emerson's contemporaries.

In Emerson's steady move toward the democratization of poetry, he recognized oratory as a model not only for direct personal engagement but also for a fullness of expressive gesture beyond the printed word. He exclaims in "The Poet": "What a little of all we know is said! . . . Hence the necessity of speech and song; hence these throbs and heart-beatings in the orator, at the door of the assembly, to the end namely that thought may be ejaculated as Logos, or Word" (*W*, III, 39-40). The sensed presence of the individual, in a form of address that preserved the live palpitations of the speaker, Emerson saw as a virtue excluded by written forms. Sherman Paul, with characteristic insight, related Emerson's enthusiastic regard for oratory to what we have seen as his theoretical insistence on man's obligation to act: "With the spoken (or acted) word he not only showed his magnetic force, his true alignment with the spiritual pole, but discharged its power by electrifying the listener. This was the total circuit of thought as the conversion of power that he never felt satisfied he achieved in the written word. The desire for action was thus in a way the need for an audience, for social response."[21] Matthiessen's observation accurately suggested the intensity with which Emerson viewed the possibilities of oratory for effecting a deep reconciliation between expressive forms of language and actual human needs: "he believed that the orator could speak both most directly and most deeply to men, breaking down their reserves, tugging them through the barriers of themselves, bringing to articulation their own confused thoughts, flooding them with sudden surprise that the moment of their life was so rich."[22]

For Emerson oratory was a dynamic form, capable of capturing the world and the mind in motion together, and conveying this circuit as if spontaneously out of the individual man thinking at the center of his world. In 1832, Emerson considered the subjective element's necessity: "What we say however trifling must have its roots in ourselves or it will not move others. No speech should be separate from our being like a plume or nosegay, but like a leaf or a flower or a bud though the topmost and remotest, yet joined by a continuous line of life to the trunk and the seed" (*JMN,* IV, 36-37). By 1839 his theoretical base was explicit: "Why should we write dramas, and epics, and sonnets, and novels in two volumes? Why not write as variously as we dress and think? A lecture is a new literature, which leaves aside all tradition, time, place, circumstance, and addresses an assembly as mere human beings, — no more — It has never yet been done well. It is an organ of sublime power, a panharmonicon for variety of note. But only then is the orator successful when he is himself agitated and is as much a hearer as any of the assembly. In that office you may and shall (please God!) yet see the electricity part from the cloud and shine from one part of heaven to the other" (*JMN,* VII, 224-225). Two years later, following a lyrical passage in his journal on the fullness of sensual response, he wrote: "I think now that the very finest and sweetest closes and falls are not in our metres, but in the measures of eloquence, which have greater variety and richness than verse" (*JMN,* VIII, 97).

Emerson's insistent attempts to eliminate the conventional qualitative distinctions between poetry and oratory expressed his profound sense that a new sincerity and extemporal power were now available outside constricted poetic form. A similar necessity has led other poets to a new regard for the inherent resources of language aside from generic sets. Hopkins, for example, sought that liberation in sprung rhythm: "Why do I employ sprung rhythm at all? Because it is nearest to the rhythm of prose, that is the native and natural rhythm of speech, the least forced, the most rhetorical and emphatic of all possible rhythms, combining it seems to me, opposite, and one would have thought, incompatible excellences, markedness of rhythm — that is rhythm's self — naturalness of expression." Indeed, he called his rhythm "oratorical."[23]

Of his admired Montaigne Emerson said much the same that he had said of the ideal orator: "the sincerity and marrow of the man reaches to his sentences. I know not anywhere the book that seems less written. It is the language of conversion transferred to a book. Cut the words and they would bleed; they are vascular and alive." Elsewhere in the essay he associates Montaigne's writing with the straightforward talk of blacksmiths and teamsters whose speech is "a shower of bullets" quite unlike the expression of "Cambridge men," who "pun and refine too much, and swerve from the matter to the expression" (*W,* IV, 168). *To seem less written* is of course the whole intent of Emerson's move away from genre traditions as he sought an expression that released his imagination into an active, sensational world.

"All good conversation, manners and action come from a spontaneity which forgets usages and makes the moment great," Emerson said in "Experience" (*W,* III, 68). He had come to epitomize conversation as possessing in an intimate and concentrated way the freedom, inventiveness, and thaumaturgic power of oratory. The assertion is from the 1844 essay, but some years earlier, in his journal, he had praised Carlyle's absorptive, animated, and plain-dealing style in terms of conversation. "I think he has seen as no other in our time," wrote Emerson, "how inexhaustible a mine is the language of Conversation . . . his paragraphs are all a sort of splendid conversation" (*JMN,* V, 291). The origin of Emerson's admiration for conversation as an art form and its public adaptation as oratory was now in the nineteenth century a necessity for Americans, as it had been for Wordsworth and, in the line of originating artists, back to Homer. Emerson meant to reassociate the written word with the act of speech. He sought a language form of intensive gesture that would be not so much *written* or even *spoken* as *talked*—a sort of splendid conversation.

There was also a practical objective in adopting the tonalities and modes of the orator. By the speaker's direct address and apparent rejection of literary affectations, he was preparing a taste for public acceptance of new writing with comparable qualities. As Yeats believed at the end of the nineteenth century that the moral ideas in poetry made it accepted in society, Emerson saw the growing public interest in a stage presence, a personality shaping the expression, a prosaic quality in the language and the element of personal enthusiasm in a face-to-face meeting. He knew these leveling aspects create wider acceptance by the American audience. The confirmation of his beliefs came from Carlyle, who had written to him in the 1830s: "My view is that now at last we have lived to see all manner of Poetics and Rhetorics and Sermonics . . . as good as broken and abolished . . . and so one leaves the pasteboard coulisses, and three unities, and Blair's Lectures quite behind; and feels only that there is *nothing sacred,* then, but the *Speech of Man* to believing Men!" (*CEC,* 103-104).

The life-giving circuit from speech to written forms has always been a matter of concern to ground-breaking poets. From Chaucer to Williams, certain poets made renewed efforts to narrow the distance between the two. Emerson's was the first major effort in America. In the theoretical mounting of his own liberation as an artist we see a movement of the modern mind: the freeing of consciousness and the coming into view of a different world. The urgency of revitalizing poetry's language fed in from cultural changes already under way. In Emerson its achievement was a matter of intellectual and imaginative survival. For this reason it has an extraordinary clarity and immediacy in Emerson that are lacking in other poets and theoreticians for whom received conventions are less antagonistic.

THE CONVERGENCE of philosophical, psychological, political, aesthetic, even scientific necessities — because each abandoned an existing formalism and indirectly encouraged an end to the elegant echoes of the literary tradition as well — opened the poetic guild to all comers, and in the end made a virtue in America out of amateurism. Thus, the relationship between the innovation we see in Emerson's aesthetic theory and the brilliant transformations of the leveling trend in Whitman and Dickinson is very close. The subject of originality and amateurism has yet to be explored adequately as it constitutes a basic element in the discontinuity of American poetry. The needs of Emerson's age for a renewed congruence between language and reality made the innovative risks of the amateur not only acceptable but inevitable. The excitement was pervasive. With the general jingoistic resistance to the supposed intrusion of European taste (more precisely, the myth of European taste) went a distrust of luxury, fancy, costume, whatever seemed frippery, ostentatious, or simply nonfunctional.[24] Leveling was involved in the distrust of impersonal science, whose practitioners seemed to a poet's mind so educated that the real world escaped them. Emerson was on the side of the primitives when he wrote in the poem "Blight": "our eyes / Are armed but we are strangers to the stars, / And strangers to the mystic beast and bird."

The culmination of this desire to flee from tradition and schooling sounded in Emerson's call for the giant of newness to destroy the old. He repeated his age's rejection of artifice when he told the young scholars at Harvard that only out of savage nature, out of terrible Druids and Berserkirs, would come the new world's Shakespeare. Out of that treasured primitivism, of course, came the barbaric yawp of Whitman and the dissenting New England wit of Emily Dickinson. These two exemplary amateurs disrupted the more complacent ways of American poetry. Continuity was utterly broken, and the complex forces that helped effect this break converged in Emerson. In his consciousness the problem of his literary age was worked out, for it was he who escaped from the deforming confinements of poetry *in extremis* and emerged with a yielding instrument of expression resonant with personal energy. The ultimate shape of that theoretical arrangement was *the form of an attitude* which, almost predictably in the Oedipal history of literature, in the twentieth century lost the Emersonian idealism and confronted a world seemingly without principle.

Emerson's aesthetic speculations reached a practicable conclusion because they were driven by an enormous frustration. His was a caged poetic imagination spinning free into a congenial new integrity of language. That radical movement toward an anti-literary and heuristic structure to replace the inherited and monumental forms came of his personal need to animate the verse which, measured by his own aspirations, he recognized as a failure. In the end Emerson strove to restore his poetic imagination to himself. It had labored in the service of rationalistic ideals with formulaic diction and rhythms and a structure based on the transforming poetic imagination. His frustration over his inability to preserve in his expression the integrity of his imagination is poignantly set out in the motto taken from Plato which he wrote alongside "Bacchus" in his own copy of *Poems:* "The man who is his own master knocks in vain at the doors of poetry" (*W*, IX, 443). In this telling comment are compacted all the defeats Emerson felt in his personal struggle for adequate expression.

He required more than adjustments along the surface of his poetry. He had to occupy a position fundamentally alien to the voices of convention. This was a poetry not identified by rhyme or meter or any other prosodic feature, but rather by *its raw power to take up the world into adequate language.* He sought a text that would give voice where "fancy . . . is silent, in the presence of great passion and action." And then, also in "Poetry and Imagination," under the heading "Veracity," he set out his credo in its hundredth version:

> I do not wish . . . to find that my poet is not partaker of the feast he spreads, or that he would kindle or amuse me with that which does not kindle or amuse him. He must believe in his poetry. Homer, Milton, Hafiz, Herbert, Swedenborg, Wordsworth, are heartily enamoured of their sweet thoughts. Moreover, they know that this correspondence of things to thoughts is far deeper than they can penetrate, —defying adequate expression; that it is elemental, or in the core of things. Veracity therefore is that which we require in poets, — that they shall say how it was with them, and not what might be said. (*W*, VIII, 29-30)

It was a colossal necessity. But we mistake its focal point if we do not see that his main concern was form, an arrangement of language that would feel and yield fully. At base it was a search for a scheme faithful to the habitual gesture of liberation that was the motor principle of his existence. Stephen Whicher penetrated to that center when he said, no doubt too darkly, of Emerson of the early years, "beneath his surface passivity a deep revulsion against his servitude to a world he never made and did not accept was slowly gathering force."[25] As the artist, Emerson required a form equal to the infinite demands he put upon the Soul. Gilman saw what it was that overshadowed his aesthetics, that is, how he wanted to be in the world. "Most of all, he tried to be the active soul, with a sensibility so fine that no experience could possibly be empty of meaning" (*SW*, viii). The enterprise of finding a form to match this ideal capacity of the Soul and reconciled at the same time with a manifold reality is the aesthetic obsession established early by Emerson.

He was unique among his contemporaries in his engagement with original artistic form and the aesthetic possibilities for truth. This necessity drives the plea in the famous opening lines of the poem "Bacchus": "Bring me wine, but wine which never grew / In the belly of the grape." The blunt cry for release into new anatomies of perception kept coming. In his verse-book, in a version of the poem "Merops," he wrote this unmasked complaint:

> What care I so the things abide
> Things of the heavenly mind,
> The rich and enriching presences,
> How long the power to give them form
> Stays behind;
> If they remain to me
> I can spare that,
> I can wait
> Till the stammering fit of life is past
> Till the soul its weed has cast
> And led by desire of these heavenly guides
> I have come into a free element
> And won a better instrument
> They taught me a new speech
> And a thousand silences
> For as there is but one path for the sun
> So is there ever but one word for me to say
>
> (Verse-Book X)

Crowded here in considerable ambiguity is much that we have discerned in Emerson's structure of thought. He attends to "one word," which is the single goal of his theoretic imagination, the transfer of the factual world into the aesthetic and moral, and is thus the subject of his poems and the cause of their perceptual limitations. But here too in these lines is Emerson the artist straining for release, for a new expression that will make audible the silences that surround his active poetic imagination. Though the lines about hope for release into "a free element" where he will have "won a better instrument" are broad allusions to immortality, they are manifestly a statement about crossing a threshhold from a "stammering fit" into "a new speech." In his mature prose, Emerson achieved that release and that new language. The prosaic freedom and wide resonance broke open the oppressive balance of his verse. The movement made visible the possibilities for the poet's mind to seek its whole life and the language to see its contemporary world.

By putting into the foreground of discussion Emerson's long meditation on poetic form, I have meant to draw attention to his powerful aesthetic yearnings that were often concealed. In the light of these artistic needs and the breakthrough he made into theoretic spaciousness and a renewed joining of poetry and the world's reality, it is not surprising to find his essays despite their avowed topics moving over the philosophical ground of this new aesthetic. In the essay "Experience," which has received so much attention as a philosophical shift toward skepticism, we now can see a nexus of his major aesthetic positions obliquely but incomparably well expressed.

If the essay has a principal moral account, it is summed up halfway through in its declaration of "this irreducibleness of the elements of human life to calculation." But beneath the explicit moral imperatives for existence in this gliding, unintelligible world ("there is that in us which changes not") rests another plane of discourse, of surpassing importance to Emerson. That is the level at which, with an artist's perception, he composes the world by metaphor. Here is the inchoate ground of Emerson's aesthetics of form, the deeper imperative that paralleled his philosophy and faith. Here operates, in a system of symbols that Lawrence conceived as the language of artistic energy, the artist's concern with the signifying power of his art.

What emerges then from "Experience" is the structural principle of art that had propelled Emerson's breakthrough. It was not a spatial concept of a field of action so much as a formal possibility of irregular tempo. It was the free-form dance of the thinking mind as Emerson thought of its being in the world. The qualities of this rhythmic and artfully self-concealing structure are the ones we have seen: spontaneity and surprise, a form of thought that is in the mind, a form of discovery that is unpredictable, and all of this tempo possessed of wide roving absorption like the humble-bee. A substantial quotation from the heart of the essay is necessary to show the cumulative build-up of terms beginning with the word *power,* which have implicit in them the design of a new aesthetic of form. (The italics are mine.)

> How easily, if fate would suffer it, we might keep forever these beautiful limits, and adjust ourselves, once for all, to the perfect calculation of the kingdom of known cause and effect. In the street

and in the newspapers, life appears so plain a business that manly resolution and adherence to the multiplication-table through all weathers will insure success. But ah! presently comes a day, or is it only a half-hour, with its angel-whispering, — which discomfits the conclusions of nations and of years! To-morrow again every thing looks real and angular, the habitual standards are reinstated, common-sense is as rare as genius, — is the basis of genius, and experience is hands and feet to every enterprise; — and yet, he who should do his business on this understanding would be quickly bankrupt. *Power* keeps quite another road than the turnpikes of choice and will; namely *the subterranean and invisible tunnels and channels of life.* It is ridiculous that we are diplomatists, and doctors, and considerate people; there are no dupes like these. Life is *a series of surprises,* and would not be worth taking or keeping if it were not. God delights to isolate us every day, and hide from us the past and the future. We would look about us, but with grand politeness he draws down before us an impenetrable screen of purest sky, and another behind us of purest sky. "You will not remember," he seems to say, "and you will not expect." All good conversation, manners and action come from *a spontaneity which forgets usages* and makes the moment great. Nature hates calculators; her methods are *saltatory* and *impulsive.* Man lives *by pulses;* our organic movements are such; and the chemical and ethereal agents are *undulatory* and *alternate;* and the mind goes *antagonizing* on, and never prospers but *by fits.* We thrive *by casualties.* Our chief experiences have been casual. The most attractive class of people are those who are *powerful obliquely* and *not by the direct stroke;* men of genius, but not yet accredited; one gets the cheer of their light without paying too great a tax. Theirs is the beauty of the bird or the morning light, and *not of art.* In the thought of genius there is *always a surprise;* and the moral sentiment is well called "the newness," for it is never other; as new to the oldest intelligence as to the young child, — "the kingdom that cometh without observation." In like manner, for practical success, *there must not be too much design.* A man will not be observed in doing that which he can do best. There is a certain magic about his properest action which stupefies your powers of observation, so that though it is done before you, you wist not of it. *The art of life has a pudency,* and will not be exposed.   (*W,* III, 67-69)

A selection of the figures of motion here emphasizes how each one has a formal corollary, and together they create what I have just called a form of spontaneity and discovery: power, the subterranean and invisible tunnels and channels of life, a series of surprises, a spontaneity, saltatory and impulsive, undulatory and alternate, antagonizing, by fits, by casualties, powerfully oblique, not by the direct stroke, not of art, not of too much design, not to be observed, a pudency, uncalculated and uncalculable. My concentration of these terms defines the form that Emerson sought and that we, using his words, can alternatively call saltatory and impulsive. It is instinctive, but being the artist's construct it is conscious and self-fulfilling. It is ardent and exact, it is Dante and Newton together. It involves, in terms Emerson would use six years later in the essay on Montaigne, "volitant stabilities" and "elastic steel."

Debilitated by closed poetry forms, Emerson's poetic sensibility required new possibilities of motion. Some of the pressures of his culture and his own philosophy made this release inevitable. Oratory was a crucial model since it demonstrated a powerful way by which a growing audience was forming its ideas and hearing its own voice, and thus seeing its world. Not less important was the private agony of Emerson the artist as he strove to integrate his imagination, experience, and voice. In seeking a radical reconciliation between experience and expression, undoing that old divorce, Emerson was led inevitably to a unique prosaic form, and thus he set about to pull down the prevailing distinctions between poetry and prose and, in the modernist way, between words themselves and action.

CHAPTER 7

Apologia for Prose

HAD THE NEED for a renewed integrity of mind and voice not been focused by an uncompromising theoretic imagination, Emerson's effort might not have advanced to a resolution. The preparations for that assault, as I indicated at the beginning of Chapter Six, gathered from reflections everywhere in his writing, and in no orderly sequence. His habit of mining his journals for his public writing created an extraordinary intertextual mesh most effectively approached as a network with many crossings (I used the word *solution* before) rather than as a chronological unfolding. We face the inescapable fact that the major poems occupy, with massive ambiguity, the same relatively limited period as the major essays. Much of what he said shows as a typology for what he accomplished. The important conceptual sortings behind the aesthetic search disclose the contours of what for him was a first necessity.

EMERSON'S ARTISTIC instincts took two main forms: the movement toward liberation from the debilitating strictures of conventional forms; and the enormous production of tropes which both rationalized his being in the world and implied the energy-absorbing language patterns that would take up that world in forms less pretending than the strictly "literary." These two necessities moved against the rigid formulas in the poems which prevented their full consciousness of the world's sensations, the "enriching presences" as he called them.

The marks of that counter movement appear widespread through the poetry. The imperative at the end of "Brahma" calls for the rejection of all limiting forms — single forms of worship, philosophical conception, perception even, and single notions of poetry. All are implicated in the heretical admonition "turn thy back on heaven." Emerson's preoccupation with freedom informs eight crisp lines of "Forbearance," a poem cataloguing the qualities of humility in a desired friend. What links those qualities is the single virtue of independence in the person who refrains from doing the conventional, unthinking act in a situation. The same impulse is basic in "Woodnotes II," where, as in "Bacchus," "The Humble-bee" and many other poems, the voice reporting what the pinetree said exhorts his listener, bankrupt of spirit, to quit the crowd and reach for the radicals of life:

> Behind thee leave thy merchandise,
> Thy churches and thy charities;
> And leave thy peacock wit behind;
> Enough for thee the primal mind
> That flows in streams, that breathes in wind.

In these iconoclastic lines we hear the "helpful giant" destroying old and false habits. Emerson the Platonist distinguishes between the seer's perception and the artifice of surfaces: "All the forms are fugitive, / But the substances survive." Wallace Stevens observed that experience always exceeds its expression in language, but that some collocations transfer more reality than others. The plum survives its poem, but the obsessive seeking for Emerson as well as Stevens was to make available a fuller experience of reality, to increase the capacity of the imagination, and to make the language take a supple motion from reality. For Emerson the need was defined by the interval through which the imagination moved between the going of the half-gods and the arrival of the gods, between the partial vision and the full one.

Emerson asks in the motto poem "Culture," referring to the poet as a half-divinity, "Can rules or tutors educate / The semigod whom we await?" Out of the stock Romantic disdain of the forms of learning by genius, he wrests a poetic self-reliance that combines openness with the discipline of the artist, the sensitive with the "fast." The whole poem is worth quoting because it is Emerson the theorist explicitly conjoining freedom and form:

> Can rules or tutors educate
> The semigod whom we await?
> He must be musical,
> Tremulous, impressional,
> Alive to gentle influence
> Of landscape and of sky,
> And tender to the spirit-touch
> Of man's or maiden's eye:
> But, to his native centre fast,
> Shall into Future fuse the Past,
> And the world's flowing fates in his own mould recast.

The lines directly treat of the process of Becoming within form, the world's flowing in the poet's mold, which we discern as Emerson's contemplation toward new fusions. In his poems, which everywhere bear the debilitating signs of received conventions of poetry and his theory of mind, at the deepest level there moves the more insistent gesture toward release and openness. He employed the very structures of moral allegory that his stronger artistic cravings were working to displace.

Reinforcing his own need for openness was the culturally sanctioned belief in the virtue of the plain and the uncultivated. That single homely attitude in poem after poem summons images for Emerson's imaginative movement into prosaic forms. Particular landscapes in Emerson stand as *prose settings* for the performances of the poetic imagination. The poem with the ironic title "My Garden," in which Emerson describes in inflated pastoral terms the woodlot he owned at Walden Pond, celebrates with intermittent sincerity and plainness the natural layout: "In my plot no tulips blow, — / Snow-loving pines and oaks instead." This is essentially the prose-seeking attitude, cherishing not delicacy or design but plainness, variety, and natural order. But even in the stanza that sets out a poetics of natural free-form art, Emerson's inversions, forced rhyme, and archaic use of *flow* as a transitive verb cry *artifice* the louder.

> The sowers made haste to depart, —
> The wind and the birds which sowed it;
> Not for fame, nor by rules of art,
> Planted these, and tempests flowed it.

The poem "Musketaquid," little regarded by readers despite its strong blank verse and its importance in Emerson's poetics, asserts the uncommonly rich experience available to the man in the prosaic setting:

> Because I was content with these poor fields,
> Low, open meads, slender and sluggish streams,
> And found a home in haunts which others scorned,
> The partial wood-gods overpaid my love.

Here once again is the open, plain setting congenial to the style of his own mind. To the farmer-poets (the identification is unmistakable) "the landscape is an armory of powers" which, one by one, they draw from the common air and ground and convert to practical, sometimes quite magical, use. The catalogue is impressive, leading to faintly metaphysical woods and meadows:

> They harness beast, bird, insect, to their work;
> They prove the virtues of each bed of rock,

And, like the chemist 'mid his loaded jars,
Draw from each stratum its adapted use
To drug their crops or weapon their arts withal.
They turn the frost upon their chemic heap,
They set the wind to winnow pulse and grain,
They thank the spring-flood for its fertile slime.
And, on cheap summit-levels of the snow,
Slide with the sledge to inaccessible woods
O'er meadows bottomless.

The men become the land and the land men in a sudden vision of total reconciliation within this allegorical poetics of the Concord fields: "(one
would say, meadow and forest walked, / Transmuted in these men to rule
their like)."

Whitman has lines that characteristically take such a vision literally and
then inflate it. The passage in "By Blue Ontario's Shore" is quite as remarkable às Emerson's:

Growths growing from him to offset the growths of
    pine, cedar, hemlock, live-oak, locust, chestnut, hickory,
    cottonwood, orange, magnolia,
Tangles as tangled in him as any canebrake or swamp,
He likening sides and peaks of mountains, forests coated with
    northern transparent ice,
Off him pasturage sweet and natural as savanna . . .

Emerson's ideal translation of the landscape of consciousness into aesthetic
form never called up a more apt trope than when he wrote that by "the
order in the field" these men "disclose the order regnant in the yeoman's
brain." The parallel in the twentieth century of this aesthetic openness and
consequent freeing of the poetic imagination appears in Olson's passages
on kinetics and field compositions in the essay "Projective Verse," as noted
earlier, and more subtly in William Carlos Williams' autobiography. Emerson's aesthetics in "Musketaquid," an equally valuable document in
American poetic theory, equates the simple with the free. His are archetypal American lines:

found I true liberty
In the glad home plain-dealing Nature gave.

Little effort is needed at this point to translate such lines into the aesthetics
by which Emerson conceived the circuit between freedom of perception
and expression, between spontaneity and the creative act, and between
power and the seemingly artless arrangements of the common human
tongue. The parable of Emerson's own translation of simplicity and com-

mon resources into power and art exists unobtrusively in the two lines that begin the final section of the poem and link him to those lowland Concord farmers: "What these strong masters wrote at large in miles, / I followed in small copy in my acre."

His exuberance in this aesthetics based on a love of his countryside turns up repeatedly, as here (Fragment on Nature):

> they who truliest love her, heralds are
> And harbingers of a majestic race,
> Who, having more absorbed, more largely yield,
> And walk on earth as the sun walks in the sphere.

The fullest absorption of resources, the largest yield: these are the goals of Emerson's farmers and poets. "Musketaquid" brings into the foreground two of the principal elements structuring his aesthetics of form: composition by low but open fields and the full joining of the form with manifold reality. That revealing metaphor for a theory of natural arrangement in "Musketaquid" focused his aesthetic musings. They had taken many forms. "There is no beauty in words," he wrote in 1831, "except in their collocation. The effect of a fanciful word misplaced, is like that of a horn of exquisite polish growing on a human head" (*JMN*, III, 271). The poem "Each and All," a bit later, is a paradigmatic statement of the same. In 1834, Emerson declared summarily: "I learned that Composition was more important than the beauty of individual forms to effect" (*JMN*, IV, 291). Matthew Arnold, though he found Emerson no great poet, saw his exemplary quality in remarkably similar terms, that is, as a force field. His central gift was the ability to join ideas and personal strength in a holding pattern. Arnold praised Emerson's clear perception of man's shortcomings and absurdities: "Truly, his insight is admirable; his truth is precious. Yet the secret of his effect is not even in these; it is in his temper. It is in the hopeful, serene, beautiful temper where-with these, in Emerson, are indissolubly joined; in which they work, and have their being."[1]

To see how important the prosaic terrain of "Musketaquid" is to Emerson's poetics is to penetrate to one of the basic metaphorical structures of his aesthetics. Stevens understood the inescapable connection of attitude and place. He believed that a unique American character distinguishes our writers from the English if only in the fact that the two groups live in two different physical worlds and, as he says, it is not nonsense to think that that matters. Emerson's intimacy with landscape and his use of the metaphors of landscape as aesthetic models are repeatedly revealed. He said of reformers and partisans, for example, that they fail of a redeeming concert with fact if they ignore the demands of reality: "the existing world is not a dream, and cannot with impunity be treated as a dream; neither is it a disease; but it is the ground on which you stand, it is the mother of whom you were born. Reform converses with possibilities, perchance with impossibilities; but here is sacred fact" (*W*, I, 303). The farmer is merged in the life of his place, absorbing it fully, yielding it back fully. The poet is to do the same, for, as Emerson wrote years later, their untrammeled exchange outlasts time.

> When I read Plutarch, or look at a Greek vase, I incline to accept the common opinion of scholars, that the Greeks had clearer wits than any other people. But there is anything but time in my idea of the antique. A clear or natural expression by word or deed is that which we mean when we love and praise the antique. In society I do not find it, in modern books, seldom; but when I come into the pastures, I find antiquity again. Once in the fields with the lowing cattle, the birds, trees and waters and satisfying curves of the landscape, and I cannot tell whether this is Thessaly and Enna, or whether Concord and Acton . . . A man of genius or a work of love or beauty will not come to order, can't be compounded by the best rules, but is always a new and incalculable result, like health.   (*W*, XII, 304-305)

To feel fully and to yield fully: these were for Emerson the ultimate aims of the soul in action; translated into his poetics they were the aims of the poet and his prosaic forms. Look anywhere in Emerson for that parable of fertile land. It is in an 1833 journal, a curious prefiguring of the darker dialogue of "Threnody." "The rocky, dry, fallow ground says 'I can produce nothing — nothing will grow — yet I see the sun and feel the rain as much as you.' 'Aye,' replies the cornfield, 'but they have plucked away my stones and turned up my surface and let in the watercourses and now the sun and the air, the heat and the snow all serve me' " (*JMN*, IV, 88).

The crucial dissociation in Emerson's early maturity was consistent with this need to renew arid ground, open brittle forms, and avoid infertility. He had acted decisively and at a great price in emotional depletion when he left the pastorate in 1832. His journal of July 15, recording his "hour of decision" in the White Mountains, a powerful and desperately serious meditation, has its roots in the obsessive need for freedom from life-robbing forms. Equally important to an understanding of the ground of his libertarian aesthetics is his awareness of the need to preserve proportion and of the essential life at stake. It is a profound reach to the ultimate convergence of morality and aesthetic need.

> The hour of decision. It seems not worth while for them who charge others with exalting forms above the moon to fear forms

themselves with extravagant dislike. I am so placed that my aliquid ingenii [something of genius] may be brought into useful action. Let me not bury my talent in the earth in my indignation at this windmill. But though the thing may be useless and even pernicious, do not destroy what is good and useful in a high degree rather than comply with what is hurtful in a small degree.

(*JMN*, IV, 30)

Liberation meant power. It was no abstract equation but the very principle upon which Emerson acted. In 1839, midway in the period of his most active poetry writing, he ruminated still, and his own poetry might well have been his subject: "The objection to conforming to usages that have become dead to you, is, that it scatters your force: loses your time, blears the impression of your character. If you maintain the church, join the Bible society, vote with the Whig or Government party, spread your table like other housekeepers, under all these screens I have difficulty to detect the precise man you are. Do your thing and I shall know you" (*JMN*, VII, 225).

The courage required for escape from the old ways is measured by the prim reaction to Emerson's address to the Harvard divinity students in 1838. His unofficial neglect by that institution for many years afterward indicates the level to which the foundations of the forms of religion reached. The forms of literature, in his view, were no less stolid. Emerson's revulsion for boundaries that limited the individual's fulfillment activated both of these crucial personal gestures, the one an act that changed his career, the other its long-meditated verbal equivalent. The Divinity School address actualized Emerson's need to stand outside the inherited rituals of the imagination. Though bound as a poet by his own system of viewing the imagination, Emerson at Harvard issued the call to give feeling and body to the hollow forms of devotion so as to make vocal the unritualized, sensuous abundance in each individual. The call had profound implications for the nature of reality outside Cambridge. With complexity recognized in the individual, an increased mystery was to become apparent in the perceived world. But Emerson in no way denied the moral seal of his beliefs, even though he had chosen in his opening paragraph to emphasize sensations. "One is constrained," he said at once, "to respect the perfection of this world in which our senses converse."

In the address, contrary to the impoverishment of the senses in the poetry and to the theory of the imagination and the formulas of revelation it engendered, there pulses the strong feeling of blooded reality. Emerson's rhetoric of intimacy, the studied exposure of a man's imaginative processes to his audience and his dramatization of the passion with which one's penetration of the world ought to be pressed, gives an ardent temper to parts of that address. Out of his terms he meant to make an intoxicating blend of stimuli from religious faith, from friendship and moral fervor, and from the speaker's manual. Rejecting the religious mission that had "petrified into official titles," Emerson declared that the language in which Christ exists for Europe and America is not one "of friendship and enthusiasm to a good and noble heart, but is appropriated and formal" (*W*, I, 130-131). He objected that historical Christianity taught accomplished revelation, the very monumentality that marked his own verse. He sought for himself and proposed to his listeners a form that would permit heuristic discovery, that would yield meaning in the very process of becoming form and language. The identical aim momentarily, almost casually, became clear to Whitman years after *Leaves of Grass* had stopped "growing," when he called that great indeterminate word secretion "a language experiment."

Emerson's own movement into the new consciousness so confidently outlined for the divinity students took him inevitably to prosaic forms. That crucial coming-into-being of an understanding and execution of a basic literary innovation enters most of his writings. He plumbed his theoretical imagination to a level of primary possibilities and aesthetic attitudes. At that depth originates a radical apology for prose. His defense must take its place as one of the credoes of the modern poetic sensibility in America and a design for a new rationale of expression. The poetic enterprise in this country was not to be the same after this transformation, which is dramatized so clearly in Emerson's struggle to make his art, like his senses, conversant with a refulgent world.

He demanded a new objectivity, summoning up Chaucer and Shakespeare as examples to follow. He urged American poets to read them in order to achieve a faithful presentation of reality which would replace "what is almost a national quality, the inwardness or 'subjectiveness' of our lyrics." In visionary clarity and the absence of ego Emerson discerned the real strength that distinguished poetry. Men of mere talent attempt to conceal the poverty of their insights by the distractions of elaboration, hiding their lack of genius behind a show of dexterity. "Foxes are so cunning," Emerson wrote, "because they are not strong" (*W*, IX, 291). No parlor verse will satisfy, but rather "Power, new power."

Emerson was remarkably precise in this poetics of personal integrity. Writing to a Mrs. Woodbridge in 1841, about some verses she had submitted to *The Dial*, he dwelt on the necessary equation of form and experience:

> I believe I am very hard to please in the matter of poetry, but my quarrel with most of the verses I read, is this, namely, that it is conventional; that it is a certain manner of writing agreed on in

society, — (in a very select society if you will) and caught by the ear; but it is not that new, constitutional, unimitated and inimitable voice of the individual which poetry ought always to be. I think I ought always to be apprised by any person's poetry, of that individual's private experience. The imagery ought to reveal to me where or with whom he or she has spent the hours, and ought to show me what objects (never before so distinguished) his constitution and temperament have made affecting to him. In short, all poetry should be original and necessary.   (*L*, II, 415)

Emerson commended the poetry of the younger Channing for similar virtues: its sincerity and honesty, its strong facts, its courage and intellectual candor. The poet, he said in his review, "should tell us not what men may be supposed to feel in the presence of a mountain or a cataract, but how it was with him" (*L*, III, 197).

Against this background, the selection of terms with which Emerson praised Whitman in his famous letter of 1855 is perfectly consistent. It is especially significant that the single word Emerson underlined in that first enthusiastic response was the term that referred to Whitman's mode. Emerson praised *Leaves of Grass* for its "great power," its "free and brave thought," and its "courage of *treatment*." He commended its "large perception" and judged the poetry "fortifying and encouraging" (*SW*, 165). The connection in Emerson's mind between free form and power, on the one hand, and closed conventions and diminished effect, on the other, was plainly drawn. In his genuine enthusiasm at first reading Whitman, the obsessive terms of his theoretical concerns came crowding forward to be expressed.

His own rationalizing of an open text capable of taking hold of more power obliged him to blur the old distinctions between prose and poetry. The discrimination was conveniently parallel to the hierarchical nature of Platonism that underlay the transcendentalist faith. But Emerson was dissolving the distinctions in concert with the general social background of impatience with all artificial barriers. Coleridge and Wordsworth had already argued that much good poetry could be, as Wordsworth said in the 1800 Preface, the language of prose when prose is well written. Emerson, however, for the constellation of reasons now apparent, pursued the ways in which prose as a protean mode enabled the poet to find a fuller being in the world. As one excellent observer of literary taste in nineteenth-century England has written, the distinction between poetry and prose "was being broken down, from the one side by Wordsworth, from the other by Lamb and De Quincey. But there was little accompanying revaluation of the peculiar stylistic possibilities through which the art of prose might rank in absolute worth with that of verse."[2]

Emerson's special strength is that he deliberately and with uncommon persistence applied himself to the practical development of a new form. He not only explored theoretically the possibilities of experience moving through a text but in the performance of his own work, which positioned itself between conversation, oration and poems, he was opening up the new territory. Emerson's criterion of how a poetic text met its highest calling came to be based on its depth of vision and on how completely the form took up the complex encounters of man thinking, man acting. The difference between poetry and stock-poetry, we recall he said, is that in the latter the rhythm is given and the sense adapted to it, while in the former the sense dictates the rhythm. At base, what evolved in the long meditation behind Emerson's famous dictum that poetry is a meter-making argument is not so much the design of possible meters but the intricacy of the argument. Compromised sense is all that can be gripped by received forms, whereas a new voice, making word strings out of a new recognition of the texture of the world, will take its shape and sound in forms at once original and necessary.

He did not shift abruptly to an explicit declaration of the poetic value of prose. Though he more and more conceived that end in some of the essays, he never totally rejected the distinction he had made that "the poet affirms the laws, prose busies itself with exceptions, —with the local and individual" (*W*, VIII, 32). Rather, he envisioned a form that would combine the two levels. Out of the knowledge of the local and the individual, the bits of life strewn outside the neat abstracting systems, would come the synthesis. Thus the prosaicizing of poetry allowed a descent into existence and, instead of moral over-views, a mode of insight.[3] Because he made no distinction between poetry and philosophy, since both aimed ideally toward gnostic experience, he opened the possibility of seeing prosaic forms as valid poetry. But his Platonism reached deeper than this, holding that, at the origin of the forces of the universe, the distinctions between mere *forms* or *genres* were irrelevant. At that level, the structure of nature and the structure of its poetic text coincide:

> By and by, when [people] apprehend real rhymes, namely, the correspondence of parts in Nature, —acid and alkali, body and mind, man and maid, character and history, action and reaction, —they do not longer value rattles and ding-dongs, or barbaric word jingle. Astronomy, Botany, Chemistry, Hydraulics and the elemental forces have their own periods and returns, their own grand strains of harmony not less exact, up to the primeval apothegm that "there is nothing on earth which is not in the heavens in a heavenly form, and nothing in the heavens which is not on the earth in an earthly form." They furnish the poet with grander

pairs and alternations, and will require an equal expansion in his metres.   (*W*, VIII, 48-49)

Here is the morphological stratum of Emerson's apology for prose and ultimately for his defining of his own art form. If we are to understand how Emerson came to find his voice and to make the authentic confession for his own age, we must be aware how deep the level is at which he forged the rationale for his prose structure. Emerson dealt with the *radical* forms of literature from the very beginning, and not its fashions, the ding-dongs, as he says. The famous letter to his second wife declares his own poetic qualities to be not in the music of the verse but in the rhyme of ideas: "I am born a poet, of a low class . . . My singing be sure is very 'husky' . . . Still am I a poet in the sense of a perceiver and dear lover of the harmonies that are in the soul and in matter, and specially of the correspondences between these and those" (*L*, I, 435).

He admired Milton for the poetry of his argument in prose: "The lover of Milton reads one sense in his prose and in his metrical compositions; and sometimes the muse soars highest in the former, because the thought is more sincere. Of his prose in general, not the style alone but the argument also is poetic" (*W*, XII, 277). Not at all curiously, Matthew Arnold praised Emerson for these same qualities. Holmes was wonderfully accurate in saying that Emerson admired in Milton his own virtues, in particular his championing of liberty and the passionate humanistic tone that controlled his discourse. Arnold's judgment closely echoes what Emerson said of Milton: "He is identified in the mind . . . with the supreme interests of the human race . . . few men ever possessed so great a conception of the manly character. Better than any other he has discharged the office of every great man, namely, to raise the idea of Man in the minds of his contemporaries and of posterity . . . exhibiting such a composition of grace, of strength and of virtue, as poet had not described nor hero lived" (*W*, XII, 254).

Indeed, there is delightful irony when Emerson defends Milton against the obloquy leveled against his name for the pamphlets on divorce, arguing that Milton meant to create an ideal world. "It was," the author of the notorious Divinity School address wrote, "a sally of the extravagant spirit of the time, overjoyed . . . with the sudden victories it had gained, and eager to carry on the standard of truth to new heights" (*W*, XII, 278).

This Miltonic quality of "higher insight," of which Emerson said "This was his poem," allowed Emerson himself to move with some confidence into the opening field of his own expression. What controlled the new freedom and gave it direction in the absence of formal conventions was his steady tone, the "temper" Arnold singled out in his assessment. It was that "conception of manly character" which presided over the selection of the varied elements to be incorporated. Emerson had fixed on the virtues of originality and necessity in the letter to Mrs. Woodbridge. In his essay "Intellect," he called for control to balance spontaneity. And in "Art and Criticism" he wrote: "Classic art is the art of necessity . . . modern or romantic bears the stamp of caprice or chance. One is the product of inclination, of caprice, of haphazard; the other carries its law and necessity within itself" (*W*, XII, 303-304). Tone, that is, became a formal but not generic principle because it allowed variety, contradiction, nuance, and personality to move freely within its arching intention. When Strauch points out to us that Emerson rarely made a flat assertion without implying its qualification, we are face to face with Emerson's first priority. He sought to follow the play of an altogether receptive mind traversing the whole scale of experience as opposed to a philosophical consistency. This is to say, Emerson's primary concern was aesthetic and not philosophical. When he speaks about a radical reconciliation in art, he means both its vertical and its horizontal reach: "The balance must be kept, — the power to generalize and the power to individualize must coexist to make a poet, Will and Abandonment, the social and the solitary humor, man and opportunity" (*JMN*, VII, 439). In that dynamic nexus of extremes resided the characteristic genius of nature and poet. Poetry, we find him saying a bit condescendingly at one point, proceeds in most peoples' view by a clever adjective here and there and not by mass and relationship. "In prose, there must be concatenation, a mass of facts, and a method. 'T is very costly; only a capitalist can take hold of it; but in poetry, the mere enumeration of natural objects suffices. Nay, Tennyson is a poet, because he has said, 'the stammering thunder,' or 'the wrinkled sea beneath him crawls'; and Longfellow, 'the plunging wave' " (*J*, IX, 56).

Emerson's theory was based on the idea of composite beauty, and prose best provides it. Thus his journal definition of composition by interaction is also a definition of ideal poetry: "a poem . . . that shall thrill the world by the mere juxtaposition and inter-action of lines and sentences that singly would have been of little worth and short date. Rightly is the art named composition and the composition manifold the effect of the component parts" (*JMN*, V, 39). He demanded of his text the possession of elemental forces. In the search for that form which "Musketaquid" metaphorically envisioned he was reestablishing a reciprocity of prose form and reality. The process required a new breadth of mind that itself came to perceive an altered world. As Flaubert exuberantly said at the mid-point of the century, "Prose was born yesterday—this is what we must tell ourselves. Poetry is preeminently the medium of past literatures. All the metrical combinations have been tried but nothing like this can be said of prose."[4]

SEEN THUS from the inside, Emerson's extensive remarks on poetry are fundamentally the poetics of his prose. As T. S. Eliot said of the poet who formulates an *art poetique*, he may think he is establishing laws for all poetry but what he has to say that is worth saying has its immediate relation to the way in which he himself writes or wants to write.

Emerson's prose *is* his power, far more than the Platonist idealism of his thought. Clearly, his theory of form possessed a basic validity. The poetics of his prose sanctioned texts with the special movement—self-discovering, seemingly spontaneous—of his own intelligence acting in the reality about him. More than this, the flowing form was able to take hold not simply of pastoral emblems but the complicated, jarring realities of the city. The pastoral poetics was passing out, and Emerson the artist set himself to devising a poetics of tempo and variegated vision, a poetics we might say of modern urbanism. When he wrote as early as 1837 that Carlyle's genius is the redolence of London, he had already become a modern of the twentieth century, intuitively grasping the poet's new challenge. His admiration for Carlyle's absorptive genius is an artist's ebullient glimpse of the possibilities of form: "So vast, enormous, with endless details, and so related to all the world, is he. It would seem as if no baker's shop, no mutton stall, no Academy, no church, no placard, no coronation, but he saw and sympathized with all, and took all up into his omnivorous fancy, and hence his panoramic style" (*JMN*, V, 291). That list is a world away from another Emerson made in the same year: "violets and bilberry bells, maple-sap and daffodels, grass with green flag half-mast high, succory to match the sky, Columbine with horn of honey, scented fern, and agrimony" (from "The Humble-Bee"). There was between the theory and the practice, then, the strongest possible link. The argument leading to the renewal of poetry by way of prose shows us Emerson at his most original as an artist. As Poe said, the poetic art succeeds or fails according to whether the theory behind it is valid or invalid.

We can see how adroitly Emerson ascribed to poetry the qualities he invested in his prose. The progress of the man as he (to use the terms from his "Merops" notes) passed into a freer element and won a better instrument —a new speech and a thousand silences—required a rejection of poetic conventions, the reduction of literariness, an emphasis on truth. George

Seferis has said in our day that poetry is the place where one cannot lie. Emerson's vulgar forms, the secularizing of the sacred station of the poet, the disparagement of jingling "talent" — all these attitudes had to be asserted if Emerson was to make room in the poetic tradition for his prose essays. For if the age was to make an honest confession of its experiences, that confession would have to be made in prose.

But Emerson's quest and his achievement were not as clear-cut and absolute as this discussion might suggest. He did not abandon his moral imperatives. He suggested to Whitman that he excise the "Children of Adam" poems from *Leaves of Grass,* though they seem to have been the inevitable outcome of the new Emersonian candor. Always in his mind was the knowledge that what was crass and soiled and sensual and corrupting could cling like barnacles to prose, unrefined by the poetic alembic. "Even partial ascents to poetry and ideas are forerunners, and announce the dawn. In the mire of the sensual life, [the people's] religion, their poets, their admiration of heroes and benefactors, even their novel and newspaper, nay, their superstitions also, are hosts of ideals, — a cordage of ropes that hold them up out of the slough" (*W*, VIII, 73-74).

The ambiguity of Emerson's suspension between the poles of his persuasions is clear here. Even as he relishes the primitive validity and truth-bearing capacity of the folk pulps, he does not see them on a moral plane with poetry. Still Emerson recognizes two inescapable facts: the prosaic level of the common imagination and the way this shared consciousness is reached by the prose of the novel and the newspaper. If *some* moral cordage is available to prose, why not more of it? Emerson drew direct comparisons between the great prose writers and poets. Both are philosophers, both converse with the "elemental forces," he said. He cites Augustine and Sir Thomas Browne and others as *prose* poets. In one of his earliest lectures Emerson went well below matters of form to find the equation: "He who perceives [the relation between thought and the world], and every man, whilst he perceives it, is a poet, is a philosopher" (*EL*, I, 226).

With *Nature* in 1836, his first important published work and the manifesto for the transcendentalist faith, he went beyond mere nationalistic chauvinism to set the philosophical basis for aesthetic independence. The power of his reasoning lay in its simplicity. "Why should not we . . . enjoy an original relation to the universe?" he asks there, reaching to the central problem of the integration of imagination, language and reality: "Why should not we have a poetry and philosophy of insight and not of tradition?" (*W,* I, 3). This is essential Emersonian aesthetics. The equation of poet and philosopher, and the implied diminishment of the supremacy of poetic art, prepares us to follow in Emerson the development of an aesthetics from an undefined advance toward liberation, to the leveling of poetic prominence, to the emergence of his own poetics of prose.

The essay codifies attitudes of Emerson's own time which also tended to subsume generic distinctions under first moral and then rhetorical principles. An anonymous commentary in the *Democratic Review* of 1838 on *Nature*, for example, declares with singular unoriginality that "the only true and perfect mind is the poetic . . . the poet alone is the man—meaning by poet, not the versifier, nor the painter of outward nature merely, but the total soul, grasping truth, and expressing it melodiously, equally to the eye and heart" (*VP*, 209). Emerson himself was similarly to draw such a capacious figure of the American scholar that the poet was contained within it. Indeed, Emerson's commentary throughout on the literary man defines him so widely that linguistic crafts of every kind are accommodated, new freedom of subject recognized, and new democratic forms of literature envisioned. The anatomies of perception and expression were changing to bring the world as it actually was into the active imagination. Emerson's journal note on the purpose of his American Scholar address is worth recalling in this context because it extends definitions even further. "Literary duties" slip down in the transcendental hierarchy establishing the preeminence of the poet and are placed lower than the task of inspiring the audience and nourishing the philosophical temper. The passage is notable even for Emerson for its nonliterary definition of literary duties: "The hope to arouse young men at Cambridge to a worthier view of their literary duties prompts me to offer the theory of the Scholar's function. He has an office to perform in society. What is it? To arouse the intellect; to keep it erect and sound; to keep admiration in the hearts of the people; to keep the eye open upon its spiritual aims" (*JMN*, V, 364-365).

THE CONSISTENT movement of Emerson's mind toward the accommodation of prose as the form of the new confession is still apparent in the late composite essay "Poetry and Imagination." In it he disassembled the popular myth that acclaimed merely talented poets who relied on the stock material of poetic conventions. Emerson announced his disappointment in the accomplishment of the poets around him. "We want an architect, and they bring us an upholsterer," he declared. It was a clearing away of the opposition and the creating of what politicians call a grass-roots draft. Emerson was making a place in the tradition for his own work and, more than that, striving to see that it was accorded a position superior to the poetry he and his contemporaries produced. The very survival of his creative intellect depended upon his carving a space for the work that made up the main body of his art. It was not altogether a self-serving campaign, but there was none more resourceful in the emergence of the modernist literary voice than Emerson's.

Except for Ezra Pound's, perhaps no other campaign made such inflated claims. Here is Emerson: "The high poetry which shall thrill and agitate mankind, restore youth and health, dissipate the dreams under which men reel and stagger, and bring in the new thoughts, the sanity and heroic aims of nations, is deeper hid and longer postponed than was America or Australia, or the finding of steam or of the galvanic battery. We must not conclude against poetry from the defects of poets" (*W*, VIII, 73). The relationships are there, remarkably modern, between Emerson's poetics and the national interest, in the invocation of technology, and between the corruption of language and the disabling self-deceptions of the society. Inspired poetry: a national patent medicine! But Emerson demands here nothing less than the marriage of the modern mind with the actual world as a way to the restoration of sanity; nothing less than a poetry to "dissipate the dreams under which men reel and stagger." He was a long way from this in his poetry, impacted as it was by its moral agenda, abstract ideas, and narrow set of language. It was in his prose that the possibility existed of an arresting fidelity.

In the process, there were ambiguities, conflicting values, and ritual repetitions of the conventions about poetry articulating "the best thoughts" by prescriptive right, with prose taking care of the menial and "material necessities." Yet Emerson's exasperation over that division of literary worth is audible. It is part of the confusion of aesthetic advance and indicative of the drama by which Emerson's imaginative power passed through the barriers of traditional form. We can see the modernist temper struggling to be born in this mildly sardonic passage from "Poetry and Imagination": "You shall not speak ideal truth in prose uncontradicted [by the literary arbiters]: you may in verse. The best thoughts run into the best words; imaginative and affectionate thoughts into music and metre. We ask for food and fire, we talk of our work, our tools and material necessities, in prose; that is, without any elevation or aim at beauty; but when we rise into the world of thought . . . speech refines into order and harmony" (*W*, VIII, 52).

Here we are at the convergence of tradition and individual need, where new aesthetic necessities are moving toward birth. For Emerson this was a crucial personal labor, but he also presents us with the figure of *the individual artist working out the literary and imaginative problems of his age.*

He turned as other fleers of tradition did before and after him to the primitive. He meant to rediscover the original sources of the language and thereby to justify the use of new strata of dictions. It was a turning, as Wordsworth had proposed, to the language really used by men. There, Emerson knew, lay the power to make visible the prose of the world. "The metallic force of primitive words makes the superiority of the remains of the rude ages," he wrote. "It costs the early bard little talent to chant more impressively than the later, more cultivated poets. His advantage is that his words are things, each the lucky sound which described the fact, and we listen to him as we do to the Indian, or the hunter, or miner, each of whom represents his facts as accurately as the cry of the wolf or the eagle tells of the forest or the air they inhabit. The original force, the direct smell of the earth or the sea, is in these ancient poems" (*W*, VIII, 57). Contained in the primitivist cliché is Emerson's belief that diction not yet sanctioned for poetry could be taken into his prose. I said earlier that Emerson had a poetic imagination without the language. We see in a passage such as this, hesitant, unsure of the details but confident in the central vision of its need, the artist's imagination in search of its own language and form.

So we come to the most familiar document in Emerson's poetics, the essay "The Poet," able to see that it too, like the Phi Beta Kappa and Divinity School addresses, attacks a cherished institution. But "The Poet" is less overt in its assault on the poetic establishment. The result, however, is more than mildly heretical, for even as Emerson acknowledged traditional poetic values, marching out all the Romantic clichés, he presents there — almost aside from the explicit language — the high claims of a poetics of prose.

Emerson is not only defending the art of the prose essayist, but he is at the same time proposing the exploitation of the many resources of prose for taking up, like Carlyle's "panoramic" style, the reality of his own time. Emerson claims for this practical, secular form the status of poetry, heretofore situated solitary in the highest literary place. This is his radical departure and it happens with considerable concentration under the disarming title "The Poet." Every serious reader must allow that, conventionally read, "The Poet" is of limited relevance to modern generations. It is filled with hyperbole and the easy phrases of inflated Romanticism, not to mention an essential patchiness of argument. It has in its argument no cut of originality like Coleridge's *Biographia Literaria*. Some of it is simply cant: the poet "knows why the plain or meadow of space was strewn with these flowers we call suns, and moons, and stars"; "Genius is the activity which repairs the decay of things"; "when the soul of the poet has come to ripeness of thought, she detaches and sends away from it its poems or songs, —

a fearless, sleepless, deathless progeny, which is not exposed to the accidents of the weary kingdom of time." The essay's high-blown rhetoric prompts even Emerson at one point to confess he is using "the old largeness" on his errand from the muse.

But Emerson's real objective in the essay touches the core of the artistic enterprise. It is the desire to come upon the voice of his own age and to render contemporary experiences in their universal significance. This is what Emerson meant when he declared that the experience of each new age requires a new confession, and the world seems always waiting for its poet. Emerson recognized the intimate connection between the experience and its expression, how new experience is discerned only through the perceiving instrument of a new language. And so, with a remarkable inward attention to the significance of form, though almost everywhere concealed behind Romantic trappings, Emerson set about his task of subverting the poetry establishment. He referred to his essay as "my errand from the muse to the poet concerning his art." We see now that Emerson is far more concerned with aesthetic and formal concerns than with moral preachments and divine afflatus, or with self-reliance and other American cultural themes that readers have so often noted. This Emerson of the intense, precise, technical aesthetic is not the familiar figure.

In the necessity for a reconciliation between the elemental forces he responded to in the world and the voice that could discover them, he inevitably began to disintegrate the old forms of thought. He begins the essay with a single sentence that rejects fashion, denigrates elegance, and dismisses the arbiters of art as shameful. It is a bold opening shot: "Those who are esteemed umpires of taste are often persons who have acquired some knowledge of admired pictures or sculptures, and have an inclination for whatever is elegant; but if you inquire whether they are beautiful souls, and whether their own acts are like fair pictures, you learn that they are selfish and sensual." He does not find among his contemporaries any but poets of decorative fancy. We hear, he says, "through all the varied music, the ground-tone of conventional life. Our poets are men of talents who sing, and not the children of music. The argument is secondary, the finish of the verses is primary." He sets about erasing the distinctions between poets and other great public men, summoning the prose masters into the pantheon. Much conventional wisdom falls to the full thrust of Emerson's need to destroy the old and build the new. He invokes the purity of a beginning before man's fall from grace into language. "Words and deeds are quite indifferent modes of the divine energy," the essay ardently declares, opening as wide as could be conceived the reception of all voices including the primitive, which could join the task of saying the world. "Words are also actions, and actions are a kind of words."

Emerson pulls down distinctions by focusing not on aspects of talent, the surface signs of literariness such as skill in prosody, but rather on the ability of the person to transform experience into idea. Conversion is the mark of the poet, not his formal manipulations. "He is a beholder of ideas, and an utterer of the necessary and casual. For we do not speak now of men of poetical talents, or of industry and skill in metre, but of the true poet." Thus Emerson dismantled the genre of poetry as the privileged form of disclosure.

He insists on dissolution. Part of his strategy is the democratizing of the entire poetic venture, discovering — not inconsistently with the doctrine of the self-reliant man — the elements of poetic imagination in all men: "If the imagination intoxicates the poet, it is not inactive in other men." It is the poet, he says in the most famous passage, who shows through his language the essential world. Not through the skills of rhyme and meter and other marks of talent do men hear the reality of their world, but through symbols. We see now how much leveling of rank is assumed in the Shelleyesque lines that are so often quoted as the heart of Emerson's poetic creed. The emphasis is on rhetoric and not rhyme: "The use of symbols has a certain power of emancipation and exhilaration for all men . . . This is the effect on us of tropes, fables, oracles, and all poetic forms. Poets are thus liberating gods." Other dissolutions proceed, including that of the axiom that the true poet dwells only in the sublime. One long section on spurious exhilaratives like narcotics leads to this passage: "the poet's habit of living should be set on a key so low, that the common influences should delight him." In that leveling movement of Emerson's imagination as it moved toward the design of a new poetics, he dismisses five centuries of English poets. "These are wits, more than poets," he declares, and allows in the same moment of ardor that "we have our difficulties even with Milton and Homer."

There are other less marked evidences of Emerson's subversive thinking. In almost every aspect, the high station of the poet is carefully lowered. The absence of the term "poem" is conspicuous at one point by its inclusion in "paper": "If a man is inflamed and carried away by his thought . . . which holds him like an insanity, let me read his paper, and you may have all the arguments and histories and criticism." Even wider implications open out from a passage parallel to the liberating-gods pronouncement, except that the idea of a poem is now swallowed up by the idea of *any* expressive form. "We love the poet, the inventor, who in any form, whether in an ode, or in action, or in looks and behavior, has yielded us a new thought. He unlocks our chains, and admits us to a new scene." Much of what we have noted of Emerson's poetics of prose is quietly compacted into that passage. There is the controlling metaphor of liberation and the equating of any man with the poet provided he exercises the converting power; there is the collapse of distinction between word and action and a tacit recognition of the orator as one of the gifted poets; finally, there is the radical recognition that the world is inseparable from and exists in the text that describes it.

Liberating insight will come in new forms — in Emerson's own essays, the reader may expect. Here he prepares the way: "We know that the secret of the world is profound, but who or what shall be our interpreter, we know not. A mountain ramble, a new style of face, a new person, may put the key into our hands." The new forms will tally better with experience: the poet "resigns himself to his mood, and that thought which agitated him is expressed,' but *alter diem,* in a manner totally new. The expression is organic, or, the new type which things themselves take when liberated." All the essential marks are in that passage too: the liberation by a new interpenetration of language, form, and reality. He insists on the flowing quality of this new writing, its openness and resilience. The terms can be extracted from the essay: "The largest power to receive and to impart," a "body overflowed by life," "the ravishment of the intellect by coming nearer to the fact," and the summary assertion that the poet "uses forms according to the life and not according to the form." Here designed in metaphor was the theoretical liberation from the hampering duality, linear plot, and pretending formality of his verse. Here was a way out, taking direction with a purpose that only a poet who felt the radical correlation of form and perception could posit. The now familiar structuring figures of release and conversion recur: "As the eyes of Lyncaeus were said to see through the earth, so the poet turns the world to glass, and shows us all things in their right series and procession . . . [He] sees the flowing or metamorphosis . . . that within the form of every creature is a force impelling it to ascend into a higher form; and following with his eyes the life, *uses the forms which express that life, and so his speech flows with the flowing nature.*"

The reconciliation is complete. Unrestricted form both releases and gives voice to the flowing figures of nature. It is a form moral in its synthesizing truth because not only is it capable of transferring an enormously expanded field of energy taken in from the world, but, since all men — poets, philosophers, politicians, yes, even nations — are inwardly poets, the form also speaks in a democratic voice to all men. This, then, to feel fully and to yield fully, is the significant form for democratic man and the democratic age.

The prose argument, though for the most part only implied, remains coherent throughout the essay. Emerson's insistence on scope, motion, and unrestrained performance of the imagination joins the fullness of life with the form of its perception and expression. The demand applies to all artists and, by implication, to the prose writer. Emerson's list was inclusive: "The painter, the sculptor, the composer, the epic rhapsodist, the orator, all partake one desire, namely, to express themselves symmetrically and abundantly, not dwarfishly and fragmentarily." If one ambitious goal were to possess in language and therefore in consciousness the essential significance of the whole American experience, a freedom of voice is being demanded that no present poetic form, least of all Emerson's, could accomplish. If "America is a poem in our eyes," as Emerson declares in the essay, then anything is a poem. We recall the full coincidence of the prosaic landscape and the poetic imagination in the poem "Musketaquid." A reader has only to extrapolate to see how expansive and necessarily prosaic a form Emerson assumes for the purpose of possessing and giving voice to the entire nation.

The way is open for the prose essayist to provide the new voice of the new age, indeed of the new world, and to attain lasting fame. Emerson again is careful to make his terms include *all books* and *every verse or sentence* of imagination. "This emancipation [into a new thought] is dear to all men, and the power to impart it, as it must come from greater depth and scope of thought, is a measure of intellect. Therefore all books of the imagination endure, all which ascend to that truth that the writer sees nature beneath him, and uses it as his exponent. Every verse or sentence possessing this virtue will take care of its own immortality."

Perhaps we can see now that in Emerson's famous statement of organic form in this essay lie the root terms of his ambivalent performance as an artist. Although his conversion argument in the poems made their "architecture" rigid and formulaic, as the statement seems unintentionally to suggest, his emphasis thereafter on means and the promotion of this "new thing" contains the apology for prose which the essay in its entirety presents. In the next chapter I shall trace the design of the "architecture of its own" that Emerson accomplished in his prose practice. But note here how in the basic ambivalence of his well-known pronouncement we can discern the doctrine of the essayist as poet:

> it is not metres, but a metre-making argument that makes a poem, — a thought so passionate and alive that like the spirit of a

plant or an animal it has an architecture of its own, and adorns nature with a new thing.

The terms that, in the disarmingly lyrical close of the essay, Emerson uses as he renews the assault on the poetry establishment now take on special formal significance: "I look in vain for the poet whom I describe. We do not with sufficient plainness or sufficient profoundness address ourselves to life, nor dare we chaunt our own times and social circumstance." In the new prose structures of *plainness* and *profoundness* were poised far greater resources of language than Emerson was able to command in his poetry.

A SUMMARY and a look ahead are in order. Emerson of all the American theorists from Bryant to Lowell, with the exception of Poe, related the aesthetic and moral aims of art directly to the problem of form. Benjamin Spencer has written that what the Transcendental group contributed to the development of the national literature "was not an arresting inventory of novel themes and modes, but rather a sustained aesthetic based on a coherent metaphysical structure."[5] As basically useful as this statement is, it neglects Emerson's unique achievement. He was in fact the radical innovator in *mode*. He reattached language to process rather than to conclusion, to the action of the mind wonderfully finding the words adequate to its experiences. Most commentary treats Emerson's ideas and themes, and of course, as Spencer says, they were not novel. But Emerson was an aesthetic adventurer of an independence we have not sufficiently appreciated before. His aesthetics aimed at an integration more complicated and inclusive even than Strauch suggests in the matter of diction traceable to Sampson Reed's early influence. Reed developed a poetics, Strauch says, of "fastening words to things and hence in elevating the importance of the single word in the creative act" and this, he concludes, "constituted a revolution embracing Emerson and his immediate heirs, Whitman and Emily Dickinson."[6] The undertaking was more complex than this, for his whole effort led Emerson to diminish the literariness of the poetic enterprise in one way after another so that the coalition between texts and things would be complete.

What he did not foresee was that, once his own animating idealism was subtracted, the new prosaic forms became morally inert. That fact more than any other accounts for the deeply ironic shift by which the descendental prose textures we see developing in Emerson under the strong holding pressure of idealism became, in a later age, the forms that equally naturally perceived a chaotic world without a dominant philosophy. The

altered signification of language forms in later American poetry is beyond
the scope of my discussion, but it will be the splendid subject for a new kind
of study alert to the inherent perceptual qualities of artistic structures, to,
that is, the history of their forms. Prosaicized poetry became the perceiver
and container of an intractable reality, things without belief, tactile experience without spiritual dimensions. The worm of despair lay concealed
in the dynamic forms that Emerson opened up. He lowered the chimes and
the cozy rhythms so that complex reality could stand out from behind the
conventions of perception. This inaugurated a basic estrangement from
the conception of an organic and purposeful universe, an alienation by
which reality in modern poetry is impervious to a converting imagination,
much less capable of being "turned to glass." In our own day the further
collapse of formal conventions in art has made familiar critical terms of
structured opposition quite obsolete. Michael Polanyi has described both
visual and language art as "the integration of incompatibles." In repre-
sentational painting, the illusion of perspective competes with our awareness of the flat canvas. In poetry, the rational content contends with the
artificial frame of rhyme, meter, and so on. The harmonious compound
formed by the elements of an attempted communication and an artistic
structure that contradicts the communication, Polanyi says, has qualities
found neither in nature nor in human affairs.[7] Like the post-modernists,
however, Emerson knew that the incompatibility of content and form
could be reduced if the artist abandoned convention or, conversely, exploited the convention of form as part of the content itself.

   The great innovation of Cubism, for example, was its willingness to go,
as Polanyi says, to "rock bottom" by reducing simulation and increasing
the part played by flatness. Emerson's new prosaicism was equally literal:
flattening literature by reducing its conspicuous signals and employing the
structure in the process of discovering its own content. The ultimate hazard
(and temptation) of Emerson's principle of reconciliation is the sort of
short circuit between life and language that flashes in "happenings" or in
the seemingly unconducted rantings of certain Sixties poets. In their work
the indiscriminate confounding of action, language, and artistic form
makes a hash of the imagination. There is no distance or perspective maintained. There is no syntax, no mediation, no moral or intellectual filter, no
taboos. This may be the ultimate working out of the revolution that began
with Emerson. His own idea of the reconciliation of language and reality,
on the other hand, envisioned the purity of action in silence. He could posit
an identification so complete that the last vestige of form would disappear.
He asks himself in a journal entry of 1834: "[Is it not true] that whenever

we live rightly thought will express itself in ordinary action so fully as to make a special action, that is, a religious form impertinent?" (*JMN*, IV, 313). Four years later he described the final linguistic gesture: "The only speech will at last be Action such as Confucius describes the Speech of God" (*JMN*, VII, 106).

The Emersonian aesthetic extended, of course, beyond Whitman to Eliot's *The Waste Land* and after. The prose quality of that poem and one of its central concerns, the caged sensibility, are elaborations of Emerson's doctrine of liberation. Eliot's prosaicism has been traced to the influence of Joyce, James, and Conrad, but Emerson stands before them all as the American artist who altered the frontier. The great irony is that, in opening up poetic space, he intended to demonstrate "the cheerful hint" in all things "of the immortality of our essence" (*W*, III, 31). With the disappearance of that faith, what remained was an open form crowded with intractable experience, manifesting more clearly than ever the multitudinousness of experience and the failure of idealistic philosophy. The form was capable of a great gathering up of life without any certain way to understand it. Seen thus from our later perspective, Emerson's poetics of release led to a poetics of disjunction. Picasso said that "once a form has been created, then it exists and goes on living its own life." And Charles Olson described in "Projective Verse" how form itself ultimately shapes attitude: "From the moment the projective purpose of the act of verse is recognized, the content does — it will — change."[8] In the evolution of Emerson's poetics of realization and reconciliation into a poetics of disconfirmation, the process had to do with the form advancing by its own intrinsic development to deny the idealism that first sanctioned it. The open form that was a heuristic transport for Emerson and Whitman becomes the vehicle of atomization for twentieth-century poets. Once the dissonant sounds of the real world were brought in, poetry could no longer without pretense tune a harmonious ideal. First affirming life, the open form produced afterward a style of formlessness, dissonance, and jarring surprise. Emerson's poem "Each and All" provided the inescapable logic: when the idea of the perfect whole, which exists only in the mind, collapses, the discrete elements are viewed in their own right, "poor, unsightly, noisome things."

The essays "The Poet," understood as a defense of prose, and "Poetry and Imagination," rightly seen as the poetics of that form, stand with Wordsworth's Preface to *Lyrical Ballads* as disclosures of a new consciousness in literature. The essays stand too with *Biographia Literaria* as the impassioned working-out of a practical new aesthetic.

These works codify revolutionary poetics that turned English-language poetry to the actual world of experience. One developmental line of the form Emerson hoped would convert the world in all its variety ended by accommodating all the discrete parts that clutter a faithless existence. But the beginnings were noble. William Gilman said with clear insight into Emerson: "except for Whitman, perhaps no American in the nineteenth century was so responsive to all experience, all occupations, all interests and powers of the body, soul, and mind" (*SW*, vii). What we have seen in the essays is the brilliant theorizing by which Emerson conceived a language commensurate to that extraordinary responsiveness.

CHAPTER 8

"Inward Skill": An Armory of Powers

EMERSON SAW BETWEEN his own art and the welfare of men a relationship as decisive as the shot fired at Concord, with consequences just as revolutionary. His essential subject was modern man in the act of attaining his full potency, and his artistic aim was to make words take hold of that phenomenon. Literally, astonishingly, he invented both: the prototypical figure of an American man in the process of Becoming and the language that would enact it.

Matthew Arnold viewed only obliquely this inescapable fact that Emerson's power, which he discerned despite the lack of "whole tissue" in the writing, was in truth a matter of form. But in a telling passage in his essay, he abruptly left off what he saw as the primary virtue of Emerson—"he is the friend and aider of those who live in the spirit"—to treat the subject of Emerson's peculiar prose form. This was Arnold's immediate observation (the italics are mine): "All the points in thinking which are necessary for this purpose he takes; but *he does not combine them into a system,* or present them as a regular philosophy. Combined in a system by a man with the requisite talent for this kind of thing, they would be less useful than *as Emerson gives them to us;* and the man with the talent so to systematise them would be less impressive than Emerson. *They do very well as they now stand.*"[1] It remains a curious oversight, this matter of form, in the same essay where Arnold declares that Emerson's essays were the most important work done in prose in the nineteenth century. The form and the subject, we shall see, are the dancer and the dance.

Man was Emerson's subject because from the poet's angle of vision the world existed in man. The idea runs through Emerson's work from the earliest sermons and lectures, and it was the presiding assumption in *Nature* despite the book's title. "The power to produce . . . delight does not

185

reside in nature, but in man," he wrote, and then added, "or in a harmony of both" (*W*, I, 11). One of the essential passages that links this concentration to the art occurs in an oration Emerson delivered at Waterville College in Maine in 1841. First he declares his radical humanism: "The termination of the world in a man appears to be the last victory of intelligence. The universal does not attract us until housed in an individual." Then, in a significantly expansive metaphor, he sets up the crucial problem of a containing form: "Who heeds the waste abyss of possibility? The ocean is everywhere the same, but it has no character until seen with the shore or the ship. Who would value any number of miles of Atlantic brine bounded by lines of latitude and longitude? Confine it by granite rocks, let it wash a shore where wise men dwell, and it is filled with expression; and the point of greatest interest is where the land and water meet." The daring Emersonian synthesis centers on the miracle of immensity contained, for man himself is a form of infinite potential and activity. In the figure of a man is the ideal conjunction of Emerson's subject and his artistic goal. The metaphors bound, even collide, fairly dance: "So must we admire in man the form of the formless, the concentration of the vast, the house of reason, the cave of memory. See the play of thoughts! what nimble gigantic creatures are these! what saurians, what palaiotheria shall be named with these agile movers?" (*W*, I, 205).

Emerson sought to give a voice in his time and place to this man in the manifold and sensational world, to make the words and the man taste the world, and thus to create in language, as I said in the last chapter, the studied exposure of a man's imaginative processes to his audience. It was and remains the epitome of artistic self-consciousness. It was a focus not on meaning, as in the poems so intent upon Platonist finalities, but on happening, of a man being overflowed by life and coming into his visionary estate.

When we address this figure who speaks Emerson's most dynamic lecture-essays, we are not talking conventionally about Emerson the author but about the fictive prototype he made from words. That is, we are clear in our minds that the dynamic personality who engages the reader is not the Concord landowner, diligent lecturer, editor, or even philosopher, but the artist's creation. We make that crucial distinction as a matter of course with Whitman's Falstaffian singer, but not so, as we should, with Emerson's Platonist democrat. John Jay Chapman is useful in helping us see the cleavage between the man Emerson and the word-bred figure that is confused with him. Chapman quotes Nathaniel P. Willis, the editor and correspondent, on the historical person and the other presence that acquires life in Emerson's words. "We can imagine nothing in nature," said Willis, "like the want of correspondence between the Emerson that goes in at the eye and the Emerson that goes in at the ear."[2]

Only if we recall the preoccupation of Emerson's American contemporaries with the moral aspects of poetic theory, and indeed his own similar preoccupation, can we recognize the originality and power in this new mask and this new body of language that animated it. It was an astounding fabrication. Partly because of a facile identification of the writer with the figure he created, the specific devising that accounts for Emerson's crucial place in the poetry of America has eluded us, and just at the point of the most radical innovation in its history. The fresh labor of his genius has also been obscured by critics' fixation on the unaccountable gap supposedly created because he never showed in his verse how to execute the ideas he eloquently and with lyrical abstractness espoused in the essay "The Poet."

The mask and the style together met the imperative of reconciliation in Emerson's poetics, a new aligning of elemental nature and the poetic voice. He looked to other reformers as promoters of this same essential conjugation: "I count the genius of Swedenborg and Wordsworth as the agents of a reform in philosophy, the bringing poetry back to Nature, — to the marrying of Nature and mind, undoing the old divorce in which poetry had been famished and false, and Nature had been suspected and pagan" (*W*, VIII, 66). This poetic necessity was what Wordsworth called "the discerning intellect of Man wedded to this goodly universe."[3] Whitman literally, characteristically, in "By Blue Ontario's Shore" was to picture the poet plunging his phallus into the land in a supreme city-begetting marriage. Almost a century later, in *Paterson*, Williams intended the landscape-woman, in an elaborate metaphor, to be reality offering herself as wife to the reluctant poet. Emerson's contribution to this Romantic metaphor of generative intercourse between nature and mind was a democratic inclusiveness of subject and a democratic leveling of style. In opening form to accommodate the fullness of nature as it is drawn into the evolving mind, Emerson understood the inherent self-generating possibilities when the interconnecting life of the various elements is not frozen by hierarchical distinction. "The Muse shall be the counterpart of Nature," he asserted, "and equally rich. I find her not often in books. We know Nature and figure her exuberant, tranquil, magnificent in her fertility, coherent; so that every creation is omen of every other. She is not proud of the sea, of the stars, of space or time, or man or woman. All her kinds share the attributes of the selectest extremes. But in current literature I do not find her" (*W*, VIII, 65). In that synthesis of variety and coherence, discovery and conjugation, Emerson located the source of the converting power of literature.

The loosening of form by prosaic liberties made possible a poetry not of history or of monumental retrospect, of impressing an order on the past, but of self-discovery, heuristic advance, and the defining of meaning as the poem's materials coalesce. "The quality of the imagination," Emerson said in "The Poet," "is to flow, and not to freeze. The Poet did not stop at the color or the form, but read their meaning; neither may he rest in this meaning, but he makes the same objects exponents of his new thought" (*W,* III, 34). Fully responsive to the flowing motion of nature, the poetic form and the voice, ideally, ascend with a power commensurate to those elemental cadences, to the rhythm of the seashore, as Emerson envisioned, to the largeness of astronomy (*W,* VIII, 56-57).

This ideal movement obviously owes much to Emerson's experience of public performance, particularly in the way it accumulates power as it marshals its rhetorical forces. The aim finally is to give man's voice to Nature itself, to make Merlin heard once again from the heart of the world. *That,* Emerson assumed, would be the ultimate reconciliation of literary form. Now tinkling and feeble, poetry might yet sound the voice of Nature in man, thundering out in primary prosaic power in the place of those reported "voices" that say their lines in Emerson's poetry. "We cannot know things by words and writing," he said, "but only by taking a central position in the universe and living in its forms" (*W,* VIII, 42). This is total congruence, the goal of his poetics, where the forms of the voice and the forms of experience are identical.

This freedom made room for the Emersonian persona and brought into being a new anatomy of perception. "All language . . . stands in an active, ultimately creative, relationship to reality," George Steiner has written. "A major poem discovers hitherto unlived life-forms and, quite literally, releases hitherto inert forces of perception."[4] What we may call impulsive motion in this regard, Emerson called "the mind allowing itself range," which entails "a corresponding freedom in the style, which becomes lyrical" (*W,* VIII, 53). In that new freedom the flow of movement could exploit sudden enthusiasms or fortuitous insights, the moment could be possessed for its unanticipated energy, and the unfolding keeps pace with the exuberant play of genius as it warms to its own progress. The form, Emerson foresaw, allows life to become. Herein, so often overlooked, is the true meaning of the famous stairway of surprise: spontaneity, leaps of impulse. On a lecture sheet, Emerson asked: "Do not the great always live *extempore,* mounting to heaven by the stairs of surprise?" (*W,* IX, 442).

The agile, revelation-seeking movements of the mind rise out of a spacious prose body so flexible and resonant that readers have looked in vain for a constructed coherence. In the clustered but provisional relationships work the very significance of Emerson's form, a structural meaning quite outside the perception of the conventionally analytical eye. Firkins wrote: "The fault of the style, in relation both to reader and author, is want of relation to the processes of consciousness; it does not recognize the reader's processes; it does not reproduce the author's."[5] Carl Strauch, however, has usefully turned readers' attention from the illogic of the arguments to the felt presence in the prose, asserting that "Emerson's personality imparts movement to the essays, where we have not a philosophical confrontation of ideas, but a dramatic and personal confrontation."[6] But that personality is far more deliberate and artful. Its dynamic drawing in of the various world was equated in Emerson's mind with power. "Man is powerful only by the multitude of his affinities," he had written (*EL,* III, 249), and those relationships were precisely the conveyors of meaning, for every new relation is a new word. Impulsive graspings, one after another with little explicit connective material, like tentative lines in a pencil drawing, constitute a series of fresh acts of conceptualization. Incompleteness itself suggests the gesture of seeking. Life is reproduced by the absence of closed patterns and rigid structures of reasoning. Thus Emerson's openness paid in surface coherence what it gained more deeply in being altogether receptive. "Room! room! willed the opening mind, / And found it in Variety," wrote Emerson in his notebook (*JMN,* VIII, 431).[7]

HIS UNIQUE Man-Becoming persona first bursts out in essential outline from the stodgy, schematic prose of *Nature* in the act of crossing the cheerless common. Amid the icy puddles and under a low sky, this alter-Emerson is feeding on magnificence. The passage in its apparent intimacy arrests the most jaded reader with its clash of extremes: "Crossing a bare common, in snow puddles, at twilight, under a clouded sky, without having in my thoughts any occurrence of special good fortune, I have enjoyed a perfect exhilaration. I am glad to the brink of fear" (*W,* I, 9).

The figure appears intermittently, subdued, through the rest of *Nature,* until near the end an outside voice is beamed in, Emerson's speaker reporting what "a certain poet sang to me." The transformation of the persona into this Orphic poet is not unimaginable. The voice is passionate, the words extravagant and lyrical, but this borrowed poet-figure is also a straw man enabling Emerson, through his extraordinary mask, to make some provocatively harsh pronouncements about man blind to his instinctual power: "We distrust and deny inwardly our sympathy with nature . . . A man is a god in ruins . . . Man is the dwarf of himself" (*W,* I, 70-71). The Emerson persona returns at the conclusion of the book in the hortatory role that is a part of his created nature, but he relies again on "what my poet said," summing up: "Know then that the world exists for you . . . What we are, that only can we see" (*W*, I, 76).

Described abstractly, Emerson's invented figure is a colossal conglomerate of the qualities necessary to link man and truth. Thus the figure is grounded solidly as a common man. His fuller description can be derived almost anywhere in the canon that is his stage. For example, he is the figure that takes shape in Emerson's account of Plato: "He is a great average man . . . men see in him their own dreams and glimpses made available . . . A great common-sense is his warrant and qualification to be the world's interpreter" (*W*, IV, 61). The exemplary consciousness, besides being ideally average, possesses the illumination of innocence because he is wholly correspondent with his world. "The lover of nature," Emerson wrote in *Nature* leading up to the transport on the common, "is he whose inward and outward senses are still truly adjusted to each other; who has retained the spirit of infancy even into the era of manhood . . . In the presence of nature a wild delight runs through the man, in spite of real sorrows" (*W*, I, 9).

As a public figure, an orator before "a convertible audience," he may "lay himself out utterly, large, enormous, prodigal, on the subject of the hour. Here he may dare to hope for ecstasy and eloquence" (*JMN*, VII, 265). As always in Emerson, his figure of fundamental man is inseparable from his idealized poet. In "Poetry and Imagination" that figure is at the center of the world, his mind dancing in rhythm to the divine currents. As a literary concoction, the figure is indeed original, mythic in its proportions, colossal in its stance, infinite in its reach, and gifted with its sight of truth. "The poet is rare," Emerson wrote in the essay, "because he must be exquisitely vital and sympathetic, and, at the same time, immovably centered." His speech is inspired, forceful, unconfined by conventions, as Emerson implies in his quote from Ben Jonson:

> Not with tickling rhymes,
> But high and noble matter, such as flies
> From brains entranced, and filled with ecstasies.   (*W*, VIII, 64)

Empowered by nature, possessed of a mind of startling activity, Emerson's prose persona seems summarized in a final passage in "Poetry and Imagination": "The number of successive saltations the nimble thought can make, measures the difference between the highest and lowest of mankind. The habit of saliency, of not pausing but going on, is a sort of importation or domestication of the Divine effort in a man" (*W*, VIII, 72). These metaphors of activity and insight will be important when we consider the form in which this detached and idealized Emersonian consciousness takes on the structure of words.

The first appearance of the fully formed alter-Emerson mask occurred in *Nature* in 1836, but readers familiar with Emerson's works know that there was a longer history to this arresting voice.[8] The persona is vaguely apparent, with predictably ministerial tones, in the early sermon entitled "The Christian Minister: Part I," first delivered in 1829 when Emerson was not yet twenty-six. The private-seeming voice, though unobtrusive at this point, runs through a series of accelerating exhortatory phrases: "I know that men who do not love the Gospel do not know what it is . . . I see the grossest ignorance and the most injurious prejudices existing in regard to that which I love and honour. I grieve to see men esteem as tyranny what I feel to be a law of love . . . if I can represent the life of Christ in such vivid and true colours as to exalt your love . . . if I can persuade one young man to check the running tide of sensual pleasure by the force of moral obliga- tion . . . if I can prevail with one old man to forgive an injury that has rankled in his breast till hatred has grown into habit . . . then I shall bless God that I have not been wholly wanting to his cause, that, by me, one mite is added to the sum of happiness."[9]

The figure enters only fleetingly the first secular lecture of Emerson's career, delivered in Boston in 1833 soon after his return from Europe. The talk was on the uses of natural history and its specific theme was "the ad- vantages which may flow from the culture of natural science" to help ex- plain man to himself. At its close, as Emerson speaks of the language of visible nature, a trace of that exemplary figure of the actively aspiring man intrudes. It is hardly archetypal in stature but it is deliberately a *model* in the first person: "I wish to learn this language — not that I may know a new grammar but that I may read the great book which is written in that tongue" (*EL*, I, 26). A few weeks later, probably in early January 1834, the figure steps forward momentarily at the close of a lecture entitled "On the Relations of Man to the Globe." We recognize Emerson's words giving gesture to his mythic figure at the approach of the moment of revelation. Emerson himself, objective and remote, begins speaking the final passage ("In view of all these facts I conclude . . . "), asserting man's "accurate adjustment" to his world, the perfect symmetry of his body, and the perfect symmetry between man and the air, the mountains, and the tides. Just at that point, the persona takes over: "I am not impressed by solitary marks of designing wisdom; I am thrilled with delight by the choral harmony of the whole. Design! It is all design. It is all beauty. It is all astonishment" (*EL*, I, 49). Most of the early lectures, especially those he gave in series, are earnest, if not solemn, lacking this other-Emerson of intimate confession and intellectual thrill. Starting out on his career as lecturer, Emerson the writer doubtless felt bound to give his listeners their money's worth, and that meant giving them what they expected in straightforward, informative discourse. The same was not true when he found his style in the decade that began in 1836.

"The first impression one had in listening to him in public," Emerson's British friend Alexander Ireland wrote of him in his 1882 memoir, "was that his manner was so singularly quiet and unimpassioned that you began to fear the beauty and force of his thoughts were about to be marred by what might almost be described as monotony of expression." Yet, as Ireland discerned only partially, the forceful persona gathered in Emerson's words and stood forward beyond the retiring speaker: "The evident depth and sincerity of his convictions gradually extorted your deepest attention and made you feel that you were within the grip of no ordinary man, but of one 'sprung of Earth's first blood' with 'titles manifold' . . . you could no longer withstand his 'so potent spell' . . . he grew . . . steadily increasing, until he became a Titan . . . The moment he finished he took up his MS. and quietly glided away" (*W*, IV, 297-298). The implied being assumed form as the lecture-essays were written and took on its most vigorous life, after its birth in *Nature* in 1836, for about a decade.

Very deliberately in "The American Scholar" address of 1837, Emerson turns away from an objective description of this heroic figure ("But I have dwelt perhaps tediously upon this abstraction of the Scholar. I ought not to delay longer to add what I have to say of nearer reference to the time and to this country") and projects the figure itself into the texture of his words. Now the persona as archetypal ordinary man speaks: "I ask not for the great, the remote, the romantic; what is doing in Italy or Arabia; what is Greek art, or Provençal minstrelsy; I embrace the common, I explore and sit at the feet of the familiar, the low. Give me insight into to-day, and you may have the antique and future worlds" (*W*, I, 111). In the Divinity School address of the next year, the titanic alter-ego takes form almost literally before our eyes (or within our ears). At the opening, the "I" is an exemplary fiction, a representative of humanity, a rhetorical figure rather than a human actor: "What am I? and What is? asks the human spirit with a curiosity new-kindled, but never to be quenched. Behold these outrunning laws, which our imperfect apprehension can see tend this way and that, but not come full circle . . . I would study, I would know, I would admire forever" (*W*, I, 120). The same generalized speaker returns later on: "Truly speaking, it is not instruction, but provocation, that I can receive from another soul" (127). Midway in the address, then, the engaging presence of the heroic improvisation appears briefly: "To this holy office you propose to devote yourselves. I wish you may feel your call in throbs of desire and hope" (135). And now, startlingly, the prototypical iconoclast stands forth in words from the most serene of speakers to tell the divinity students and the nation that their religion and the institution of religion itself are near death. "It is my duty to say to you," come the words of the persona out of the mild man, "that the need was never greater of new revelation than now. From the views I have already expressed, you will infer the sad conviction, which I share, I believe, with numbers, of the universal decay and now almost death of faith in society . . . The Church seems to totter to its fall, almost all life extinct" (135). The mask of ancestral consciousness comes to an end with a now characteristic prophetic and self-reflective vision, summoning at the same time the ideal in others: "I look for the hour when that supreme Beauty which ravished the souls of those Eastern men, and chiefly of those Hebrews, and through their lips spoke oracles to all time, shall speak in the West also" (151).

Improbably complete self-possession, bordering on narcissism, is an aspect of this fictive temperament created by Emerson's dramatic art in prose. Not surprisingly, it is this figure, so fanatic as to be a contrast to the gentle Emerson himself, which dominates the essay "Self-Reliance," in *Essays* of 1841. The noble instinct, potent and proud, changes to bombast: "I am ashamed to think how easily we capitulate to badges and names, to large societies and dead institutions . . . I ought to go upright and vital, and speak the rude truth in all ways . . . I would write on the lintels of the door-post, *Whim*" (W, II, 51). A figure outrageously and single-mindedly assaulting conformity, this constellation of Emerson's invention thinks in unbecoming absolutes. "Let us never bow and apologize more," the alter-ego says. "A great man is coming to eat at my house. I do not wish to please him; I wish that he should wish to please me. I will stand here for humanity, and though I would make it kind, I would make it true" (60). Further along in the essay, the figure has heated to a harshness rarely matched in Emerson's private journals:

> Live no longer in the expectation of these deceived and deceiving people with whom we converse. Say to them, "O father, O mother, O wife, O brother, O friend, I have lived with you after appearances hitherto. Henceforward I am the truth's. Be it known unto you that henceforward I obey no law less than the eternal law. I will have no covenants but proximities. I shall endeavor to nourish my parents, to support my family, to be the chaste hus-

band of one wife, — but these relations I must fill after a new and unprecedented way. I appeal from your customs. I must be myself. I cannot break myself any longer for you, or you.

(W, II, 72-73)

Imagine how such lines would be received or who, indeed, would deliver them at a college commencement today. It is this fictive mask of radical dissent and not the historical Emerson who occupies our American imaginations.

The figure plays a succession of roles in "The Over-Soul," each of them representing an element in the conglomerate make-up of Emerson's detached performer. He is a man in the holy place, a solitary wonder-worker, a reporter of the vision and the ecstatic experience, a dissolver of time and matter, and the Platonic central man who forages like the humble-bee. He is, as well, a plain man, a father, and all together an example of self-contained power. In "The Poet" essay from *Essays, Second Series* of 1844, the Emersonian speaker sets out at first as a representative "I" of vague definition: "I remember when I was young how much I was moved one morning by tidings that genius had appeared in a youth who sat near me at table"; "I shall mount above these clouds and opaque airs in which I live . . . and from the heaven of truth I shall see and comprehend my relations" (*W*, III, 10, 12). It is transformed, however, into the noble figure of vast vision. Read aright, I believe, this astonishingly prideful figure presents itself unabashedly as the very figure of the ideal poet for which it calls. *It summons itself.* Not the least of its show is the intensity of passion in its summons: "I look in vain for the poet whom I describe. We do not with sufficient plainness or sufficient profoundness address ourselves to life, nor dare we chaunt our own times and social circumstance . . . We have yet had no genius in America, with tyrannous eye, which knew the value of our incomparable materials . . . Banks and tariffs, the newspaper and caucus . . . Our log-rolling, our stumps and their politics, our fisheries" and so on, the list continues (*W*, III, 37). This gigantic, immovably centered figure, in effect, says let there be a poet equal to the task, and there, in the rush of words, is the poet.

Perhaps the epitome of the mythlike speaker occurs in the essay "Experience," also from *Essays, Second Series*. Again it is a composite figure in which we see the father, quite outrageously concocted, who seeks reality so intently he cannot grieve his son's death; we see also a commoner familiar with the streets and a waiter for the light; we see the figure of a man aspiring and finding. Early in the essay the ideologue appears who courts reality: "An innavigable sea washes with silent waves between us and the things we aim at and converse with . . . In the death of my son, now more than two years ago, I seem to have lost a beautiful estate, —no more. I cannot get it nearer to me" (48). The figure shades into the volatile waiter for revelation with whom we are familiar: "I saw a gracious gentleman who adapts his conversation to the form of the head of the man he talks with! I had fancied that the value of life lay in its inscrutable possibilities; in the fact that I never know, in addressing myself to a new individual, what may befall me. I carry the keys of my castle in my hand, ready to throw them at the feet of my lord, whenever and in what disguise soever he shall appear. I know he is in the neighborhood, hidden among vagabonds" (53-54). But again the figure changes form before us into a man of extreme aspiration who wrests illumination from the most banal circumstances. "Leave me alone," the over-stater says, "and I should relish every hour and what it brought me, the potluck of the day, as heartily as the oldest gossip in the bar-room. I am thankful for small mercies . . . I begin . . . expecting nothing . . . If we will take the good we find, asking no questions, we shall have heaping measures" (61-62).

The invented alter-Emerson, then, is the very model of a man winning through to the vision. He is the noble spirit Matthew Arnold cherished, the inspirer in the collocation of words, and only indirectly the American author that Arnold crossed the ocean to pass judgment on. Here is that mask in "Experience," wholly living in the future, not in America but in the possibility of America:

> Underneath the inharmonious and trivial particulars, is a musical perfection; the Ideal journeying always with us, the heaven without rent or seam. Do but observe the mode of our illumination. When I converse with a profound mind, or if at any time being alone I have good thoughts, I do not at once arrive at satisfactions, as when, being thirsty, I drink water; or go to the fire, being cold; no! but I am at first apprised of my vicinity to a new and excellent region of life . . . every insight from this realm of thought is felt as initial, and promises a sequel. I do not make it; I arrive there, and behold what was there already. I make! O no! I clap my hands in infantine joy and amazement before the first opening to me of this august magnificence, old with the love and homage of innumerable ages, young with the life of life, the sunbright Mecca of the desert. And what a future it opens! I feel a new heart beating with the love of the new beauty. I am ready to die out of nature and be born again into this new yet unapproachable America I have found in the West.   (*W*, III, 71-72)

Finally, in "Experience," an essay all the more powerful for its diminished rapture, we hear the disengaged and now quieting voice of the persona in solemn, uncharacteristic retrospect, the seemingly completed creation of the quiet man from Concord who was himself at the time only forty years old:

> A wonderful time I have lived in. I am not the novice I was fourteen, nor yet seven years ago. Let who will ask, Where is the fruit? I find a private fruit sufficient. This is a fruit, —that I should not ask for a rash effect from meditations, counsels and the hiving of truths . . . When I receive a new gift, I do not macerate my body to make the account square, for if I should die I could not make the account square. The benefit overran the merit the first day, and has overrun the merit ever since. The merit itself, so-called, I reckon part of the receiving.   (83-84)

Taken together, this composite figure was a potent insertion, Titan as Ireland said, into the American literary imagination. Emerson's persona was Man Thinking, Man Becoming, and the style and form were the motion of the mind's discovery. The saltations of his nimble thought, his *going on,* as Emerson said, made him no ordinary man. But in dramatizing a brain "entranced and filled with ecstasies," there was an order necessary in the unfolding, in the domestication of the divine effort in a man; otherwise it would be willful, whimsical, fragmented, unintelligible. The prose that was the authentic vehicle of this imaginative complex of occasions took its form from Emerson's modernist aesthetics of glimpses.

We misjudge the discipline of Emerson's theorizing unless we recognize that he did not throw the intellect out with the old rationalistic forms. Emerson never abandoned his faith in the ordering power of the mind. He was a fierce preserver of the hard center of intellect, as Eliot was also to be, those qualities of sharp and deliberate intellection that until the recent past have marked the literary expression of the modern poetic imagination. Emerson conceived of a form that would hold poised both the transporting metaphysical impulse and the controlled act of the mind: "Poetry is the perpetual endeavor to express the spirit of the thing, to pass the brute body and search the life and reason which causes it to exist . . . Its essential mark is that it betrays in every word instant activity of mind, shown in new uses of every fact and image, in preternatural quickness or perception of relations" (*W*, VIII, 17).

All of these considerations of affective power of form Emerson distilled to the primary aesthetic question for his age as he worked to free its poetic imagination, discover the abundant world, and give it an authentic voice. Emerson's proposition warrants a second reading: "The problem of the poet is to unite freedom with precision; to give the pleasure of color, and be not less the most powerful of sculptors. Music seems to you sufficient, or the subtle and delicate scent of lavender; *but Dante was free imagination, —all wings,—yet he wrote like Euclid"* (*W*, VIII, 72; italics mine).

Neither the philosopher nor the mystic speaks here but the aesthetician, the artist concerned with form and with holding in the lines of the mind the play of experience. The problem as Emerson defined it became the central problem of the modern imagination, seeking structures for a new veracity and reconciliation with experience. Emerson was aware of the intimate interplay of the imagination and the form in which it finds its voice. Thus his prose was a transforming of an aesthetics of impulses, discovery, and becoming. In his speculation on this aesthetic phenomenon, he forced his thought to the center, holding simultaneously the idea of a new imagination confronting a new world, in effect, and searching for a new voice. The aesthetic truths he won in his own prose are indeed part of the poetics of the modern age.

EMERSON MADE extravagant claims for the saltatory style. In that progressive form he saw the promised conversion of the world. Homer and Milton would sound like tin pans—like talents merely—when the imagination of modern man danced with the voice of the new age, whose language would "open the eye of the intellect to see farther and better" (*W*, VIII, 68). Language was the single instrument and man the single repository that could effect the conversion of the world into its spiritual meaning: "There is a great deal of spiritual energy in the universe," Emerson maintained at the end of his career, "but it is not palpable to us until we can make it up into man" (*W*, X, 276). Power will issue from the art form itself, for therein will occur the synthesis of the abundant materials the poet-prosaicist brings to his creation: "Ever as the thought mounts, the expression mounts. 'T is cumulative also; the poem is made up of lines each of which fills the ear of the poet in its turn, so that mere synthesis produces a work quite superhuman" (*W*, VIII, 54). Cumulative power is a function of the spontaneous form Emerson has posited in his theory. In his public addresses, he was able to convey this impulsive style with consummate art, as Lowell attested: "how artfully (for Emerson is a long-studied artist in these things) does the deliberate utterance, that seems waiting for the first word, seem to admit us partners in the labor of thought, and make us feel as if the glance of humor were a sudden suggestion; as if the perfect phrase lying written there on the desk were as unexpected to him as to us!" (*W*, VII, 342).

The prose form that actualized Emerson's theory was various and adaptable on its surface. Within, it had a structure associated with the act of metamorphosis that moved at the center of Emerson's thought. The form he devised was not a shape of deliberate figuration but rather a process and a passage along which the reader was conveyed. This new structure — distinct from the stiff linearity of his verses — was a *rhythm of ideas.* Emerson suggested its insubstantial nature when he talked about rhyme as the transparent frame that allows "the pure architecture of thought to become visible to the mental eye." In Emerson's prose the hidden tendency artfully enacts the rhythm of a man's imaginative processes, and thus carries the reader's imagination from the familiar to the unfamiliar. That aesthetics of discovery, as Chapman observed, was Emerson's unique exploitation of the orator's art: "It was the platform which determined Emerson's style. He was not a writer, but a speaker . . . The pauses and hesitation, the abstraction, the searching, the balancing, the turning forward and back of the leaves of his lecture, and then the discovery, the illumination, the gleam of lightning which you saw before your eyes descend into a man of genius, — all this was Emerson."[10]

One of the terms by which he referred to this concealed principle was "inward skill." The structure is implied, accessible to the intellect and not on the visible surface. It is a construction not of rhetoric but, much deeper, a structure of the imagination. Like Pound's work in which form follows intellect, the Emersonian essay is constructed on an armature of beliefs patterned on the elemental forces of nature: symmetry and abundance in a spiraling moral arrangement. The essay once composed, the armature disappears, its shape existing only by implication or glimpses. Emerson's sprung form, as we have already seen, allowed for sudden enthusiasms, the exploitation of the extemporaneous and the seizing upon fortuitous crests of passion. On the structure of thought, whose sense dictates rhythm, Emerson declared: "I might even say that the rhyme is there in the theme, thought and image themselves" (*W*, VIII, 54). Here again is the extreme reach of Emerson's poetics. He has substituted for the conventional prosodic qualities of poetry the intellectual arrangement of ideas and images. This was to define poetry in a new way, by its configuration of relationships and "saliencies."[11]

Emerson equated that internal associative and shaping force with touchstones of the Romantic and Platonist vocabularies. It is associated with the "soul" that animates the "body"; it can be thought of as "inspiration," the animating force of poetry or music. Emerson believed that this internal movement was capable of transforming the familiar into something else. The poet, "by an ulterior intellectual perception, gives [emblems, symbols, and thoughts] a power which makes their old use forgotten" (*W*, III, 20).

Paradoxically, but consistently Emersonian, this insubstantial rhythm of thought discloses the "firm" truth of nature. The rhythm of ideas is the artist's counterpart to the invisible force that swings the elements of the universe into harmony. The passage about Spenser, Marlowe, and Chapman which served us as a gloss on the poem "The Snow-Storm" also describes Emerson's persona: "In their rhythm is no manufacture, but a vortex, or musical tornado, which, falling on words and the experience of a learned mind, whirls these materials into the same grand order as planets and moons obey, and seasons, and monsoons" (*W,* VIII, 50).

Emerson's formal principle reflects these invisible laws, holding not planets but experience in a dynamic order, aligning and realigning, reconciling its field constantly with the variety of nature itself. The conception is traceable to Emerson's identification (like Coleridge's) of the poetic craft with divine creation. As Sherman Paul says, "The logic he wanted for his literary method had to be the silent logic of creation itself."[12] Emerson meant the artistic imagination always to be receptive to that natural ordering. If left alone, domesticated in the mind, thoughts would take their own order, and this order was divine. It was "God's architecture" (*JMN,* III, 316). In Shakespeare he found that natural identification of idea and aesthetic form: "If I could write like the wonderful bard whose sonnets I read this afternoon I would leave all and sing songs to the human race. Poetry with him is no verbal affair; the thought is poetical and Nature is put under contribution to give analogies and semblances that she has never yielded before" (*JMN,* IV, 286). In the end, the reconciliation of art with experience depended upon the formalizing of the natural rhythm of ideas. Emerson said of "the eloquent man," a model of his fictive speaker, "The possession by the subject of his mind is so entire, that it ensures an order of expression which is the order of nature itself, and so the order of greatest force and inimitable by any art" (*JMN,* IX, 280). Emerson designed his prose, in effect, to provide a language in which this natural order could evolve.

"Read his prose, and you will be put to it to make out the connection of ideas," wrote John Jay Chapman, saying in homely terms what Arnold called the want of "an evolution sure and satisfying."[13] Certainly the structure of the most forceful essays is faintly adumbrated, often concealed, rarely very explicit, and contributes to the indeterminacy we experience in reading them. In this respect they relate to some of his strongest poems.[14] But the works that seem inexplicit at the same time make us sense the presence of a person in them and, more than this, a person spontaneously coming upon the words adequate to his meaning. It seems to be the language of the vital process of being fully in the world. The prose follows the high-intensity, diverse movement of the intelligence that the verse conventions usurped. It is Emerson's second invention, a language body, devised to hold his first original creation, the event of Man-Becoming in the world.

The terms that animate his great essay "Experience" come back to us as the terms of this language structure: impulsive and casual. Emerson's naming there of the lords of life ("I dare not assume to give their order, but I name them as I find them in my way" [*W*, III, 83]) emphasizes the deliberate randomness that invites attention and forces participation: "Illusion, Temperament, Succession, Surface, Surprise, Reality, Subjectiveness." This knowingly casual mode contrasts with the mode of the poetry, which is *written*, conveys *meaning*, and stands for *Being*. The prose of motion is *talked*, conveys *activity*, and gives voice to *Becoming*. Whereas the poetry has the marks of being composed line by line, the prose comes on in large gestures, paragraph waves of inspired process. Like the snowstorm, the prose is a body whirled into existence, all the underlying structures obscured.

Emerson's various terms for the state of full human receptivity metaphorically describe the condition of this prose construct as a sensual body: it manifests "the rhythmical structure of man," "the mind allowing itself range," a "succession of experiences so important that the new forgets the old," "a complex of occasions," "a body overflowed by life," "the largest power to receive and to impart," "poetry which tastes the world." Feeling fully and yielding fully are ideal qualities of Emersonian man, and this is the single metaphor that captures the significant elements of the prose method: improvisational, of irregular tempo, with "the form and gait of the body," unpredictable, ejaculatory, a field of temperament, fecund— in Emerson's marvelous term, a "volatile stability." Arnold declared that Emerson could not construct a philosophy, but Emerson's intention was not to build a system but to follow an event, not to make the requisite wholeness of good tissue but to make words activate new relationships and thus enact discovery, domesticating the divine effort in a man.

"Organic form," a concept I find generally irrelevant, is not an issue here. The concept remains a metaphor, rarely examined objectively in practical execution, based upon an imagining of perfectly integrated living cells—which is a condition quite impossible with words because language has structure that is imposed and not organic. With Emerson's prose we are closer to his mode if we call the enveloping form a holding force, an intellectual temperament as Arnold might have said. As in a novel and as we saw in the list of the lords of life in "Experience," substitutions can be made, one serving as well as another. The work is not seamless; the quality of the interaction and, often, the effect of abruptness carry the force. This linguistically created quality of a single man planted in the world, moving spontaneously, accumulating sensations, and converting them to ideas, accounts for the indeterminacy in Emerson's essays. It is characteristic for the direction of the essays to be vague, to take form only as the paragraphs proceed, and to have a dynamic quality of discovery. Emerson's way in the prose, after all, was not a mode of sculpting, not even a way of arguing a case, but a way of thinking. His persona was the projected figure in whom, seemingly, this occurred.

What this apparent vagueness accomplished is inclusion. Emerson's language body made a difficult unity, for it gave form to the action of a person in the process of Becoming in the complicated world. Close linguistic analysis will discover the syntactical and structural choices that enabled Emerson to give form to this condition in prose. Indeed, analysis is already revealing how Emerson's syntax created the condition of agentless process and power that attracted Nietzsche so strongly. A passage in *The Genealogy of Morals* effectively defines the philosophical meaning of Emerson's language field. It is only the snare of language, the arch fallacies of reason petrified by language, Nietzsche argued, that presents the process of power as a causal chain beginning with a subject. "There is no 'being' behind the doing . . . 'The doer' is merely a fictitious addition . . . the 'doing' is all."[15] Emerson's prose created a comparable vision, but his strategies were conscientiously submerged.

"INWARD SKILL" is the term Emerson used for the artistic faculty thàt can raise the rhythm of thought to revelation. The expression names the technique that derived from his aesthetic of glimpses, which in turn reflected his ideal of writing informed by activity of mind everywhere. These objectives are implicit in passages in "Poetry and Imagination" where Emerson labored to define this admired skill. He sought a form capable of sustained vitality, with no lagging, each element building in affective power upon the ones before it. Here is the full passage:

> a verse is not a vehicle to carry a sentence as a jewel is carried in a case: the verse must be alive, and inseparable from its contents, as the soul of man inspires and directs the body, and we measure the inspiration by the music. In reading prose, I am sensitive as soon as a sentence drags; but in poetry, as soon as one word drags. Ever as the thought mounts, the expression mounts. 'T is cumulative also . . . mere synthesis produces a work quite superhuman.
> (*W*, VIII, 54)

If we attend to these words, we see two principal criteria: writing should show everywhere an activity of mind; it should possess a sure sense of building and discovery. He quotes as an example the nineteen lines of Beaumont and Fletcher in _The Nice Valour_ (III, 3), beginning "Hence, all ye vain delights" and ending "Nothing's so dainty sweet as lovely melancholy." The qualities Emerson admired are those that progressively heighten expression. The images quickly follow one upon the other and sound repetitions punctuate the onward movement, which culminates in the final hyperbole, by this time fully earned: "Nothing's so dainty sweet as lovely melancholy." It is an Emersonian passage. We see devices he habitually employed, but we recognize especially the deliberate building movement from tentative beginnings to the epigram at the end where the conversion is complete: melancholy is not what you thought, but something other. Emerson gives further examples of the same effect: "Keats disclosed by certain lines in his Hyperion this inward skill; and Coleridge showed at least his love and appetency for it. It appears in Ben Jonson's songs, including certainly The Faery beam upon you, etc., Waller's Go, Lovely Rose! Herbert's Virtue and Easter, and Lovelace's lines To Althea and To Lucasta, and Collins's Ode to Evening, all but the last verse, which is academical" (_W_, VIII, 55-56).

Inward skill involved placing words, lines, and images so as to define indirectly by their relationship the "soul" of the poem. Images well chosen, like those of Keats and the others, create a mounting gesture both of emotion that enlists the reader's acquiescence and of the trajectory of the argument. As Emerson says of the bard in "Merlin," "Leaving rule and pale forethought, / He shall aye climb / For his rhyme." That heuristic thrust first of excitement and then revelation must be spontaneous, forged in the transporting passion. "Shun manufacture or the introducing an artificial arrangement in your thoughts," Emerson said, "it will surely crack and come to nothing, but let alone tinkering and wait for the natural arrangement of your treasures" (_JMN_, V, 92). In his poetics that natural arrangement, by flexibility and seemingly casual advance, reproduces the singularity, the variety, and the waiting revelation of inspired individual experience.

Because Emerson's aesthetic concepts turned consistently on a pair of ideas — the converting imagination and the free movement that gesture required — his thought contains numerous analogues of inward skill. It is fundamentally the same tendency of sudden discovery implied by the stairway of surprise in "Merlin." Both the philosophy and the style are cumulative, rising together in the dramatic experience of Emerson's Man-Becoming. "In proportion as a man's life comes into union with truth, his thoughts approach to a parallelism with the currents of natural laws, so that he easily expresses his meaning by natural symbols, or uses the ecstatic or poetic speech. By successive states of mind all the facts of Nature are for the first time interpreted" (*W*, VIII, 68). Not surprisingly, the principal analogue for inward skill is Nature itself. The association was deeply set in Emerson's thinking, informing much of what he wrote, including the epigraph to *Nature:*

> A subtle chain of countless rings
> The next unto the farthest brings;
> The eye reads omens where it goes,
> And speaks all languages the rose;
> And, striving to be man, the worm
> Mounts through all the spires of form.

The rhythm of intent is a kind of aesthetic gravitation like the holding forces of the universe. He drew a direct analogy between cosmic laws and aesthetic laws when he concluded that Spenser, Marlowe, and Chapman whirled their materials, vortex-like, into the same grand order that the planets and moons and seasons obey. Emerson conceived a wild yet purposeful aesthetic engine that drives the poetic imagination as it does nature.

Literature, thus, could also seek its revelatory ways in the inductive ways of science. Emerson said that the poet follows "true science" in using forms according to the life and not according to the form. He admired in *Morte d'Arthur* the Merlin passage he described as "a height which attracts more than other parts, and is best remembered." In the poem "Merlin" he listed the world-embracing range of the elements of inward skill: the natural rhyming of ideas and images, peremptory chords that match nature's tones, men's hearts and orators', the din of cities and wars, and prayers; rhythms free of conventional meters; works not dutifully produced but impelled by need; subtle rhymes that carry Fate's undersong. As an encompassing symbol, "Musketaquid" illuminates once again the character of the form Emerson associated with the concept of inward skill, especially the artist's resources by which the form could draw on almost all of man's experience. The landscape, he wrote there, "is an armory of powers, / Which, one by one, they know to draw and use." Chiefest prize, he concluded, was "true liberty / In the glad home plain-dealing Nature gave."

An essential part of Emerson's poetics rests in that simple-seeming image: the broad resourceful landscape has all the elements of its own cultivation and in this self-generation the purpose of the whole is manifest. To Emerson, whose early sermons were closely argued along definite lines, that purposeful new artistic freedom followed an inherent necessity characteristic of classic form. He compared his own heterogeneous compositions to George Sand's, which, like Walter Scott's and Shakespeare's, unfolded to inevitable ends. "Mme George Sand, though she writes fast and miscellaneously, is yet fundamentally classic and necessitated: and I, who tack things strangely enough together, and consult my ease rather than my strength, and often write *on the other side*, am yet an adorer of the *One*. To be classic, then, *de rigueur*, is the prerogative of a vigorous mind who is able to execute what he conceives" (*J, IX*, 25). Thus his own conscious purpose held, despite the apparent structural miscellaneousness. His concentration on the inmost structure of conversion rather than on formal harmonies has misled generations of his readers. Carlyle nowhere discovered signs of design or coherence. Rather than holding solidly like a "beaten *ingot*," each paragraph, he wrote to Emerson, was "a beautiful square *bag of duck-shot* held together by canvas" (*CEC*, 371).

Firkins was similarly critical. Emerson's "aptitude for method was mediocre, permitting him, in lucky subjects and genial moods, to approach excellence, and in refractory subjects or unruly moods, to sink to the plane of badness. At its lowest, however," he concluded, "it is far above chaos."[16] Norman Foerster saw no organization in Emerson's form. "It is true that in his own writing, his own practice of art, Emerson was notoriously deficient in the organic law in its formal aspect; his essays and poems are badly organized, the parts having no definite relation to each other and the wholes wanting that unity which we find in the organisms of nature. Rarely does he give us even a beginning, middle, and end, which is the very least that we expect of an organism, which, indeed, we expect of a mechanism."[17]

For Emerson there was no distinguishing between revelation and freedom of form. That is his artistic truth. "If you desire to arrest attention, to surprise, do not give me facts in the order of cause and effect," he wrote in his journal, "but drop one or two links in the chain, and give me with a cause, an effect two or three times removed" (*JMN*, VII, 90).[18] In the Shakespeare lecture in *Representative Men*, Emerson was also explicit on the art of hiding structure: "all the sweets and all the terrors of human lot lay in his mind as truly but as softly as the landscape lies on the eye. And the importance of this wisdom of life sinks the form, as of Drama or Epic, out of notice. 'T is like making a question concerning the paper on which a king's message is written" (*W*, IV, 211). The conversational freedom of his own prose is the manifest evidence of this aesthetic truth. What seemed to readers a compositional grab bag was by conscious endeavor a supple prosaic body to contain his unique persona, to address the modern experience of an urban variousness, and to give off a contemporary dynamism: spontaneity and the tempo of the responsive mind.

THE MAJOR elements in his armory of powers were grounded in the natural rhyme of elemental forces. The correspondence of Emerson's aesthetics, man's everyday affairs, and the abiding structures of nature is absolute. As the imagination ascends to visions of immutable truths, so do the rhythms of the language. "Of course rhyme soars and refines with the growth of the mind," Emerson said, tracing an analogy from the child's drum to the adult's jews'-harp, and distinguishing the "melodies" in daily affairs. In man himself there is an instinctive rhythm that such things as anniversaries demonstrate: "Omen and coincidence show the rhythmical structure of man." By and by, he added, men will apprehend the real rhymes, "namely, the correspondence of parts in Nature" (*W*, VIII, 48-49). That vision of a natural pattern of correspondence is the source, to shift to Emerson's architectural metaphor, "from whence we get tiles and copestones for the masonry of today" (*W*, I, 98).

Emerson is explicit with examples of those rhymes in nature. In the poem "Woodnotes II," he pairs sound and echo, land and water, body and shadow, man and maid, and many others in a veritable compendium. To his mind those visual rhymes presented as natural an attraction as rhymes in the ear and explain man's impulsive response to them. A reflection in water "is rhyme to the eye, and explains the charm of rhyme to the ear" (*W*, VIII, 45). He cites shadows as paired correspondence, also colonnades, rows of windows, the symmetry of gardens; in men's social affairs, the couples in a bridal company, in a company of soldiers, in a funeral procession. Not only is pairing in nature a visual symbol of inspired unity, but in reflections there is a compounding of beauty: a bush reflected in water becomes "beautiful by being reflected" (*W*, VIII, 45). Visual rhymes constitute a major element in the armory of powers that Emerson described in his poetics and employed in his writing.

He drew, then, a direct correspondence between visual rhymes and the rhyme of ideas, that is, a conceptual dialectic between whose boundaries lay truth and in whose natural ascension ideas reach insight into nature. Reflections and shadows, nature's repetitions, form a cosmic system of symmetry based on visual rhymes. To break that correspondence is to destroy the rhyme of nature. Such a rupture constitutes the subject and dramatic structure of "Each and All." The catalogue at the end of the poem provides a list of nature's rhymes: pairing, symmetry, and a soaring visual result. In short, there is natural rhyme.

Translated into language, natural rhymes take the form of iteration. Emerson quotes with approbation in "Poetry and Imagination" this passage: "At her feet he bowed, he fell, he lay down: at her feet he bowed, he fell: where he bowed, there he fell down dead" (*W*, VIII, 47). The interplay of slightly altered phrases, together with alliteration, are linguistic reflections of nature. Similarly, Emerson repeated syntax, diction, and images. Each strategy was capable of many permutations, so there occurs in the prose a continual play of echoes and shadows.

Emerson quotes with admiration several reflecting lines from Milton, including these from *Comus*:

> Was I deceived, or did a sable cloud
> Turn forth its silver lining on the night?
> I did not err, there does a sable cloud
> Turn forth its silver lining on the night.

And this from *Samson Agonistes*:

> A little onward lend thy guiding hand,
> To these dark steps a little farther on.

Emerson's own iterative manipulations are far more subtle in the essay in which these quotations appear. They accumulate power subliminally, as Gertrude Stein knew. He wrote, for example, in "Poetry and Imagination," this paragraph about how rhythm affects human feeling—a simple enough paragraph with an intricate network of synonyms and repetitions.

> Young people like *rhyme, drum-beat, tune*, things in *pairs* and *alternatives*; and, in higher degrees, we know the instant power of *music* upon our *temperaments* to change our *mood*, and give us its own; and human *passion*, seizing these constitutional *tunes*, aims to fill them with appropriate words, or *marry music* to *thought*, believing, as we believe of all *marriage*, that *matches* are made in heaven, and that for every *thought* its proper melody or *rhyme* exists, though the *odds* are *immense* against our finding it, and only genius can rightly say the *banns*.
>   (*W*, VIII, 47; italics mine)

Not only is there repetition of sound and phrase but a cumulative clustering of images and trains of analogies, all of which limn the single idea at the invisible center.

Symbols are another and well-known element in this armory of language powers. They are to Emerson veritable touchstones, clarifying and persuading as they fall in deliberate alignment toward the climactic revelation. By embodying visual aspects of nature (the Papacy "is a stone in the body of Italy"), these symbols become mnemonic touchstones, and they stand for thoughts, which form in turn individual elements of the rhythm of ideas in the writer's system. Nature, converted by the poetic imagination and translated into elements of language, becomes another thing. He described the conversion this way, with an example we have encountered before: "Nature offers all her creatures to him [the poet] as a picture-language. Being used as a type, a second wonderful value appears in the object, far better than its old value; as the carpenter's stretched cord, if you hold your ear close enough, is musical in the breeze" (*W*, III, 13). Such pairings in the poetry created an oppressive duality in both thought and sound, but in Emerson's "strangely tacked together" prose they allowed the full activity of the ideally centered consciousness. "I am a complex of occasions," Emerson wrote. His translation of the rhymes of nature into the syntactic and symbolic layout of language created a universal prose based on a radically correspondent poetics. Here are not tinklings, as he said, but language equivalents of the immutable correspondences and cadences of the physical world.

In his prose we can trace by linguistic analysis his stylistic choices at the phonetic, syntactic, and semantic levels, and plot how they create a dramatic texture. There is an astonishing variety of logic-confounding structures that, in combination, mimic the mind's excursions of discovery: agent deletion, nominalization that projects supposition as fact, *there*-insertion that does the same, conflation of apparent opposites, chiasmus, clefting that fragments assertions, switching of tenses that blurs time distinction, interchanging of singular and plural entities, transforming of multiples to single elements in defiance of syntactic logic, and word-order inversion. In addition, there is redundancy almost of an incantatory nature, violations of subject-verb convention ("mountains migrate"), abrupt and unannounced shifts from cause to effect, agent to receiver (Arnold had remarked "the want of clearly-marked distinction between the subject and the object"), passivization, mixing of abstract and concrete imagery, paradox, pun, riddle, aggression and docility of tone, and comedy.

In Emerson's poetry this energy quotient was sapped by formalities. His composition of the poem "Seashore" demonstrates how that armory of powers in the prose was stifled as it passed into poetry. "Seashore" is closely related to its prose origin in Emerson's journal of 1857. The germinal prose impulse compactly embodies the concealed armature of inward skill, building toward revelation by the interactions of sound, syntactical choice, and diction. Emerson cast the prose version with complete naturalness in that characteristic dissociated voice which sounds much like the deep Heart of nature we encountered in "Threnody." But, being less strident, it is more closely related to the Emerson persona. Faithful to the idea of inward skill, the journal entry proceeds directly, but unobtrusively, along the conversion axis of not-this-but-that, ending appropriately in the insightful paradox that, though the sea is alive and active, it hints of unchanging perfection. Edward Emerson's account of the poem's germination is revealing:

> In July, 1857, Mr. Emerson, induced by Dr. Bartol, took his family to spend two weeks at Pigeon Cove, on Cape Ann. The day after our return to Concord, he came into our mother's room, where we were all sitting, with his journal in his hand, and said, "I came in yesterday from walking on the rocks and wrote down what the sea had said to me; and to-day, when I open my book, I find it all reads as blank verse, with scarcely a change."
>
> Here is the passage from that journal, as he read it to us: July 23. "Returned from Pigeon Cove, where we have made acquaintance with the sea, for seven days. 'T is a noble, friendly power, and seemed to say to me, Why so late and slow to come to me? Am I not here always, thy proper summer home? Is not my voice thy needful music; my breath thy healthful climate in the heats; my touch thy cure? Was ever building like my terraces? Was ever couch so magnificent as mine? Lie down on my warm ledges and learn that a very little hut is all you need. I have made this architecture superfluous, and it is paltry beside mine. Here are twenty Romes and Ninevehs and Karnacs in ruins together, obelisk and pyramid and Giant's Causeway; here they all are prostrate or half piled. And behold the sea, the opaline, plentiful and strong, yet beautiful as the rose or the rainbow, full of food, nourisher of men, purger of the world, creating a sweet climate and in its unchangeable ebb and flow, and in its beauty at a few furlongs, giving a hint of that which changes not, and is perfect."
>
> (*W*, IX, 484-485)

The rhyme of ideas, deployed along the plot of not-this-but-that, proceeds briskly through the early lines: *my* becomes *thy, voice* becomes *music, breath* becomes *climate, touch* becomes *cure,* and so on. Implied parallels set up visual and then conceptual rhymes: rock ledge-architecture-obelisk; ruins-Rome-Nineveh-Karnac; rose-rainbow; unchangeable ebb-flow. The submerged not-this-but-that paradox lies in the juxtaposition of the dead temples and the life-giving sea. The paradox is all but lost in the slackness of the contrived poem, and the idea-rhymes, reflections, and even the final revelation (what ebbs and flows shows what changes not) are obscured by Emerson's pompous formality. Several lines of the poem are worth quoting for their squandering of possibilities from the plain-dealing prose original.

I heard or seemed to hear the chiding Sea
Say, Pilgrim, why so late and slow to come?
Am I not always here, thy summer home?
Is not my voice thy music, morn and eve?
My breath thy healthful climate in the heats,
My touch thy antidote, my bay thy bath?
Was ever building like my terraces?
Was ever couch magnificent as mine?
Lie on the warm rock-ledges, and there learn
A little hut suffices like a town.

I make your sculptured architecture vain,
Vain beside mine. I drive my wedges home,
And carve the coastwise mountain into caves.
Lo! here is Rome and Nineveh and Thebes,
Karnak and Pyramid and Giant's Stairs
Half piled or prostrate; and my newest slab
Older than all thy race.

                          Behold the Sea,
The opaline, the plentiful and strong,
Yet beautiful as is the rose in June,
Fresh as the trickling rainbow of July;
Sea full of food, the nourisher of kinds,
Purger of earth, and medicine of men;
Creating a sweet climate by my breath,
Washing out harms and griefs from memory,
And, in my mathematic ebb and flow,
Giving a hint of that which changes not.
Rich are the sea-gods:—who gives gifts but they?
They grope the sea for pearls, but more than pearls:
They pluck Force thence, and give it to the wise.
For every wave is wealth to Dædalus,
Wealth to the cunning artist who can work
This matchless strength. Where shall he find, O waves!
A load your Atlas shoulders cannot lift?

The poem displays Emerson's bad habits, including periphrastic expansion to make meters and a fundamental confusion in the speaker's identity. There are crisp passages added in the poem, but these sharper edges are pillowed in the wordiness and the clichés.

Not aphoristically cramped as his early verse, this poem still binds its possibilities, failing to transfer intact the bold patterns of paradox that went spontaneously into the prose version. Other instances abound where Emerson's prose, in contrast to the poetry, captures intensity in its freedom of movement. A good example is the first part of the "Morals" section of

"Poetry and Imagination," a portion of which I cited earlier. Here is the inward conversion of appearances Emerson strove to attain, the cumulative passion of thought and insistent conceptual rhyme, and the elements of rhetorical power: repetition of phrase and sound, chiasmal build-up, homely and exotic symbols, allusion, more repetition — rising in incantatory fashion to a climactic unity. It has a modernist paste-up diversity:

> Is not poetry the little chamber in the brain where is generated the explosive force which, by gentle shocks, sets in action the intellectual world? Bring us the bards who shall sing all our old ideas out of our heads, and new ones in; men-making poets; poetry which, like the verses inscribed on Balder's columns in Breidablik, is capable of restoring the dead to life; — poetry like that verse of Saadi, which the angels testified "met the approbation of Allah in Heaven;" — poetry which finds its rhymes and cadences in the rhymes and iterations of Nature, and is the gift to men of new images and symbols, each the ensign and oracle of an age; that shall assimilate men to it, mould itself into religions and mythologies, and impart its quality to centuries; — poetry which tastes the world and reports of it, upbuilding the world again in the thought; —
> "Not with tickling rhymes,
> But high and noble matter, such as flies
> From brains entranced, and filled with ecstasies."
> (*W*, VIII, 64)

Perhaps the most splendid performance of Emerson's aesthetics of discovery was "The American Scholar." Carlyle said, "God be thanked for it, I could have wept to read that speech; the clear, high melody of it went tingling through my heart" (*CEC*, 173). It provides us with concentrated examples of the powers available to Emerson when his poetic imagination was first darting freely into the space that his new aesthetic excursions were creating. Indeed, one scholar has called the essay "frenzied speech of the prophet."[19] We can trace in it his raw materials, the interior movement of the argument from the homely to the universal, the discovery as it proceeds, its repetitions in manifold forms, the numerous variations on the theme, and the periodically arresting presence of that unique persona. In short, it is a model of Emerson's rhetorical movement and the accumulation of conviction.

The essay is a series of liberations. Its theme is the freeing of men from conceptual systems into truth. At every step the essay ushers the reader through appearance to Emersonian reality. This aim determines the local architecture of the piece and directs the powerful rhythm of the core idea. We go from the "sluggish mind" of America to the noble model of Man-

Becoming, and to a general call for enlistment in the conversion of the world. It is the scholar-poet's task to reveal the promise. Much later Emerson quoted Zoroaster to this effect, that the poet's employment is "in producing apparent imitations of unapparent natures, and inscribing things unapparent in the apparent fabrication of the world." So the poet's strategy is "to make appear things which hide" (*W*, VIII, 19). Images in this essay range with extraordinary diversity (a list would run into the dozens), aphorisms stand as intellectual touchstones in the unity-seeking thought; rhetorical questions hammer as the persona reaches out to engage the reader; sentences syncopate rhythmically in length and sharply in tone as the poetic imagination moves across its flexible prose; repetitions keep up the incessant rhyme of ideas.

Emerson is dislodging and then opening the mind. The effect is direct upon readers. Ralph Rusk said of the essay, "Its broad basis in common sense made this one of Emerson's most powerful writings. It was alive with rhetoric that went home to the hearer" (Rusk, 265). Jonathan Bishop has traced more closely than most what he calls the "moral adventure" in the essays, "the stringency, the vital demand" as we follow "the leaps of the pen from word to word, from phrase to phrase."[20]

The intricacy of Emerson's devices can be shown in selected passages. In paragraph eight of "The American Scholar," the focus is on man thinking his way into the shared structural unity of nature, his own body, and his perceiving consciousness. It is a slow-motion replay of the transparent-eyeball revelation. The long rhythms of nature are set up rhetorically beginning in sentence two by enumeration, repetition, alliteration, and opposition. The cadence momentarily accelerates ("so entire, so boundless . . . system on system . . . upward, downward") until, initiated by the single two-word sentence, "Classification begins," the synthesis begins. In one long inclusive sentence, then, the fragments of experience are followed to their "one stem." The syntax — arranged by conjunctions, parallel main clauses ("it finds," "it goes"), and significant verb roots ("join," "see," "tie," "discover," "cohere," "flower") — bonds stylistically what is coherent philosophically. Here is the first half of the paragraph:

> I. The first in time and the first in importance of the influences upon the mind is that of nature. Every day, the sun; and, after sunset, Night and her stars. Ever the winds blow; ever the grass grows. Every day, men and women, conversing — beholding and beholden. The scholar is he of all men whom this spectacle most engages. He must settle its value in his mind. What is nature to him? There is never a beginning, there is never an end, to the in-

explicable continuity of this web of God, but always circular power returning into itself. Therein it resembles his own spirit, whose beginning, whose ending, he never can find, —so entire, so boundless. Far too as her splendors shine, system on system shooting like rays, upward, downward, without centre, without circumference, —in the mass and in the particle, Nature hastens to render account of herself to the mind. Classification begins. To the young mind every thing is individual, stands by itself. By and by, it finds how to join two things and see in them one nature; then three, then three thousand; and so, tyrannized over by its own unifying instinct, it goes on tying things together, diminishing anomalies, discovering roots running under ground whereby contrary and remote things cohere and flower out from one stem.

(*W*, I, 84-85)

At the point where Emerson insists that the scholar is a man of action, the direct-speaking "I," the action verbs (run, grasp, suffer, work, pierce, dissipate, dispose, vanquish, plant, extend) and the cluster of polysyllabic words of eloquence come together and, in the resulting wave of linguistic particles, the Emersonian persona takes fictive shape. Whitman's invention is prefigured, to be sure.

The world, —this shadow of the soul, or *other me*, —lies wide around. Its attractions are the keys which unlock my thoughts and make me acquainted with myself. I run eagerly into this resounding tumult. I grasp the hands of those next me, and take my place in the ring to suffer and to work, taught by an instinct that so shall the dumb abyss be vocal with speech. I pierce its order; I dissipate its fear; I dispose of it within the circuit of my expanding life. So much only of life as I know by experience, so much of the wilderness have I vanquished and planted, or so far have I extended my being, my dominion. I do not see how any man can afford, for the sake of his nerves and his nap, to spare any action in which he can partake. It is pearls and rubies to his discourse. Drudgery, calamity, exasperation, want, are instructors in eloquence and wisdom. The true scholar grudges every opportunity of action past by, as a loss of power. It is the raw material out of which the intellect moulds her splendid products. A strange process too, this by which experience is converted into thought, as a mulberry leaf is converted into satin. The manufacture goes forward at all hours.   (95-96)

The pulsations of nature are drawn into paragraph twenty-five by the series of compounds, with the unifying label "Polarity" gathering them up conceptually for the eyeball experience at the close, a not-this-but-that revelation, the paradoxical insight that laws of spirit determine the laws of matter.

But the final value of action, like that of books, and better than books, is that it is a resource. That great principle of Undulation in nature, that shows itself in the inspiring and expiring of the breath; in desire and satiety; in the ebb and flow of the sea; in day and night; in heat and cold; and, as yet more deeply ingrained in every atom and every fluid, is known to us under the name of Polarity, — these "fits of easy transmission and reflection," as Newton called them, are the law of nature because they are the law of spirit.   (98)

Insistent imperatives string one homely image after another along the argument of not-this-but-that in paragraph thirty-nine; an extremely diverse range of particulars is taken up into its body, but the world is no dull miscellany as it appears, not a puzzle, but in the consciousness of the Man-Becoming persona it becomes one single dignity-conferring design:

Give me insight into to-day, and you may have the antique and future worlds. What would we really know the meaning of? The meal in the firkin; the milk in the pan; the ballad in the street; the news of the boat; the glance of the eye; the form and the gait of the body; —show me the ultimate reason of these matters; show me the sublime presence of the highest spiritual cause lurking, as always it does lurk, in these suburbs and extremities of nature; let me see every trifle bristling with the polarity that ranges it instantly on an eternal law; and the shop, the plough, and the ledger referred to the like cause by which light undulates and poets sing; — and the world lies no longer a dull miscellany and lumber-room, but has form and order; there is no trifle, there is no puzzle, but one design unites and animates the farthest pinnacle and the lowest trench.   (111-112)

Emerson's final paragraph, two and a half pages in length, is a tour de force. Taking as his beginning point the insulated individual, he activates yet again the not-this-but-that conversion ("The world is nothing, the man is all"), reaching the single focal question of men's failure to reach their potential: "What is the remedy?" The conversion act hums again ("They did not yet see . . .") and then the shot is fired: the rightful work of a man is nothing less than the conversion of the world. A rhetorical question abruptly brings the listener-reader over to the persona's side, and *American* Man-Becoming declares the common adventure — "We will walk . . . we will work . . . we will speak." That summons sweeps effortlessly into the terminal equation:

What is the remedy? They did not yet see, and thousands of young men as hopeful now crowding to the barriers for the career do not yet see, that if the single man plant himself indomitably on his instincts, and there abide, the huge world will come round to him.

Patience, —patience; with the shades of all the good and great for company; and for solace the perspective of your own infinite life; and for work the study and the communication of principles, the making those instincts prevalent, the conversion of the world. Is it not the chief disgrace in the world, not to be an unit; —not to be reckoned one character; —not to yield that peculiar fruit which each man was created to bear, but to be reckoned in the gross, in the hundred, or the thousand, of the party, the section, to which we belong; and our opinion predicted geographically, as the north, or the south? Not so, brothers and friends, —please God, ours shall not be so. We will walk on our own feet; we will work with our own hands; we will speak our own minds. The study of letters shall be no longer a name for pity, for doubt, and for sensual indulgence. The dread of man and the love of man shall be a wall of defence and a wreath of joy around all. A nation of men will for the first time exist, because each believes himself inspired by the Divine Soul which also inspires all men.   (114-115)

Emerson's text was indeed a complex of occasions, fulfilling the credo he set in "Poetry and Imagination": "The problem of the poet is to unite freedom with precision . . . Dante was free imagination, —all wings—yet he wrote like Euclid."

"HE IS THE only writer we have had who writes as he speaks, who makes no literary parade," wrote John Jay Chapman in 1899. More than three quarters of a century later we cannot usefully alter that acute observation.[21] Emerson drew into his art some elements that were not in the art of his predecessors, things present but never examined: an eye for the diversity of life in America, its extraordinary energy, and the quiescent but gigantic idealizing intellect that could turn it into language and truth. It was an explosive synthesis, this encircling theory of Emerson's and his practice of it in the great prose works, and we cannot lose sight of its audacity if we care about how art and the imagination change. "American life storms about us daily, and is slow to find a tongue."

A single metaphor will not hold the distinction between Emerson's poetry and prose. Both derived from the same set of mind: the conception of an infinitely various but rhyming universe for man and the objective of converting that world of matter and spirit into its divinity-conferring truth. The simultaneous existence of the famished poetry and the vital prose may call to mind D. H. Lawrence's figure for a comparable division in James Fenimore Cooper: "as an American citizen he lived correct, impeccable—a clock-work man. Yet his living soul moved on in passional progress."[22]

Though Emerson's poetry remained linear, retrospective, and closed, a system of Platonic parables, the prose spread irregularly but fully dimensional, improvisational, and charged with personality and intimate demands. The intricate prose texture achieved a new self-consciousness that was a revolutionary break from a form of literature which was about something else. The new form was about itself, a complex of occasions holding a full and seemingly unrehearsed dramatic life. The principle of conversion had been for Emerson an instrument of constraint in the poetry, but the vision of reconciliation of literature and life, in the prose, became the instrument of freedom. This is the dynamic figure of aesthetic vision and language form I have tried to precipitate out of the whole body of his work. In the end I hope I have answered the profound question Hyatt Waggoner posed: "He published just two slim volumes of new poetry during his lifetime . . . If he really was, as he told [his second wife] Lidian, 'born a poet,' why was he so easily distracted from his real vocation? If the sense of vocation was really strong in him, why did he spend most of his time the rest of his life writing prose?"[23] I answer that the prose did what the impacted poetry could not: it put him in contact with the broad and deep American reality he sought and thus restored his art to his passional self.

By his self-promoted prosaicism, Emerson devalued the accepted counters of literariness. What emerged from behind the distractions of artifice were the sounds and possibilities of Man-Becoming in a rushing and complex world. Emerson conceived this encounter as the main undertaking of the poetic imagination in his age. Nothing less than its exemplary dramatization would suffice. To the extent that he opened literary form to the heuristic movements of the active mind, he made possible the modern multidimensional poetic imagination that relies not on past revelations or single assumptions, but on the poetic imagination seeking its own meaning in the art it creates.

Emerson's action "upon the Public," as he defined the American Scholar's obligation, is perfectly direct where it is most forceful. Here are no impatiently formulaic methods involving dissociated voices brought in from the outside, but the Earth's first blood speaking out from a text, to use his own term, of ejaculatory body and confronting the lords of life. The action was the form itself. Something better than speech, as he said, seemed at last identical with the thing itself spoken of. That power and that liberation would endure.

His formal innovation showed how a radical reconciliation was possible between the imagination and the inescapable world. Emerson had written in *Nature* that wise men pierce the rotten diction they inherit and fasten words again to visible things. This was a way of returning the world to the artist and the artist to himself. Like Hart Crane, an equal in high artistic self-consciousness, he never doubted that words in a certain order could reach final visions and thereby liberate men.

Because his prose was heuristic and conversational, a form more of talking than writing, concerned with process instead of meaning, it seemed indeterminate. In reality, it held new power and new perceptions. That liberation into the resources of reality, the self, and language allowed what was previously absent — the mind's infinite activity in a world of matter — to enter the modern consciousness. This literary epicenter and its aftershocks have never been charted.[24] The process of form determining attitude is a complicated and ironic transaction: Emerson's radical departure from restrictive form, set in train by his need to overcome the impoverishment of his poetry, produced a prosaic aesthetic that inverted idealism, clouding the glass of philosophical Platonism. In the twentieth century, the boundary between life and art began to collapse, with neither philosophical nor aesthetic belief to buttress it. With casual, seemingly talked form there came disconfirmation of the sustaining unitary vision.

Because art is a hypothesis about reality, the onset of a prosaic form in which elements do not fall into line according to convention or belief leads to a kind of philosophical cubism that breaks the nostalgia for rhyme in nature. The encompassing in art of more and various and dissociated experience performs the break. Lawrence believed that such a rejection of supernaturalism was a sign of maturation. "The mystic passion for infinitude is the ultimate of all our passion for love, oneness, equality . . . But it is no goal. The individual must emerge from this bath of love, as from the baths of blood in the old religions, initiated, fulfilled, entering on the great state of independent maturity."[25] In this light, it seems to have been Emerson who faced head on "the problem of the poet," as he called it, and first turned along the passage to poetic maturity.

The new idiom no longer rose vertically in moral abstraction but opened out horizontally, democratically, a democratic art of prose, to traverse the whole scale of experience. In the interstices left in that inclusive form by the disappearance of a unifying faith, the first glimpses of the wasteland were to come. The opening occurred a century and a half ago, when Emerson disengaged his liberating theory from his poetry and gave it body instead in his prose. That struggle holds all the drama for us and provides an unparalleled view into how a culture changes its voice and its mind.

Notes

Index

Notes

Introduction

1. James, *Memories and Studies* (New York: Longmans, Green, 1934), 22.

2. Bishop, *Emerson on the Soul* (Cambridge: Harvard University Press, 1964), 102. Much Emerson scholarship argues the contrary. "Whatever Emerson's methods, one must admit that the essays do lack 'art,' in the sense of aesthetic . . . form . . . And this lack of art may be related to Emerson's basic training and purpose: he was primarily a man of religion, a philosopher, or a moralist, before being an artist"—Frederic Carpenter, *Emerson Handbook* (New York: Hendricks House, 1953), 77. "Although Emerson is not, on the whole, a great poet, he belongs to that rarest class—the poets of ideas"—Carl F. Strauch, "The Year of Emerson's Poetic Maturity: 1834," *Philological Quarterly,* 34 (October 1955), 353. "Emerson's neglect of the element of technique was based not merely upon lack of interest, but upon his conviction that the theorists of his day exaggerated the importance of external form"—Vivian Hopkins, *Spires of Form* (Cambridge: Harvard University Press, 1951), 60. For more recent judgments, see R. A. Yoder, "Toward the 'Titmouse Dimension': The Development of Emerson's Poetic Style," *PMLA,* 87 (March 1972), 255, and Hyatt H. Waggoner, *Emerson as Poet* (Princeton: Princeton University Press, 1974), 51 and passim (see especially the introduction, which surveys one hundred years of Emerson criticism). The general judgment is summarized in Lawrence Buell's excellent survey, *Literary Transcendentalism: Style and Vision in the American Renaissance* (Ithaca: Cornell University Press, 1973), 1-2: "undoubtedly Emerson and his circle *are* more important for historical reasons than for the quality of their achievements in art, philosophy, and theology." Finally, for a discussion of Emerson as "the crucial figure in the continuity of the culture," see Sacvan Bercovitch, *The Puritan Origins of the American Self* (New Haven: Yale University Press, 1975), 163.

3. References to the standard editions of Emerson's works and biography appear throughout the text in this parenthetical form. A list of abbreviations follows the Preface.

4. Composed evidently in Autumn 1833. Strauch's gloss advises that this couplet may refer to Emerson's trip abroad following the death of his first wife.

Lionel Trilling observed a long time ago that a large proportion of American writers have embodied the dialectic of their age.

5. Vivian Hopkins said tentatively: "perhaps Emerson's own great essays come closest to the new and dynamic creation which he sought for New England's literature." *Spires of Form,* 145.

6. Matthiessen, *American Renaissance* (New York: Oxford University Press, 1962), 5.

7. Bishop, *Emerson on the Soul,* 7.

8. Studies yet to be published by Brian Fitzgerald and Gayle Smith, former graduate students of mine, will contribute to this revealing work. Particularly valuable symposia that have appeared in the journals *ESQ* and *American Transcendental Quarterly* are cited elsewhere in the notes.

1. Poetry Warps Away from Life

1. Arnold, *Discourses in America* (London: Macmillan, 1885), 153. My chapter title derives from a passage in Emerson's essay "Poetry and Imagination" which is characteristically self-revelatory and supremely demanding in its poetic standard: "Literature warps away from life, though at first it seems to bind it. In the world of letters how few commanding oracles! Homer did what he could; Pindar, Aeschylus, and the Greek Gnomic poets and the tragedians. Dante was faithful when not carried away by his fierce hatreds. But in so many alcoves of English poetry I can count only nine or ten authors who are still inspirers and lawgivers to their race" (*W,* VIII, 65).

2. Emerson criticism is surveyed in Strauch, *A Critical and Variorum Edition of the Poems of Ralph Waldo Emerson* (Ann Arbor: University Microfilms, 1971), and in Waggoner, *Emerson as Poet,* 3-52. Selections from the criticism itself are to be found in Milton R. Konvitz, ed., *The Recognition of Ralph Waldo Emerson: Selected Criticism since 1837* (Ann Arbor: University of Michigan Press, 1972), and Thomas J. Rountree, *Critics on Emerson* (Coral Gables, Fla.: University of Miami Press, 1973).

3. Burke, "I, Eye, Ay—Emerson's Early Essay 'Nature': Thoughts on the Machinery of Transcendence," *Transcendentalism and Its Legacy,* ed. Myron Simon and Thornton Parsons (Ann Arbor: University of Michigan Press, 1966), 23.

4. Arnold, *Discourses in America,* 154, 158-159.

5. Santayana, *Winds of Doctrine* (New York: Scribner's, 1926), 192. For a similar evaluation, see Seymour Gross, "Emerson and Poetry," *South Atlantic Quarterly,* 44 (January 1955), 82-94.

6. Carl Strauch, "The Mind's Voice: Emerson's Poetic Styles," *ESQ,* 60 (Summer 1970), 43-59. See also Albert Gelpi, *The Tenth Muse: The Psyche of the American Poet* (Cambridge: Harvard University Press, 1975), 92-105, for his essay, the shorter version of which appears in *Emerson: Prophecy, Metamorphosis, and Influence,* ed. David Levin (New York: Columbia University Press, 1975).

7. Merton Sealts, "Emerson on the Scholar, 1833-1837," *PMLA,* 85 (March 1970), 193.

8. See M. H. Abrams, *The Mirror and the Lamp* (New York: Norton, 1958), 160. Walter Ong calls this dominance "hypervisualism of the sensorium."

9. Lawrence, *Phoenix* (New York: Viking, 1968), I, 335.

10. Mailer, *The Presidential Papers* (New York: Putnam, 1963), 282.

11. Reed, *Observations on the Growth of the Mind* (Boston, 1859), 49.

12. Pearce, *The Continuity of American Poetry* (Princeton: Princeton University Press, 1961), 431.

13. Stein, *John Ruskin and Aesthetic Thought in America, 1840-1900* (Cambridge: Harvard University Press, 1967), 30.

14. Quoted in Frank Kermode, *Romantic Image* (New York: Chilmark, 1961), 162.

15. Lawrence, *The Symbolic Meaning* (New York: Viking, 1964), 232.

16. Orestes Brownson admired the literary merit of Emerson's poems but because of their antidoctrinal cast he thought them "hymns to the devil." Strauch writes: "Longfellow's golden praise [in a letter to Emerson, December 27, 1846] hardly prepares us for the conclusion at which we must arrive: that Emerson's *Poems* [1847] was the most controversial book of verse published in America before Whitman's *Leaves of Grass*" (*VP*, 197, 190).

17. Davie, *Articulate Energy* (London: Routledge and Kegan Paul, 1955), 112.

18. Nowottny, *The Language Poets Use* (London: Athlone, 1965), 143.

19. See my essay "Emily Dickinson: The Poetics of Doubt," *ESQ*, 60 (Summer 1970), 86-93.

20. See Sheldon W. Liebman, "The Origins of Emerson's Early Poetics: His Reading in the Scottish Common Sense Critics," *American Literature*, 45 (March 1973), 23-33.

21. Davie, *Articulate Energy*, 60.

2. "Threnody"

1. Thoreau, *A Week on the Concord and Merrimack Rivers* (Boston: Houghton Mifflin, 1906), 323-324.

2. Eliot, "Baudelaire," *Selected Essays* (New York: Harcourt Brace, 1950), 378-379.

3. See Yoder's excellent discussion of Emerson's stylistic compression as "the titmouse dimension," in the article cited above.

4. Bishop, *Emerson on the Soul*, 189.

3. The Act of Imagination

1. See Abrams, *The Mirror and the Lamp*, 69. My chapter title is from a passage in "Poetry and Imagination": "The act of imagination is ever attended by pure delight. It infuses a certain volatility and intoxication into all Nature."

2. Basic studies of Emerson's beliefs and their derivation are Sherman Paul, *Emerson's Angle of Vision* (Cambridge: Harvard University Press, 1965), and Kenneth W. Cameron, *Emerson the Essayist*, 2 vols. (Raleigh, N.C.: The Thistle Press, 1945). See also Jeffrey L. Duncan, *The Power and Form of Emerson's Thought* (Charlottesville: University Press of Virginia, 1973).

3. See Sealts, "Emerson on the Scholar, 1833-1837," cited above.

4. See also *JMN*, V, 249-250.

5. See Stuart M. Sperry, Jr., "Keats and the Chemistry of Poetic Creation," *PMLA*, 85 (March 1970), 269.

6. Abrams, *The Mirror and the Lamp*, 56.

7. See Paul, *Emerson's Angle of Vision*, 149ff.

8. See Harold Bloom on the Bacchus-Merlin dialectic in *The Ringers in the Tower* (Chicago: University of Chicago Press, 1971), 290-321.

9. Poirier, *A World Elsewhere* (New York: Oxford University Press, 1966), 56.

10. See also Channing's "Remarks on National Literature" (1830) for evidence of his great influence on this and other aspects of Emerson's thoughts. See Paul, *Emerson's Angle of Vision*, 53-55, and Strauch (*ESQ*, vol. 70) for other sources, including Sampson Reed.

11. I rely to a considerable extent on the essay "Poetry and Imagination," though its exact provenance is unclear (see my Preface). Although Perry Miller said of the essay that "there is no more precise summation of the poetic program to which the [Transcendentalist] group as a whole had dedicated themselves in the 1830's" (*The American Transcendentalists* [Garden City: Doubleday, 1957], 196), it is uniquely Emerson's thought in the essay's most significant aspects. On the element of conversion, see J. A. Ward, "Emerson and 'The Educated Will': Notes on the Process of Conversion," *ELH*, 34 (1967), 495-517.

12. Spencer, *The Quest for Nationality*, 13.

13. Bishop, *Emerson on the Soul*, 49.

14. See Hopkins, *Spires of Form*, 8, 32, and Henry Nash Smith, "Emerson's Problem of Vocation," *NEQ*, 12 (March-December 1939), 66.

15. See also Emerson's letter to his brother Edward, May 31, 1834 (*L*, I, 412-414), his journal covering the summer of 1835 (*JMN*, V, 46ff), and the poem "Empedocles" (*VP*, 299). Sherman Paul is useful on these terms (*Emerson's Angle of Vision*, pp. 220-224). For a larger context, see the discussion of the concept of genius in Charles R. Metzger, *Emerson and Greenough* (Berkeley: University of California Press, 1954).

16. Sperry, "Keats," 272, 273.

17. Ibid., 270. He traces the figure to Sir Humphrey Davy's science discourses.

18. Very, *Poems and Essays* (Boston: Houghton, 1886), 20, 22-23.

19. Paul, *Emerson's Angle of Vision*, 223.

20. See Hopkins, *Spires of Form*, 9.

21. Kermode, *Romantic Image*, 48.

22. Stevens, *The Necessary Angel* (New York: Random House, 1965), 96.

23. For a full discussion of these sources, see Hopkins, *Spires of Form*, 17ff.

24. Pearce, *The Continuity of American Poetry*, 34.

25. Spencer, *The Quest for Nationality*, 22.

26. For a useful discussion of this organic supposition in Emerson see Norman Foerster, "Emerson on the Organic Principle in Art," *Emerson: A Collection of Critical Essays*, ed. Milton Konvitz and Stephen Whicher (Englewood Cliffs: Prentice-Hall, 1962), 108-120.

27. Arnold, *Discourses in America*, 203.

28. Steiner, "The Language Animal," *Encounter*, 33 (August 1969), 16.

29. Gombrich, *Art and Illusion* (New York: Pantheon, 1961), 30.

30. Sherman Paul paraphrases Emerson (*J*, III, 292-293) and Coleridge: "The idea is a *way* of contemplating, that is, a form of intuition or direct perception through which what is revealed is always the Absolute Reality." Elsewhere Paul says, "Emerson took the static idea [of correspondence] and fitted it to the demands of spirit-piercing perception. It was the prism (idea or law of first philosophy) through which he saw the universe. It was the perception of correspondence itself that for him made perception 'the armed eye.' " (*Emerson's Angle of Vision*, 44, 70.)

31. Waggoner writes: "Community, friendship, love, grief, tragedy—these are all effectively absent from . . . Emerson's vision, and together they encompass no insignificant slice of human experience," but he does not attempt to explain why (*Emerson as Poet*, 200).

32. Barthes, *Writing Degree Zero* (Boston: Beacon, 1970), 86.

33. Stevens, *The Necessary Angel*, 56.

34. Paul, *Emerson's Angle of Vision*, 34-35.

35. Ohmann, *The Art of Victorian Prose*, ed. George Levine and William Madden (New York: Oxford University Press, 1968), 295, 308.

36. Strauch, "The Mind's Voice," 53.

4. The Muse Has a Deeper Secret

1. Oscar W. Firkins, *Ralph Waldo Emerson* (Boston: Houghton Mifflin, 1915), 287, and Rusk, 321-323. My chapter title is taken from a letter uncollected in *Letters* quoted by Strauch in "The Date of Emerson's *Terminus*" *PMLA*, 65 (June 1950), 369-370, from A. Warren Stearns, ed. "Four Emerson Letters to Dr. Daniel Parker," *The Tuftonian*, 1 (November 1940), 9.

2. Bishop, *Emerson on the Soul*, 23.

3. Levine, ed., *The Art of Victorian Prose*, 297.

4. Cf. Yoder, 262. For an indirect gloss on the distinction, see *Young Emerson Speaks*, ed. Arthur C. McGiffert, Jr. (Boston: Houghton Mifflin, 1938), xxxix-xl.

5. For an indispensable discussion of "The Sphinx," see Thomas R. Whitaker, "The Riddle of Emerson's 'Sphinx,' " *American Literature*, 27 (1955), 179-195.

6. Kermode, *Romantic Image*, 2.

7. Strauch, "The Mind's Voice," 52. See also Yoder, 262,

8. See R. L. Francis, *ELH*, 33 (1966), 467, for a different emphasis: "Uriel is a mythological expression of the 'transparent eyeball,' of the poetic function in its prophetic dimension that unites heaven and earth."

9. Whicher, *Freedom and Fate* (Philadelphia: University of Pennsylvania Press, 1953), 94.

10. Holmes, *Ralph Waldo Emerson* (Boston: Houghton Mifflin, 1885), 332-333.

11. I am indebted to Brian Fitzgerald for aid in detransforming the line.

12. Paul, *Emerson's Angle of Vision*, 25.

5. Crisis

1. See "The Date of Emerson's *Terminus*," 360-370, cited earlier, in which Strauch has a fine discussion of the possible course of the poem's composition, possible dates from 1850-51 to December 1866, the personal and historical background to the poem, and the reasons to think certainly that part of the poem was meant to refer to middle life and not life's end.

2. Whicher, *Freedom and Fate*, 60.

3. Alfred S. Reid, "Emerson's Prose Style: An Edge to Goodness," *ESQ*, 60 (Summer 1970), 42.

4. The eighty-line draft of "The Discontented Poet" in verse-book *P* suggests a fairly coherent intention on Emerson's part which was subsequently dispersed in the much longer, pieced-together composition with the title "The Poet." The integrity of the text of "The Poet" is indicated by the editorial comments of both Cabot and Edward Emerson (see especially *W*, IX, v, vii, 500-501). Although present evidence is insufficient to determine if the Centenary text is of Emerson's composing in every detail, it does not seriously challenge that view. I am indebted to Carl Strauch for sharing with me his detailed knowledge of the textual problem.

5. Lawrence, *Phoenix*, I, 317.

6. A Breakthrough into Spaciousness

1. *The Dial 1840-1844* (New York: Russell, 1962), I, 220-221, my italics.

2. Proust, Stendhal, and Robbe-Grillet are Bersani's examples of such writers. *Balzac to Beckett* (New York: Oxford University Press, 1970), 333.

3. Bishop, *Emerson on the Soul*, 8.

4. Carpenter, *Handbook*, 94.

5. See Spencer, *The Quest for Nationality*, 170, Hopkins, *Spires of Form*, 68-69, and Lawrence Buell, "Reading Emerson for the Structures: The Coherence of the Essays," *Quarterly Journal of Speech*, 58 (1972), 58.

6. Miller, ed., *The American Transcendentalists*, 12.

7. Whicher, *Freedom and Fate*, 97.

8. Miller, ed., *The American Transcendentalists*, 139.

9. Pearce, *The Continuity of American Poetry*, 187.

10. Olson, *Selected Writings of Charles Olson*, ed. Robert Creeley (New York: New Directions, 1966), 16.

11. Barthes, *Writing Degree Zero*, 86. A significant part of Emerson's new reality was the growing importance of cities in America. See, for example, Michael H. Cowan, *City of the West: Emerson, America, and Urban Metaphor* (New Haven: Yale University Press, 1967).

12. Francis Murphy, "Going It Alone," *Yale Review*, 56 (Autumn 1966), 23-24.

13. Tanner, *The Reign of Wonder* (Cambridge: Cambridge University Press, 1965), 46.

14. Lawrence, *The Symbolic Meaning*, 18.

15. Paul, *Emerson's Angle of Vision*, 137.

16. Bishop, *Emerson on the Soul*, 19.

17. Metzger, *Emerson and Greenough*, 32, 51-52.

18. Miller, ed., *The American Transcendentalists*, 5-6.

19. Benjamin Spencer says of the renunciation of the ornate and the new taste for the plain in this time: "It was from the astringent cultural climate of the New Zion rather than from the neo-classic, rationalistic, or scientific atmosphere of English culture that the 'new true stile' took its cisatlantic course" (*The Quest for Nationality*, 8). The phenomenon was not solely American. In England conditions favored a similar development away from poetic formality and decorum toward a more prosaic imagination and voice. The utilitarian doctrines contributed to the shift, as did Evangelical and Puritan desires for an artless faith. Moreover, a commoner's voice was demanded by a broadening audience less well educated and possessed of a deep-rooted anti-intellectualism. See Merritt in *The Art of Victorian Prose*, 12-13.

20. See Matthiessen, *American Renaissance*, xiv.

21. Paul, *Emerson's Angle of Vision*, 163.

22. Matthiessen, *American Renaissance*, 17.

23. Quoted by Harold Whitehall in *Gerard Manley Hopkins By The Kenyon Critics* (Norfolk, Conn.: New Directions, 1945), 38.

24. See Neil Harris, *The Artist in American Society* (New York: Braziller, 1966), 32ff.

25. Whicher, *Freedom and Fate*, 13.

7. Apologia for Prose

1. Arnold, *Discourses in America*, 193.

2. Travis R. Merritt, "Taste, Opinion, and Theory in the Rise of Victorian Prose Stylism," *The Art of Victorian Prose*, 5. On Coleridge's own intentions in prose, see Bishop C. Hunt, Jr., "Coleridge and the Endeavor of Philosophy," *PMLA*, 91 (October 1976), 829-839.

3. For a full discussion of concepts of the distinction between prose and poetry, see M. H. Abrams, *The Mirror and the Lamp*. Emerson, for example, saw the relationship much more deeply than the English theorist who wrote: "The terms *poetry* and *prose* are incorrectly opposed to each other. Verse is, properly, the contrary of *prose;* and because poetry speaks the language of fancy, passion, and sentiment, and philosophy speaks the language of reason, these two terms should be considered as contraries, and writing should be divided, not into poetry and prose, but into *poetry* and *philosophy*" (*The Mirror and the Lamp*, 97).

4. April 1852. Quoted in Gerald L. Bruns, *Modern Poetry and the Idea of Language* (New Haven: Yale University Press, 1974), 140.

5. Spencer, *The Quest for Nationality*, 162.

6. Strauch, "The Mind's Voice," 43.

7. Polanyi, "What Is a Painting?" *The American Scholar*, 39 (Autumn 1970), 669.

8. Olson, *Selected Writings*, 24.

8. "Inward Skill"

1. Arnold, *Discourses in America*, 179.

2. Quoted in Chapman, *Emerson and Other Essays* (New York: Scribner's, 1899), 74.

3. See the excellent discussion of this concept in M. H. Abrams, *Natural Supernaturalism* (New York: Norton, 1971), 27-30.

4. Steiner, "The Language Animal," 19.

5. Firkins, *Ralph Waldo Emerson*, 270-271.

6. Strauch in *American Literary Masters*, I, ed. Charles R. Anderson et al. (New York: Holt, Rinehart, and Winston, 1965), 470.

7. Authorship here is disputed (*JMN*, VIII, 431, n. 274).

8. "Almost nothing has been written about the persona in Emerson's essays, because it has been almost universally assumed that there is none." This surprising circumstance is noted by Lawrence Buell in his superb discussion of the "autobiographical I" and the more generalized exemplary persona in some of Emerson's essays, as well as the apparent fading of the exemplary "I" after *Essays, Second Series,* and the increased frequency of the private "I." *Literary Transcendentalism,* 284-296. There are provocative shadowings that will surely reward a study of Emerson's essay persona compared to the American who "stands for the New World" and "intermediate selfhood," concepts that can be traced back to Cotton Mather (Bercovitch, 136, 177). R. W. B. Lewis' *The American Adam* (Chicago: University of Chicago Press, 1955) is indispensable.

9. McGiffert, ed., *Young Emerson Speaks,* 23-24, 30.

10. Chapman, *Emerson and Other Essays,* 33.

11. See *Emerson's Angle of Vision,* 112, where Paul relates Emerson's style to his first visit to Paris. "The dialectic as a natural unfolding of thought—the science of ideas he discovered in Coleridge's *The Friend*—this, too, he saw *expressed* in the natural chain of forms in the Jardin des Plantes. It was the hint he needed."

12. Ibid., 110.

13. Chapman, *Emerson and Other Essays,* 94.

14. Cf. Buell, "Reading Emerson for the Structures," 68.

15. Nietzsche, *The Genealogy of Morals* (New York: MacMillan, 1897), 47. Besides the work in progress by Brian Fitzgerald and Gayle Smith which undertakes this linguistic analysis, recent essays by Donald Ross, Jr. treat Emerson's prose with some of the methods of stylistics: "Composition as a Stylistic Feature," *Style,* 4 (Winter 1970), 1-10; "Emerson and Thoreau: A Comparison of Prose Styles," *Language and Style,* 6 (Summer 1973), 185-195; and "Emerson's Stylistic Influence on Whitman" in a most valuable essay collection, Carl F. Strauch, ed., *Characteristics of Emerson, Transcendental Poet: A Symposium* (Hartford: Transcendental Books, 1975), 41-51. Useful essays are to be found in *ESQ,* 18, 4 (1972), devoted to Emerson's rhetorical strategies. A few recent dissertations touch on this area also.

16. Firkins, *Ralph Waldo Emerson,* 238.

17. Foerster, "Emerson on the Organic Principle in Art," *Emerson: A Collection of Critical Essays,* 109.

18. Buell calls this passage "a beautiful description of the method of his best essays." *Literary Transcendentalism,* 161.

19. Reid, "Emerson's Prose Style," 41.

20. Bishop, *Emerson on the Soul,* 225.

21. Chapman, *Emerson and Other Essays,* 30.

22. Lawrence, *The Symbolic Meaning,* 86.

23. Waggoner, *Emerson as Poet,* 79.

24. Harold Bloom has discussed the debt some contemporary poets owe to "the Emersonian or American Sublime" and the "Emersonian dialectic" of Fate, Freedom, and Power. See *Figures of Capable Imagination* (New York: Seabury Press, 1976), 48, and *Wallace Stevens: The Poems of Our Climate* (Ithaca: Cornell University Press, 1976), 10.

25. Lawrence, *The Symbolic Meaning,* 38.

Index

Porter, David
Emerson and literary
change
5.00

814
PORTER
1978

DEMCO